● Colored circles indicate approximate city locations within the state.

Restaurant Index by State and City, - Eastern USA

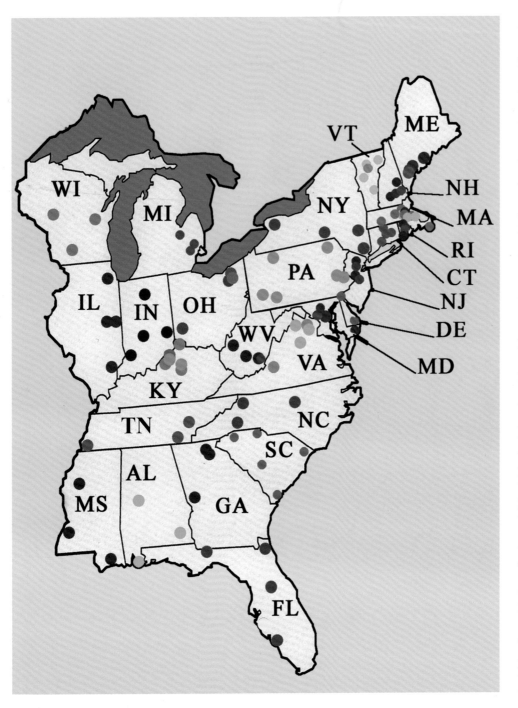

● Colored circles indicate approximate city locations within the state.

TASTE OF MAIN STREET AMERICA

Recipes from Independent and Family Owned Restaurants on Main Streets Across America

Over 200 Restaurants Throughout All 50 States

By Recipe Publishers

JEC PUBLISHING COMPANY
2049 E. Cherry Street
Springfield, Missouri 65802
(800) 313-5121
www.jecpubco.com

Copyright © 2010 by Recipe Publishers

First Edition

Library of Congress Control Number: 2010912003

ISBN: 978-0-9826424-9-8

Authors: JE Cornwell, Pam Eddings, Lisa Renee Dull

Contributions by: Gerrl Dean Tabor

Edited by: Pam Eddings

Cover and Graphics Layout by: Carolyn Cambronne

Prepared for Publishing by: JE Cornwell & Carolyn Cambronne

Printed in China

THANK YOU

Special THANKS from the Publisher:

This cookbook would not have been possible without the support from the restaurant owners, managers and chefs who appear in this book.

I would like to thank my staff, Lisa Renee, Gerrl Dean, Carolyn and especially Pam. These women worked hard and diligently on this project from start to finish. Without them, this cookbook would not have happened.

I would also like to thank my mother Judie and my two aunts, Gloria and Gail for helping me to finally get the idea for this cookbook out of my head and starting the process, and for their love and support.

And finally, a big thanks to my wife Susan and son Brandon for their love and support and for believing in me and this project.

Thanks!

JE Cornwell

JE Cornwell
Publisher

INTRODUCTION

The idea for this cookbook came about several years ago during election interviews with people across America. The term "Main Street America" seemed to generate visions of hard-working Americans in local communities across the country. In the summer of 2009, JE Cornwell called me into his office and shared his dream of putting together a cookbook featuring recipes from independent and family-owned restaurants located on "Main Streets" in all fifty states of the country. He and several family members "tested the waters" that summer by making a few calls to restaurants they found on Main Streets in several areas of the United States. However, it soon became apparent that in order for the dream to come true, someone would have to dedicate LOTS of time and research to gathering the information and calling restaurants to share the dream.

In December 2009, I came on board to begin the research and phone-calling process. After one month, JE and I realized the job needed more than one person involved, so Renee joined me. We divided the country in half and each began working 25 states. There was great rejoicing in the office the day we received our first recipe. Although JE wasn't as involved in the research and phone calling for this project, he was always available to advise us and suggest ways to get to the next level. Months went by, and JE decided to bring Gerrl Dean on board to make most of the introductory phone calls to the restaurants. Her friendly, excited manner was a blessing, and soon recipes were coming into the office almost every day. The day finally arrived when we had received recipes from restaurants in all fifty states!!

At that point, I began the process of editing the recipes and restaurant information, and then placed them in Carolyn's capable hands to begin the lay-out process. Hundreds of page proofs flew back and forth between JE and the restaurants as we worked to get everything just right. Finally, eleven months later, everything is completed.

Our thanks goes out not only to our team who prayerfully put this together, but also to all the restaurants across America who have willingly given us your favorite recipes and information about your restaurants, staff and communities for our book. Without you, this cookbook would not have been possible.

Now, our office team is looking at maps and planning vacations based on the communities and restaurants that are in our cookbook. We can't wait to meet you all in person and taste the "best recipes" from "Main Street America."

May the Lord bless you all!
Pam Eddings, Editor

Pictured left to right: Carolyn Cambronne, Pam Eddings with granddaughter Bethany Eddings, JE Cornwell, and Lisa Renee Dull. Not pictured: Gerrl Dean Taber.

TABLE OF CONTENTS

*Some of the Restaurant names have been shortened for space.

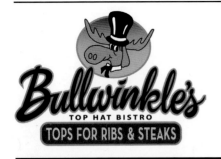

19 N. Main Street
Miamisburg, OH 45342
Phone: 937-859-7677
Fax: 937-859-996
Website: www.bullwinklestophatbistro.com
Catering website: www.bullwinklestophatcatering.com

Nestled in historic downtown Miamisburg in southwest Ohio, Bullwinkle's Top Hat Bistro has been serving great food and drinks to patrons since 1986. Known for its award-winning BBQ ribs, choice fresh cut steaks and seafood, it is the "go-to place" for gathering with friends for a casual evening out. In addition, the catering division, "Top Hat Catering," is widely known for its expertise in catering corporate events and wedding receptions. Miamisburg is known as the Miami Valley's "Star City," which inspired this dish.

Star City Scallops

10 20-30 count dry packed scallops
1/4 c. heavy cream
3 Tbsp. finely diced onion
3 Tbsp. finely diced tomato
1 tsp. fresh chopped garlic
1 tsp. fresh chopped parsley
2 slices thick sliced sourdough
1 oz. parmesan cheese, shredded
1/2 oz. olive oil
1/2 oz. butter, melted
Salt and pepper to taste

Directions:
Drizzle oil in heated sauté skillet; add onion and sauté 1 minute. Add scallops and sear on one side until golden brown; turn and repeat. Add garlic and tomatoes; sauté until tomatoes are just tender, then add salt and pepper to taste. Add half of the parsley and heavy cream, reduce by half. Place scallops on center of plate and drizzle sauce over and around. Top with half of the parmesan cheese. Brown cheese in broiler. Butter bread and brown both sides in broiler, then add remaining half of parmesan to one side of each slice and broil until brown. Cut bread into triangles and arrange the "star" around the scallops and sauce. Garnish with remaining parsley.

Appetizers   *Submitted by: John Sizemore, Executive Chef*

Hotel Julien Dubuque
200 Main Strect, Dubuque, IA 52001
Phone: 563-556-4200
Fax: 563-582-5023
Website: www.hoteljuliendubuque.com

In 1839, travelers' first sight as they crossed the Mississippi River into Dubuque was a hotel building on the corner of 2nd and Main. This old "Julien Hotel" survived a fire, hosted famous guests such as Abraham Lincoln, "Buffalo Bill" Cody and Mark Twain, gained notoriety thanks to Al Capone and was ultimately purchased by the current ownership in 1962. Now 170 years later, after a $30 million interior renovation and exterior restoration, the Hotel Julien Dubuque has redefined elegance through the blending of its rich history with modern luxury and style.

Artichoke Fritters

1 #10 can artichoke hearts
14 scallions
1 3/4 lb. cream cheese
6 3/4 oz. cheddar cheese
6 3/4 oz. parmesan cheese
5 wheels Boursin cheese
1 3/4 lb. Panko bread crumbs
5 Tbsp. salt
2 Tbsp. black pepper

Choose Caroline's Restaurant for delectable American cuisine with a twist. Indulge in a cocktail and appetizers at the Riverboat Lounge. Have your hotel event catered. Relax and order room service. There is plenty to eat, drink and enjoy when you stay at the Hotel Julien Dubuque.

Directions:
Slice scallions. Shred both cheeses using a fine blade shredder. Drain juice off of artichoke hearts. Combine all ingredients in a mixing bowl and mix until all ingredients are completely incorporated. DO NOT OVER MIX. Portion mix into 1 ounce balls. Toss in flour dip, in egg wash, then roll in Japanese bread crumbs. To cook: deep fry in 350° until golden brown. Place in 350° oven for 3-4 minutes. Serve with your favorite dipping sauce. Mayo based sauce is perfect.

Submitted by: Andrew Weis, Executive Chef

315 Main Street
Malvern, IA 51551
Phone: 712-624-8082

Classic Café is a family owned and operated restaurant in Malvern, Iowa. They have specialty coffees, smoothies, full bar, and a full service restaurant with daily specials. Darren Bartley is the owner/chef and his sister, Alicia Bartley and brother in-law, Brad Hagen are his partners. They have a large garden which produces much of the fresh produce for the café.

Fried Goat Cheese with Homemade Tomato Sauce and Grilled Bread

3 1/2 oz. portions of fresh goat cheese (local if possible)
Egg wash (1 egg with a splash of milk, whipped together with a fork)
4 oz. seasoned flour (add a pinch of salt, fresh ground black pepper, and a pinch of cayenne pepper)
3 oz. Panko bread crumbs

Directions:
Form cheese into balls and place in seasoned flour. Shake off excess flour and place in egg wash making sure to coat it well. Place in bread crumbs and coat evenly. Repeat with remaining cheese, then place in freezer for 20 minutes.

Tomato sauce
1/4 c. extra virgin olive oil
1 yellow onion, diced small
4 garlic cloves, smashed
3 Tbsp. fresh chopped thyme

1 carrot, shredded
3 1/2 lbs. (whole peeled) canned tomatoes
Salt and fresh ground black pepper to taste

Directions:
Sweat onion and garlic in olive oil until soft and golden brown. Add thyme and carrot and sweat 5 minutes. Add tomatoes with their juice and bring to a boil. Turn heat down to simmer and cook for 30 minutes. Season with salt and pepper and place in blender, blending until smooth. Yields 6 cups.
Take goat cheese out of freezer and place in hot oil (325°) and fry until golden brown. Place on paper towel. Place 4 ounces of warm tomato sauce on plate and place fried cheese on top of the sauce. Garnish with a slice of grilled sourdough bread.

Appetizers   *Submitted by: Darren Bartley, Owner/Chef*

12900 Main Street
Garden Grove, CA 92840
Phone: 714-539-4334
Fax: 714-539-4343
Website: www.dougsdowntowngrill.com

Applewood Smoked Pork Loin Dip

5-6 split pieces of applewood
1-2 (10-12 lb.) prime boneless pork loin
Fresh baguette bread
1 c. Ajus to serve
5 Tbsp. seasoned salt
5 Tbsp. granulated garlic
5 Tbsp. dark chili powder
3 Tbsp. black pepper
1/2 c. brown sugar

Doug's Downtown Grill, on Historic Main Street in Garden Grove, CA, offers the most exquisite steakhouse cuisine in the area and is quickly becoming a must stop for area locals looking for a fine dining experience in a friendly environment. Ambience and mood is serene and classy, food mouth watering.

Directions:
Soak 3-4 pieces of applewood in a bucket of water for at least one hour. Start the fire in your smoker. Mix all dry spices together. Rub all spices all over the pork loin. When coals have settled down, put pork in the smoker. Add one piece of soaked applewood to bed of coals. Add applewood pieces as needed and smoke for six hours. Thinly slice pork loin then and stack high on toasted baguette. Serve with a cup of Ajus for dipping and enjoy.

Appetizers   *Submitted by: Doug Coleman, Owner*

240 Main Street
Groveville, NJ 07728
Phone: 609-585-7085

It is with great pride that we at Family Nest offer you the finest quality of food and service. Family Nest brings together "Old World" quality and simplicity with "New World" innovation to create a menu that "tickles" a wide range of palates with our zesty sauce and traditional recipes. Buon Appetito!

Eggplant Rolatini in Vodka Sauce

1 lg. eggplant (Comes out as 8 slices)
1 plum tomato, chopped
5 Tbsp. of chopped onions
3 tsp. parmigiana cheese
1/2 c. mozzarella cheese
4 Tbsp. ricotta cheese
4 whole eggs

1/2 c. flour
1/2 c. spinach
8 oz. tomato sauce
8 oz. heavy cream
A splash of Vodka
Salt and pepper to taste
1 1/2 c. oil

Directions:

Get an eggplant and peel the skin off. Crack 3 of the eggs in a bowl and add salt, pepper and 1 teaspoon of Parmigiana cheese. Beat until everything is well mixed. Put the oil in a pan and bring to a boil. Dip the eggplant first into the flour, then into the egg mixture. Fry in the oil until it starts to turn brown; then flip it and cook until lightly browned. Remove from pan and drain on a plate covered with paper towels. In another bowl, place the ricotta, 1 egg, mozzarella, remaining 2 teaspoons of parmigiana cheese, and salt and pepper. Mix well. Take the 8 pieces of fried eggplant and lay them flat next to each other. Fill them with the prepared cheese stuffing, then roll them up.

Sauce directions:

Put some oil and a teaspoon of butter in a medium sized saucepan. When the butter and oil are hot, add the chopped onions and tomato. Continue cooking until the onions look brown. Add the splash of vodka. When you put this in, make sure there are flames coming from the side (means that alcohol has been taken away) Stir in the heavy cream, then add the cup of sauce and let it cook for a little while. You'll know it's ready when the vodka sauce is creamy. Place the rolled eggplant on an oven safe plate and bake in a preheated 350° oven for 30 minutes. When the cheese melts in the eggplant, remove from the oven, put the vodka sauce on top and serve while hot! Serves four people.

203 Main Street
Hamilton, MT 59840
Phone: 406-363-4567

Green Chili Rellenos

(Filling Station Specialty)

The Filling Station Grille is located in beautiful downtown Hamilton, Montana. Known for our authentic New Mexican Cuisine and hometown hospitality, the Filling Station features fresh Hatch green chilies to create our homemade dishes. Voted the most hospitable restaurant, and best soup in the Bitterroot Valley. While dining, our patrons enjoy the fun and nostalgic atmosphere of an old-time gas station.

10 New Mexico Hatch green chilies, roasted and peeled (canned chili may be used)
10 oz. Monterey Jack Cheese
Batter
Green Chili Sauce
Shredded Sharp Cheddar Cheese
Hot oil or lard

Batter:
1 c. all-purpose flour
1 tsp. baking powder
1/2 tsp. salt
3/4 c. cornmeal
1 c. milk
2 eggs, slightly beaten

Directions:

To make batter, combine flour, baking powder, salt, and cornmeal. Blend milk and eggs. Combine milk and egg mixture with the dry ingredients. If needed add more milk for a smooth batter. To make rellenos, slice cheese into 3/4" strips and the length of the chili. Make a small slit in the chili, just large enough to insert the cheese. Using tongs, dip the stuffed chili into the batter and fry in hot oil or lard until golden brown. Drain rellenos and serve topped with green chili sauce (see recipe below) and shredded cheddar cheese. Serve with pinto beans and Spanish rice. Garnish with lettuce and tomatoes.

Green Chili Sauce

2 Tbsp. oil or lard
2 tsp. granulated garlic
1/4 c. diced onions
2 Tbsp. flour

4 c. water
2 c. diced New Mexico hatch chili (canned or frozen diced green chili may be used)
Salt to taste

Directions:

To make Green Chili Sauce: In a heavy sauce pan sauté onion and garlic. With a wooden spoon, blend in the flour. Add green chili and water. Bring to a boil and simmer, stirring frequently until sauce thickens.

Appetizers

Submitted by: Raina Young, Owner/Chef

888 Main Street
Waltham, MA 02453
Phone: 781-894-2234
Fax: 781-891-2554

I l Capriccio serves a constantly changing Northern Italian menu featuring local products with an award winning Italian wine and Grappa list. Though long considered a local secret, Il Capriccio has been the number one Northern Italian restaurant in Zagat's over the last decade. The New York Times wrote "Il Capriccio offers consistently sumptuous northern Italian food cooked by Richie Barron, with an extraordinary list of Italian wines -- many of them hard to find outside Italy."

Steamed Mussels with White Wine

60 clean Prince Edward Island or Maine mussels
4 oz. halved cherry tomatoes
6 cloves minced garlic
5 sliced scallions in 1/4 in. pieces
1 oz. extra virgin olive oil
1 Tbsp. butter
1 c. dry white wine
Salt and pepper to taste

Directions:
In large saucepan heat the olive oil and butter together over medium flame, add garlic and scallions and sauté with no color. Add tomatoes and cook 1 minute, add mussels and toss with mixture. Add white wine, salt and pepper and cover for 3 minutes until mussels open. With tongs, place mussels open side up in 4 bowls, pour liquid over mussels and serve immediately.

Appetizers   *Submitted by: Richie Barron, Owner*

117 E. Main Street
LaGrange, KY 40031
Phone: 502-222-2286
Website: www.theirishroverky.com

Irish Rover, Too is the second location of The Irish Rover, Louisville's Irish Pub. Both pubs are owned and operated by Clare County natives, Michael Reidy and his wife, Siobhan. Now entering their seventeenth year of business, they attempt to recreate the notion of the Irish pub as a social center with authentic recipes and a relaxed but lively atmosphere. They are famous for their Fish & Chips, as well as the following recipe for Soda Bread, which is served with every meal at The Irish Rover.

Smoked Salmon Pate with Brown Soda Bread

Smoked Salmon Pate

1/3 yellow onion, chopped
2/3 lb. smoked salmon, chopped

1/2 tsp. lemon juice
1 lb. cream cheese

Directions:
Process first three ingredients in Robot Coupe food processor, then add cream cheese. Continue processing until creamy. Spread on Brown Soda Bread; garnish with diced red onion and lemon wedges.

Brown Soda Bread

1 c. white flour
2 c. whole wheat flour, preferably coarse
1/2 tsp. salt

1 tsp. baking soda
1 Tbsp. butter
1+ c. buttermilk

Photos by: John Nation

Directions:
Preheat oven to 450º. Stir dry ingredients together with a fork. Cut butter into dry mix. Make a well in the center and pour in buttermilk. Stir to mix well, making a slightly sticky dough. Turn out onto floured surface. Working the dough as little as possible, pat it into a round loaf. Place on a greased baking sheet and bake for 10 minutes. Lower heat to 375º and continue baking for 30-40 minutes. Bread is done if tapping the bottom of the loaf produces a hollow sound. (A spoonful of brown sugar may also be added to the dry ingredients for a sweeter loaf.)

Appetizers

Submitted by: Siobhan Reidy, Owner

1072 Main Street
Dubuque, IA 52001
Phone: 563-556-0505
Fax: 563-556-0200

Naming L.May after their grandmother Lillian May, sibling owners Lea and E.J. Droessler have provided patrons with a warm and friendly environment reminiscent of a family gathering while also offering an impressive selection of appetizers, gourmet pizzas, decadent entrees, and tempting desserts. Innovative nightly entree features and muddled-from-scratch cocktails are specialties at L.May Eatery, which is nestled in the historic 1000 block of Main Street, Dubuque. This pizza recipe is a twist on a classic Italian dish and a great light dinner or appetizer, featured on L.May's summer menu.

Isle of Capri Pizza

14"-16" pizza crust (thin crust recommended)
Roasted garlic*
1/2 c. extra virgin olive oil
10-12 fresh basil leaves
2 med. size beef steak tomatoes, sliced
6 oz. fresh mozzarella (buffalo, if possible), sliced
1/4 c. balsamic glaze
Sea salt
Pepper
Fresh grated parmesan

Directions:

*To roast garlic: Cut off top of garlic stalk, place in tin foil, drizzle with olive oil, and roast at 350° for 20 min. Coat your pizza crust with extra virgin olive oil and top with roasted garlic. Bake as directed until golden. Remove crust from oven; immediately top with sliced tomatoes, pieces of fresh mozzarella, and basil leaves (in that order). Drizzle with balsamic glaze, and sprinkle with sea salt, pepper and fresh parmesan to taste. Enjoy!

Appetizers   *Submitted by: Chef Juan Dorantes*

314 W. Main Street
Chattanooga, TN 37408
Phone: 423-266-7595
Fax: 423-634-0455

La Altena is locally owned and operated since 1997 by the family. This is my parents' first location. They now have two additional locations. All three are operated by the family. The name La Altena comes from the mountains of Mexico, where my parents are from. One reason that my parents started a restaurant business was because their friends loved my mom's cooking and convinced them to open a restaurant with authentic Mexican food in the southeastern region of the United States.

Chile Rellenos

2 whole tomatoes
1/2 tsp. salt
1/4 tsp. garlic powder
1 c. water

4 poblano peppers
1 liter vegetable oil
5 egg whites
Salt to taste
Garlic powder to taste
1/2 tsp. flour
8 oz. easy melt white American cheese
1 c. flour

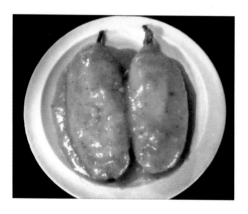

Directions:

For the sauce, pour the water into a pot and bring to a boil. Add the tomatoes, garlic and salt. Boil for 10 minutes, then place the tomatoes and a little of the boiling water into a blender and blend. You may add as much water as needed to make the sauce the thickness that you prefer.

For the Chile Relleno, pour the oil into a frying pan and heat. Once it's hot, drop one pepper at a time into the oil and flip front to back for 30 seconds to a minute. Take it out and place on a cooling rack for 5 minutes. Once the peppers are cool, peel the skin, then make an opening from top to bottom to take the seeds out. Stuff them with 2 ounces of cheese. Set aside. Place egg whites in a bowl and beat at medium to high speed while stiff peaks form. Add sprinkle of salt, garlic, and flour. Set aside. In a separate flat dish, pour the cup of flour and roll each stuffed pepper in the flour. Dip it in the egg mixture, then drop it in the boiling oil. Turn it front to back until it is golden brown. Remove and place on a cooling rack to drain the oil for 2 minutes. You can serve them as appetizers or as a meal accompanied with rice, beans, lettuce, tomato and cheese.

Appetizers

Submitted by: Maria Fuentes, General Manager

1905 Main Street
Vancouver, WA 98660
Phone: 360-571-5010
Fax: 360-571-5012
Website: www.labottegafoods.com

Spreading delectable, rich warm gorgonzola cheese and light marinara sauce over crisp, grilled bread is nothing sort of heavenly; a most original dish you're sure never to forget. The Gorgonzola Cheese Cake is only the beginning of a wondrous culinary adventure to be had for your curious taste buds at La Bottega Café.

Gorgonzola Cheesecake

Crust
    1/2 c. cornmeal
    1 1/2 c. water
    1/2 tsp. salt
    1 tsp. dry basil
    1 tsp. chopped garlic
    1/4 c. shredded parmesan

Cake
    2 1/2 lb. cream cheese
    1 lb. gorgonzola
    5 eggs
    14 cloves roasted garlic

From the remarkable Smoked Mushroom Raviolis, to the extensive, international wine list, along with professional and friendly service, you will find yourself lost in a sea of utter and complete amazement. There is certainly no room for disappointment at La Bottega Café; but be sure to leave room for the Tiramisu, or a scoop of the home-made Italian Gelato!

Directions:
Boil water in sauce pan. Slowly stir in cornmeal ensuring no lumps. Add salt, garlic and basil and allow to simmer. Cover for 20 minutes. Remove from heat and stir in parmesan. Allow to cool slightly and press into a 10"x2" round cake pan. Allow the cream cheese to soften. Beat the two cheeses together, then beat the eggs in one at a time. Pour mixture on top of polenta crust. Circle the garlic around the outside. Cover and bake in a water bath for 90 minutes at 350° or until 160° inside.

Appetizers   *Submitted by: Lisa Dougherty, Owner*

301 S. Main Avenue
Sioux Falls, SD 57104
Phone: 605-731-2384
Fax: (605) 731-2397

Leonardo's prepares an expansive menu of fresh cooked meals Monday through Thursday from 11:00 AM–2:00 PM and Friday and Saturday from 11:00 AM–4:00 PM. Kids and adults rave about the food, and we know you'll love it. Leonardo's also provides on-site catering for weddings, pre-show dinners, special holiday buffets and more. Their tasty and affordable offerings have even Mona Lisa grinning ear-to-ear! Leonardo's is conveniently located in the Washington Pavilion of Arts and Science and enhances the other exciting attractions that are offered. Come for lunch, then stay and explore the rest of the building. With three floors of hands-on science exhibits, a Cinedome theatre featuring a giant 60-foot domed screen, six art galleries, and a 1,800 seat performance hall, there is sure to be lots to keep you inspired and entertained.

Savory Southwest Cheesecake

1 springform pan, 9-12 in.	16 oz. sour cream	1 c. heavy whipping cream
Cooking spray	16 oz. chunky salsa (your choice)	1 c. shredded cheddar cheese
1 bag multi-colored tortilla chips	3 lg. eggs	1 pkg. taco seasoning
3 8 oz. pkg. cream cheese	4 heaping Tbsp. flour	

Directions:

In a mixing bowl, add cream cheese, sour cream, salsa, taco seasoning and cheddar cheese. Mix until thoroughly incorporated. Meanwhile, crunch up at least two cups of the tortilla chips and use them as your crust layer for the cheesecake, similar to the way you would use graham crackers for a crust. It should be approximately 1/4 – 1/2 inch thick in the bottom of the springform pan. In the mixing bowl, add eggs, one at a time until incorporated, then one heaping tablespoon of flour at a time until incorporated. Finally, blend in the cup of whipping cream. Spray the pan with the cooking spray, then pour the mixture into the pan, filling it approximately 3/4 full. Bake at 350° for 45-60 minutes or until top starts to set and crack open. Color should be lightly brown. It is best to turn the oven off when cooking is close to complete and leave the cheesecake in there for an additional 30 minutes for cooling. Before serving, make sure the cheesecake is cooled to room temperature. Use the remaining tortilla chips to dip into it or even celery, carrots and vegetables of all sorts. For garnishing, dollop little circles of sour cream on top and use fresh cilantro sprigs to finish. Can be served on the bottom of the springform pan. Just remove the sides and let the guests dive in.

Appetizers   *Submitted by: Paula Lechner, Manager & Rick Tobin, Chef*

7131 E. Main Street
Scottsdale, AZ 85251
Phone: 480-947-6042
Fax: 480-994-3474
Website:
www.maleesthaibistro.com

Malee's on Main opened in August of 1987. The building that is home to Malee's on Main has a fascinating story of its own. Built in 1921, it was once Miss Lillian's Tea Room, and later a French restaurant called Lucky Pierre's. For a few years it was Hugo's, an Italian restaurant named for the owner who sang opera as he served the customers. Since Malee's on Main opened, people have asked for our recipes. Our Chefs bring extensive experience and infuse it with secret techniques. We are constantly trying new ideas, even doing a little 'Thai Spy' wherever we find delicious discoveries, in places as far away as Bangkok.

Drunken Dragon Wrap

8 oz. minced chicken
1 oz. canola oil
1/4 c. diced tomatoes
2 oz. bean sprouts
1 oz. fresh basil
1/2 head iceberg lettuce
1 oz. chopped cilantro
1 Tbsp. ground roasted peanut

Seasoning
1 tsp. green curry paste
1 Tbsp. oyster sauce
1 Tbsp. fish sauce
1 Tbsp. sugar

All our meals are prepared individually in 10' sauté skillets, so four people at one table can each order the same dish, and have it prepared differently, depending on personal preference or dietary need.

Directions:
Heat sauté pan with oil. Brown chicken with seasonings. Stir, then plate. Top with diced tomatoes. Serve with chilled iceberg lettuce cups. Sprinkle ground peanuts and cilantro on top.

Over the years, we have welcomed everyone from Hollywood celebrities to high school prom dates. Our goal was to create a place where everyone feels comfortable. A place that doesn't look like a typical Thai food restaurant, but instead reflects the unique character of its location with our patios, fireplaces, and original artwork. Malee's on Main is true to the spirit of Scottsdale.

MERMAID CAFE
OLDINLET BOOKSHOP AND B&B

HOMER, ALASKA

3487 Main Street
Homer, AK 99603
Phone: 907-235-7649
Website: www.mermaidcafe.net

This is a super fun dish. It may seem over seasoned at first but as you peel the shells off, the bit of seasoning that remains on your fingers seasons the shrimp inside, and you just can't help licking your fingers and making a big ol' mess.

Prince William Sound Side-Stripe Shrimp. Spit-Fire Style

1 lb. fresh PWS shrimp
3 Tbsp. butter
1 Tbsp. garlic
2 tsp. salt

2 tsp. ground black pepper
1 tsp. chipotle powder or smoked paprika
1 Tbsp. chives or parsley
Lemons

Directions:

Sauté garlic till fragrant, then add the remaining ingredients. Sauté for just a few minutes, tossing regularly. Test one and adjust seasoning or cooking time. Serve right away with a big lemon to squeeze all over the top and lots of paper towels.

Appetizers   *Submitted by: Michael Hiller, Owner*

286 S. Main Street
Wolfeboro, NH 03894
Phone: 603-569-3662
Fax: 603-569-3677

Morrisseys' is located in Wolfeboro, NH…America's first summer resort. Chef Aaron Morrissey has been working in restaurants and hotels for over 20 years. He and his family have been operating the restaurant for 8 years. The restaurant focuses on specialty homemade recipes from scratch using the best ingredients.

Lobster Crab Cakes

1 lb. shrimp, chopped
1/4 lb. lobster, chopped
1/4 lb. butter
1/2 c. scallions
1 lb. crab claw meat
1/4 lb. rock crab meat
2 Tbsp. garlic
1/2 tsp. dill

1 Tbsp. Old Bay Seafood Seasoning
2 c. bread crumbs
1/2 c. mayonnaise
1/2 Tbsp. black pepper
1/2 Tbsp. Tabasco sauce
2 eggs

Directions:
Blanch shrimp in butter, cool and chop fine. Add all ingredients, mix well using hands, being careful not to break crab too much. Form into 16 equal 2 inch thick patties. Pan fry in clarified butter until golden crust forms on both sides. Yields 16 cakes.

Appetizers   *Submitted by: Aaron Morrissey, Owner/Chef*

1007 Old North Main Street
Clover, SC 29710
Phone: 803-222-4467

Patti-O Grill is a small, rustic Bar & Grill with a down home, comfortable atmosphere and fresh, never frozen cuisine. We remind you of the show "Cheers" because at Patti-O's you never meet a stranger.

Patti-O's Nacho Supreme

1 lb. ground chuck
1/4 c. onion
1 c. water
1/2 c. tomatoes, diced
Salt and pepper
1 Tbsp. parsley flakes
1 Tbsp. Italian seasoning
2 Tbsp. cumin
1/4 c. chili powder

8 oz. sharp cheddar
cheese, shredded
(or Velveeta cheese)
1/2 c. whole milk
2 tsp. pickled jalapeno,
finely diced

8 6-in. fresh white corn tortillas
1 c. lettuce, shredded
1/4 c. tomatoes, diced
Salsa
Sour cream

Directions:
Brown ground chuck with onion. Drain excess grease from meat. Add water, diced tomatoes, and spices. Mix and simmer for 30-40 minutes. Combine cheddar cheese (or Velveeta) with milk. Melt the mixture on low heat or in the microwave. Stir until smooth. Add pickled jalapenos to cheese mixture. Stir until smooth. Cut 8 – 6 inch tortillas into quarters and deep fry until golden brown. Place tortillas in a basket with foil lining. Pour cheese mixture over tortillas, then pour chili over tortillas and cheese. Top with lettuce, tomatoes, jalapenos, salsa, and sour cream.

Appetizers   *Submitted by: J Patti Imler, Owner*

4725 Main Street – Suite #228
Orange Beach, AL 36561
Phone: 251-224-6900
Fax: 251-224-6901
Website: www.rafterssportsbar.com

Rafters is a family oriented restaurant & sports bar specializing in seafood, BBQ, Burgers and more. Located on the beautiful Alabama Gulf Coast, we have been serving this area since 2002. This recipe is a local favorite and one I'm sure you will love also.

Blue Water Smoked Tuna Dip

3 lb. smoked tuna
1 c. sour cream
1 c. shredded parmesan cheese
1 1/2 Tbsp. paprika
1 1/2 Tbsp. Louisiana hot sauce
1/2 Tbsp. blackening seasoning
1/2 Tbsp. garlic salt
A squeeze of fresh lemon juice

Directions:

Crumble smoked tuna into a 3-quart mixing bowl. Add all other ingredients and mix thoroughly; chill for at least one hour. Dip is best served on a bed of green leaf lettuce with a salad wafer-style cracker. Makes approximately two quarts.

510 Main Street
Wellsville, KS 66092
Phone: 785-883-4119

Smokey's is family owned and operated by Darren and Renae Maples. It was started in 1999. We have 5 special sauces that are made from scratch. We are based in the Kansas City area.

Barbeque Cream Cheese Dip

3 pkg. 8 oz. cream cheese
1 c. barbeque sauce
(use your favorite sauce)
1 1/2 c. crumbled cooked bacon
1 1/2 c. shredded Monterey jack cheese
1 c. diced green onion
2 Tbsp. chipotle mix

Directions:
Soften cream cheese in mixing bowl. Add all other ingredients. Serve cold, or heated up in microwave, with chips or crackers.

Appetizers   *Submitted by: Darren Maples, Owner*

310 Main Street
Eastsound, WA 98245
Phone: 360-376-7171
Fax: 360-376-7174

Owners Steve and Monica Duthie have created an exceptional Northwest dining experience. The Madrona Bar and Grill is located directly over the water on beautiful Orcas Island in the world renowned San Juan Islands. The restaurant features fresh local seafood from the Puget Sound region as well as a variety of prime steaks and burgers. Locals and tourists alike both rave about the friendly atmosphere and stunning views along with the generous selection of northwest microbrews and creative cocktails.

Dungeness Crab Cakes with Wasabi Mayonnaise

Crab Cakes
    2 lb. fresh cooked Dungeness crab meat
    1/3 c. mayonnaise
    1/2 c. chopped green onion
    2 1/3 c. Panko bread crumbs, set aside 2 c. for dredging
    1 1/2 tsp. ground black pepper
    1 1/2 tsp. hot chili sauce
    1 tsp. Thai fish sauce
    2 Tbsp. lemon juice

Wasabi Mayonnaise
    1 c. mayonnaise
    3 Tbsp. Wasabi powder
    1 Tbsp. soy sauce
    1 tsp. fresh grated ginger
    1 1/2 tsp. granulated sugar
    1 Tbsp. lemon juice

Directions:
Drain the cooked crab, then mix all the ingredients for the crab cakes. Form into 3 ounce balls, then roll in the additional 2 cups of Panko bread crumbs to coat. Discard any remaining Panko. Form into rounded patties about 1 1/2 inch thick and chill in the refrigerator for at least one hour. To make the Wasabi mayonnaise, whisk together all ingredients. After crab cakes have chilled, sauté over medium high heat until golden brown on each side then finish in the oven at 400° for about 5 minutes. Serve with Wasabi mayonnaise on the side or drizzled over the top. Makes 12 crab cakes, or 6 servings.

Appetizers   *Submitted by: Monica & Steve Duthie, Owners*

707 Main Street
Norwell, MA 02061
Phone: 781-561-7361
Website: www.thetinkersson.com

Chefs: Brian Houlihan & Melinda Lynch

The Tinker's Son is an Authentic Irish Pub in the center of Historic Norwell, Massachusetts. The rustic interior, with large beams and hardwood floors, is reminiscent of the pubs in Dublin. The Tinker's Son prides itself on using organic, locally grown produce in its made-from-scratch Kitchen. At the Bar, built from reclaimed wood, you are sure to find inviting conversation alongside your favorite pint or specialty cocktail.

Pâté de Maison

Pâté

6 oz. butter
8 oz. chicken livers
1 shallot, thinly diced
2 Tbsp. fresh thyme, chopped
2 oz. brandy
3 oz. port
1 clove of garlic, chopped
2 oz. duck fat

Fruit Compote

Seasonal Berries
2 c. sugar
1 c. water
1 c. merlot

Directions:

Pâté - Sweat onions with thyme in a sauté pan over medium heat until onions are soft. Add chopped garlic and sauté for approximately 10 minutes. Place chicken livers in sauté pan and carefully sear all sides of livers. Deglaze pan with brandy and port, and allow livers to steam until medium-rare. Gently remove livers from pan and place directly into Robot-Coupe, and pulse until smooth. While doing so, allow contents of pan to reduce by 80 percent. Add reduction to livers in Robot-Coupe, and pulse to combine. Gradually add ice cold butter, 1 tablespoon at a time, to liver mixture; season with salt and pepper to taste. Press hot mixture through chinoise, then gently spoon into soufflé cups and allow to "set-up" in refrigerator for approximately 8 hours. When Pâté has set-up, remove from refrigerator and top with a thin layer of melted Duck Fat, (melt in saucer over low heat). Allow to chill and serve with Fruit Compote and Melba Toast.

Fruit Compote - Simmer all ingredients until they reach a syrup-like consistency and chill.

709 Main Street
Wolfforth, TX 79382
Phone: 806-866-0411

Chris and Alyssa own and operate the Tiger Drive-In and Café with their 3 boys Hunter, Cole and Griffin. Chris is the chef and Alyssa is the front house manager. Chris' passion for cooking and Alyssa's friendly smile make customers feel at home. The two believe that being a cooking-from-scratch restaurant is very important to maintain quality of food and customer service.

Cabaniss Fried Chile Peppers

6 New Mexico Hatch green chili peppers
(preferably fresh)
Olive oil
 Salt

Batter
   2 c. flour
   1 Tbsp. salt
   1 Tbsp. pepper
   1 Tbsp. paprika
   1 tsp. celery salt
   1 tsp. sugar

Egg wash
   2 eggs
   1 c. milk
   1/2 c. buttermilk

Directions:

Cut peppers in half, core and de-seed. Coat peppers with olive oil and salt. Roast in oven at 400° for 15-20 minutes. Turn over during roasting. While roasting, mix ingredients for batter and egg wash in two separate bowls. Remove peppers from oven and let cool. Peel and remove skins. Place in batter to dust peppers. Dip peppers in egg wash to coat. Dip again in batter. Fry for 2 minutes at 360°. Drain and season to taste. Serve with side of ranch for dipping.

Appetizers

Submitted by: Chris Cabaniss, Chef

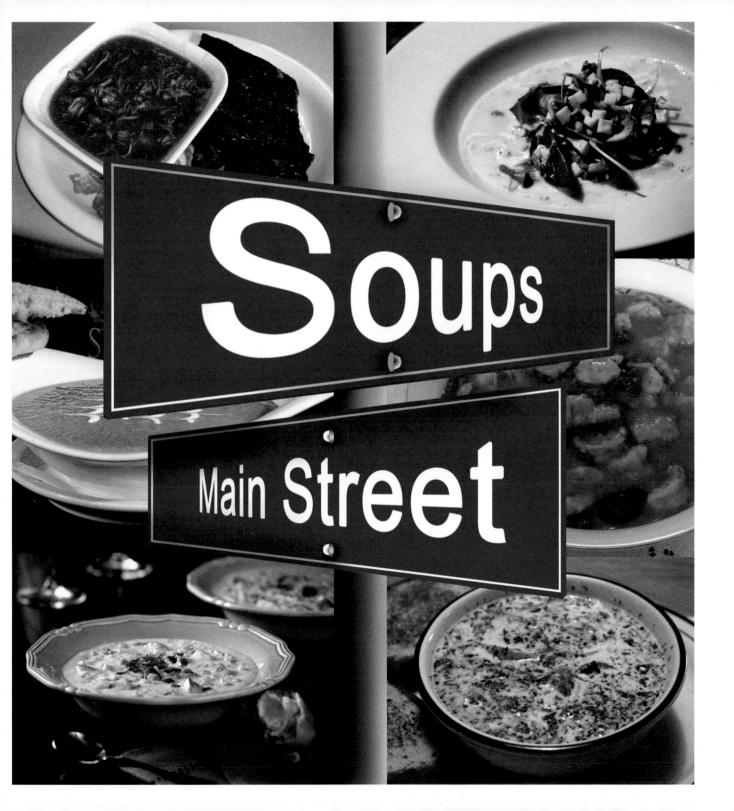

Soups
Main Street

56 Main Street
Springfield, VT 05156
Phone: 802-885-6987
Website: www.fiftysixmainstreet.com

Fifty-Six Main Street Restaurant is a very special little place in the heart of downtown Springfield, Vermont. The cozy, comfortable dining room is the perfect gathering place for friends and family to enjoy a tasty lunch or a relaxing dinner. The menu offers something for everyone...traditional American cuisine with a touch of Mexican and Italian fare, as well as vegetarian entrees. Check out the menus for yourself, and see why patrons return again and again. Great food...great service...great value. Proprietors Jerry & Robin Szawerda hope to see you soon!!

Harvest Bisque

4 oz. bacon, chopped
1 onion, chopped
2 cloves garlic, whole
1 rutabaga, peeled & diced
1 celery root, peeled & diced
   (can substitute 2 stalks celery)
2 sweet potatoes, peeled & diced
2 parsnips, peeled & diced
4 qt. chicken broth (or enough to cover)
2 c. heavy cream
Salt
Black pepper
Cayenne pepper

Directions:
In an 8 quart saucepan, sauté bacon until almost crisp. Add onions and garlic, and sauté for 2 minutes. Add next four ingredients. Cover and cook on low heat for 15 minutes. Add enough chicken stock to cover and simmer another 45 minutes. Puree. Add heavy cream. Season with salt, pepper and cayenne to taste. Bisque may be frozen in small quantities before adding heavy cream.

Soups   *Submitted by: Ross Jones, Chef*

218 N. Main Street
Springhill, LA 71075
Phone: 318-539-2284

AmJenns opened for business on November 1, 2006. It is named after our two daughters, Amy and Jennifer. We are a 50's style shop that serves hamburgers, sandwiches, the "Rueben," soups, ice cream, malts, banana splits, cobblers, and the thickest, most delicious brownies this side of the Mississippi. Everything is home made. Stop by and get your picture on the wall.

AmJenns Chicken and Sausage Gumbo

1 c. shortening
1 c. flour
3 c. chopped onions
2 c. chopped celery
1 c. chopped bell peppers (red, yellow & orange are pretty)
1 1/2 gal. chicken stock
1 bay leaf
1/8 tsp. thyme
1/8 tsp. sage

2 Tbsp. salt
1 Tbsp. red pepper
1 tsp. black pepper
3 cloves crushed garlic
8 lb. chicken (I use only the breast)
3 lb. smoked sausage
Filé (the seasoning, just enough to sprinkle on top of each bowl)
Rice

Directions:
Ahead of time boil chicken, reserving broth. De-bone and cut into chunks. Make a roux with the shortening and flour. Add onions, celery and bell peppers. Cook until onions are transparent, then add stock and bring to a rolling boil. Let boil a dew minutes and lower heat to simmer. Add bay leaf, thyme, sage, salt, red and black pepper, garlic, chicken and sausage. Let simmer about 45 minutes. Serve over hot rice, and sprinkle a little filé on top.

Soups   *Submitted by: Christine McCutcheon, Owner*

41 Main Street
Nantucket, MA 02554
Phone: 508-228-7001
Website: www.arnos.net

Arno's at 41 Main Street has been a staple on the Nantucket restaurant scene for over 50 years. Current owner, Chris Morris, brings a renewed energy to Nantucket's Main Street and a passion for matching wines from around the world with his American eclectic cuisine. Now featuring the only wine bar on Nantucket, the 41 Grill offers 41 wines by the glass, cheese plates with suggested wines, and wine flights to compare tasting characteristics.

New England Clam Chowder

3 qt. heavy cream
2 lb. cubed red bliss potatoes
1 lb. applewood smoked bacon
1/2 diced onion
1/4 stalk diced celery
1 c. roux (bacon roux preferred)
2 c. clam juice

1/4 c. clam base
3 c. chopped clams
1/2 c. fresh dill
1 Tbsp. fresh ground pepper
6 dashes chipotle Tabasco (optional)
6 dashes Worcestershire sauce

Directions:

Blanch potatoes and hold in bowl. Render bacon in large pot on medium high heat. Add onions and celery and sweat until translucent (3-4 minutes). Add cream, clam juice, cooked potatoes and base. Stir with whisk until boiling. Add roux and stir until thickened. May require more roux depending on how thick you want your soup to be. Add pepper, Tabasco, Worcestershire, dill and stir. Add clams and cook for 10-12 minutes or until thickened. Serve hot with oyster crackers and a pinch of paprika for color. Serves 4.

Serving breakfast, lunch and dinner seasonally, Arno's at 41 Main Street hopes to be your everyday dining destination. Stop by for a bountiful breakfast to start your day, a quick, fresh made lunch, including Nantucket's Best Clam Chowder, an après work appetizer at the 41, or a relaxing dinner on historic Main Street. Whatever your occasion, it all starts at Arno's at 41 Main Street.

5 E. Main Street
Chanute, KS 66720
Phone: 620-431-7733
Fax: 620-431-0026

Benchwarmers is locally owned and operated since 2005. Owners, Ken and Cathy Matney have 25 years of restaurant experience. We are Southeast Kansas' only sports Bar & Grill that puts family first. This BBQ stew is best when served with our St. Louis ribs.

BBQ Stew

1/4 lb. butter
1 3/4 c. catsup
1/4 c. French's yellow mustard
1/4 c. white vinegar
1/2 Tbsp. chopped garlic
1 tsp. coarse ground black pepper
1/2 tsp. crushed red pepper
1/2 oz. liquid smoke
1 oz. Worcestershire sauce
1/2 oz. Tabasco
1/2 Tbsp. fresh lemon juice
1/4 c. brown sugar

1/4 lb. butter
3 c. small diced potatoes
1 c. small diced onion
2 14.5 oz. cans chicken broth
1 lb. baked chicken

8-10 oz. smoked pork
8.5 oz. can early peas
2 14 oz. cans stewed tomatoes
1/4 c. liquid smoke
14.5 oz. can creamed corn

Directions:

Sauce first: In a 2 quart sauce pan over low heat, melt butter, add catsup, mustard, vinegar. Blend until smooth, then add garlic, black pepper, red pepper, liquid smoke, Worcestershire, Tabasco and lemon juice. Blend until smooth, add brown sugar. Stir constantly, increase heat to simmer (do not boil) for approximately 10 minutes. Set aside for later. The stew: In a 2 gallon pot over low heat, melt 1/4 pound of butter, then add diced potatoes, onions, chicken broth, baked chicken, and pork. Bring to boil, stirring until potatoes are near done. Then add the cans of peas, stewed tomatoes, creamed corn, the prepared sauce, and 1/4 cup of liquid smoke. Slow simmer 2 hours. Makes about 1 gallon.

Soups

Submitted by: Ken Matney, Owner

204 Main Street
New Town, ND 58763
Phone: 701-627- 3888

Better 'B' Café is located in the west central part of North Dakota. We serve a café style menu and are known for our homemade soups. We are also known for our burgers and homemade specials. Everything is made with fresh ingredients and the care of a family run restaurant.

Beef Tortilla Soup

14 c. water
3 c. diced tomatoes
1 green pepper
1 med. white onion
4 oz. jalapeno peppers
1 tsp. black pepper
4 c. diced roast beef

1 Tbsp. beef base
3 Tbsp. cornstarch
1 c. American cheese
1 c. Swiss cheese
10 oz. Velveeta cheese
2 c. shredded cheddar cheese

Directions:
Add tomatoes, green peppers, onion, jalapenos, black pepper, and roast beef to water. Bring to boil. Add beef base to beef broth. Boil for 30 minutes. Mix corn starch with cold water to make roux; mix to consistency of loose paste. Add to soup to thicken. Reduce heat. Simmer 30 minutes. Add in cheeses 1 cup at a time. Stir until melted and blended into soup. Serve in bowls with a side of your favorite tortilla style chips.

Soups   *Submitted by: Earl Fredericksen, Owner*

923 Main Street
Winfield, KS 67156
Phone: 620-221-2233

Winfield, Kansas, Rated Number 56 in The 100 Best Small Towns in America, is the home to Bl'eus Family Dining, owned and operated by Blain and Sue Evans. Our menu consists of home-style favorites featuring the town's best fried chicken and chicken fried steaks. This particular recipe came to be due to a mishap in the kitchen and became a big hit!

Cowboy Clam Chowder

1 lb. bacon, diced
2 Tbsp. granulated garlic
1/2 Tbsp. white pepper
1 Tbsp. seasoned salt
1 1/2 sticks of butter or margarine (whichever you prefer)
6 c. minced clams, drained (save the juice)
6 c. chopped onions
1/4 c. all-purpose flour
5 c. water
6 c. whole milk
12 c. diced potatoes
You will need a two gallon pot and a large frying pan

Directions:

Chop the bacon into pieces. Add to your frying pan with the butter. Sauté the bacon, then add onions and sauté until onions are limp. Set this mixture aside, but do not drain. In 5 cups of water, add potatoes, garlic, season salt, white pepper and the clam juice. Cook until potatoes are tender. Set aside and do not drain. To the bacon and onion mixture, add the flour and make a roux. Mix the roux into the potato mixture, and bring to a boil. Stir down when the boiling point is reached and add the milk and clams. Do not allow the chowder to boil again once the milk is added. Serve hot with your favorite soup crackers as an entree or a meal. Enjoy! Serves 12-14.

Soups   *Submitted by: Clayton Nearhood and Bryan Wilson, Chefs*

226 Main Street
Millsboro, DE 19966
Phone: 302-934-5160
Facebook.com: Blue Water Grill

Join Josh and Jess Wiggins at the Blue Water Grill located on Main Street in downtown Millsboro, Delaware where you will find amazing homemade creations in a fun and friendly atmosphere. They strive for perfection and to provide a wonderful experience for their guests. The menu which definitely provides something for everyone, contains over 80 items with American flare. The restaurant is housed in a historic brick building dating back to 1900 with original brick work, tin ceilings, and hardwood floors.

Wild Mushroom Soup

1/2 gal. chicken stock
2 Tbsp. minced garlic
1 qt. heavy cream
2 lb. wild mushrooms
1 white onion
1/4 lb. butter
1/4 lb. flour

The atmosphere is comfortable in its contemporary design with nostalgic undertones. The Blue Water Grill seats 120 and provides a full array of delicious local brews and cocktails from the bar. Reservations and large groups are always welcome. The restaurant is open seven days a week with extended hours from Memorial Day to Labor Day.

Directions:
Add 1 cup of chicken stock to food processor with minced garlic (roughly chopped) and half of the mushrooms. Puree then return the mixture to the chicken stock, add heavy cream and simmer. In a large sauté pan, caramelize the white onions with butter and add flour slowly.

Reduce down to a roux, then add to soup mixture and simmer until desired thickness. Serves approximately 15 people.

Soups   *Submitted by: Josh Wiggins, Chef*

1285 Main Street
Panaca, NV 89042
Phone: 775-728-4800

Cindy-Sooz is a family owned and operated restaurant in beautiful downtown Panaca, Nevada. We specialize in homemade foods from hand pressed hamburgers, fresh cut fries, homemade soups, chilies, potato salads, coleslaw and much more. We are well known for grandma's homemade pies. (But that is a little family secret.) We pride our self on our cleanliness and hospitality.

Clam Chowder

3 strips bacon
1 onion
3 6 1/2 oz. cans clams
3 Tbsp. flour
3 med. potatoes
Salt and pepper to taste
1/2 tsp. Worcestershire
1 c. evaporated milk
1 c. half & half cream
1 c. milk
1 Tbsp. Bragg liquid aminos
4 Tbsp. butter

Directions:
Drain clams. Save juice and add water to juice to equal 2 1/2 cups. Fry bacon until crisp; remove from pan, sauté onion in bacon grease and add flour to onions. Add broth and potatoes. Cover and simmer until done. Add milk and butter, salt and pepper.

Soups   *Submitted by: Susan Austgen, Owner*

51 W. Main Street
Dahlonega, GA 30533
Phone: 706-867-8551
Fax: 706-867-0144

Come and enjoy a night of delectable creations at Corkscrew Café, located in the foothills of the Appalachian Mountains, just an hour outside of Atlanta. The Curry Squash Bisque is a perfect example of why the proprietors, Rob and Coleen Rotunno deemed "dining with a twist" their signature tag line. Dining at the Corkscrew Cafe is not just a great meal; it's a great experience.

Curry Squash Bisque

4 med. zucchini
4 lg. yellow squash
4 lg. carrots
1 lg. onion
1 Tbsp. shallots
2 Tbsp. garlic

2 oz. (weighed) roasted vegetable base
4 oz. (weighed) Masman curry paste
1 1/2 c. granulated sugar
2 tsp. ground curry powder
1 tsp. cinnamon
Olive oil

Directions:

Chop peeled zucchini, squash, and carrots in large chunks. Place them in a large stockpot. Fill water to approximately halfway point of the vegetables. Bring to a boil. Cook until vegetables are fork tender. They will make their own juices during the boiling process. Do not drain. Remove from stove. Puree with hand mixer. Set aside.

In large skillet, coat lightly with olive oil, combine onion, shallots and garlic. Sauté on medium heat until onions are translucent. Add vegetable base and Masman curry paste. Continue to sauté, stirring until dissolved. Add sugar, curry powder and cinnamon. Continue stirring until dissolved.

Combine sautéed ingredients into vegetable puree in stockpot. Blend until smooth. Add heavy cream and continue blending. Reheat on low, stirring frequently. Adjust taste as desired with sugar, curry powder or cinnamon. Yields 12 servings.

Soups   *Submitted by: Coleen Rotunno, Proprietor*

528 Main Street
South Portland, ME 04106
Phone: 207-773-4913

Deb's Sandwich Shop, formally known as Brodericks, was established in 1978. This family run business has been a local favorite for many years. It features quality home cooked meals.

Haddock Chowder

1 sm. onion
1/3 c. margarine
2 lb. fresh haddock
6 med. potatoes

1/2 tsp. salt
1/4 tsp. pepper
1 qt. half and half
1 qt. whole milk

Directions:
Sauté onion in margarine. Add salt and pepper. Peel and cube potatoes and add to onions. Add just enough water to cover potatoes, cook on medium heat for 15 minutes. Lay haddock on top of the potatoes; cover and simmer for 15 minutes. Add 1 quart of half and half and 1 quart of whole milk. Cook on medium heat until hot.

Soups   *Submitted by: Deborah Carter, Owner*

925 N. Main Avenue
Choteau, MT 59422
Phone: 406-466-3311
Website: www.elkcountrygrill.com

Jesse's mom started teaching him to cook at a young age, and he was required to cook a complete meal, with his mom's help, by age 10. Most of his soup recipes are his mom's, but this one is his own. After having this soup at another restaurant, he saw where it could be improved upon. It's one of the locals' favorites.

Cream of Potato and Italian Sausage

1/ 8 c. butter
2 Tbsp. chicken base
1/4 c. potato flour, for a gluten-free soup
(or regular flour if you want gluten)
1 qt. heavy whipping cream
2 qt. half and half

2 c. diced celery
1 c. diced onion
1/4 c. diced fresh parsley

1 Tbsp. basil
1 Tbsp. Italian seasoning
Garlic salt to taste

3-4 diced or cubed, cooked potatoes, skin on
(Be careful NOT to over cook potatoes)
1 lb. good quality Italian Sausage, diced or cubed
1 c. finely diced green leaf lettuce

Directions:
Over low heat melt butter; add chicken base and mix together. Add flour and mix well. Then add heavy whipping cream and half and half. Continue cooking over low heat. If not already done, dice up celery, onions and parsley, then add to soup. Now add basil, Italian seasoning, garlic, potatoes and sausage. Cook until 165° to 170°, then remove from heat. Add lettuce and serve.

Soups   *Submitted by: Jesse Crawford, Owner*

224 S. Main Street
Naperville, IL 60540
Phone: 630-717-0777
Fax: 630-717-7770
Website: www.heavenonseven.com

In 1980, the Bannos family - Mom, Dad, Jimmy and George - opened its concept of a "neighborhood restaurant in the middle of the loop." On the seventh floor of the Garland Building, the "New Garland Coffee Shop" was born. The Bannos' love of people, along with Jimmy's skill in the kitchen drew the customers in, and got them hooked. It was in 1984, while experimenting with Louisiana recipes, that Jimmy's real passion and talent for cooking emerged.

Duck and Sausage Gumbo

2 lb. boneless, skinless duck breasts, cut into 3/4 in. cubes
4 tsp. plus 1/2 tsp. Angel Dust Cajun Seasoning***
2 Tbsp. extra virgin olive oil
1 lb. andouille, cut into 1/4 in. slices
1 c. diced yellow onion
3/4 c. thinly sliced green onion, white and green parts
1/2 c. diced red onion
2 c. seeded, diced green bell pepper
1 c. diced celery
1 Tbsp. seeded, minced jalapeno
1 Tbsp. Roasted-Garlic Puree*

1/2 tsp. dried basil
1/2 tsp. dried oregano
1/4 tsp. freshly ground black pepper
1/4 tsp. ground white pepper
1/4 tsp. crushed red pepper flakes
1 sm. bay leaf
6 1/3 c. chicken stock
1 c. Dark Roux**
1/4 tsp. filé powder (see note)
White rice

Directions:
Toss the duck and 4 teaspoons of the Cajun seasoning together in a medium-sized bowl and set aside. In a large (7-quart) heavy Dutch oven, preferably enameled cast iron, heat the oil over high heat. When the oil is hot but not smoking, add the andouille and brown for 6 minutes, stirring frequently. Add the seasoned duck and cook for 4 minutes, stirring occasionally. Mix in the bell pepper, celery, jalapeno, and garlic puree, and sauté for 2 minutes. Add the basil, oregano, ground black and white peppers, red pepper flakes, bay leaf, and remaining 1/2 teaspoon of Cajun seasoning; cook for 2 minutes more. Pour in the stock and bring to a boil. Whisk in the roux a little at a time and stir continuously for 5 minutes. Reduce the heat to low and simmer uncovered for 1 hour, stirring occasionally to prevent the mixture from sticking to the bottom of the pan. Remove from the heat and stir in the filé powder. Do not let the mixture boil once you have added the filé powder. Remove the bay leaf. Serve with cooked white rice. Serves 6 people.

Soups

Recipe continued on next page

Recipe continued

*Roasted Garlic Puree

  1 c. peeled garlic cloves
  1 c. extra virgin or regular olive oil

Directions:

Preheat the oven to 300°. Place the garlic in a small ovenproof container and pour in the oil. Use additional oil if needed to completely immerse all the garlic cloves. Cover the container with aluminum foil and roast for 1 hour, until garlic is soft and light golden brown. Strain the garlic and place in a blender along with 2 tablespoons of the oil. Puree to a smooth consistency, adding a small amount of oil if necessary. Pour into a container and cover the top of the puree with a thin layer of the oil. Cover and store in the refrigerator. Reserve the remaining garlic-infused oil in another container and refrigerate. Makes 1 cup.

***Angel Dust Cajun Seasoning

  3 Tbsp. Hungarian paprika
  1 1/2 Tbsp. Spanish paprika
  5 tsp. salt
  1 1/4 tsp dried thyme leaves
  1 1/4 tsp. dried oregano
  1 tsp. ground white pepper
  1/2 tsp. dried basil
  1/2 tsp. ground red pepper
  1/4 tsp. black pepper
  1/8 tsp. garlic powder
  1/8 tsp. onion powder

Directions:

In a small bowl, combine all ingredients. Use as needed and store in an airtight container for up to 2 months. Makes 1/2 cup.

**Dark Roux

  2 c. canola oil
  2 1/2 c. all-purpose flour

Directions:

Heat oil in a 4-quart Dutch oven over high heat until very hot, about 3 minutes. Carefully whisk in the flour a little at a time until all the flour is incorporated. (The mixture will foam up as you add the flour, so add a small amount at a time.) Reduce the heat to medium and stir continuously, preferably with a flat-edged wooden spoon, for 22 to 25 minutes, until the roux is a dark brown. To prevent the roux from cooking any further, carefully pour it into a heat-proof bowl and cool for 45 minutes. Drain off any oil that separates from the roux. Store the roux in a covered container and refrigerate. Makes 2 cups.

Soon regular customers were going crazy over Jimmy's gumbo and red beans, demanding Cajun specials year round. Feeling a true affinity for the South, something he'd had even as a little boy, Jimmy and wife Annamarie headed for New Orleans to immerse themselves in the culture. In 1985, compelled by a real love for this food, the Bannos family transformed their neighborhood coffee shop into "Heaven on Seven." Aptly named to identify its seventh floor location, and to describe the heavenly clouds of steam wafting from Jimmy's scrumptious gumbo, "Heaven on Seven" was created with heart and soul. Jimmy's goal was then and is now for "Heaven on Seven" to be the best Louisiana style restaurant outside of New Orleans. Today a visit to "Heaven on Seven" will transport you right out of Chicago and down to the bayou. Stop in and see Jimmy and George, and join the impassioned throngs who can't get enough of this heavenly food with a devilish kick!

Soups

Submitted by: Chef Jimmy Bannos, Owner

1501 S. Main Street
Crookston, MN 56716
Phone: 218-281-9912
www.IrishmansShanty.com

Irishman's Shanty

Here in Crookston, Minnesota, we value our customers at the Irishman's Shanty. Paul Gregg, owner, says, "We aren't a tourist town; we don't have new customers every day. Our customers are the people in Crookston, the surrounding areas, and our neighbors down the street." Paul has been running the place for 23 years. You will find him here daily, and he does his work hands-on.

Beer Cheese Soup

1 stalk celery
3 carrots
2 onions
1/3 c. parsley flakes
2 Tbsp. onion powder
2 Tbsp. garlic powder
Dash black pepper
1 qt. beer
1 #10 can cheese sauce
2 bags cheese powder
Milk for thinning to your liking

Directions:

Chop all vegetables and put in large pot. Add enough water to cover. Add half of beer into it and boil until vegetables are soft. Add the cheese sauce, all the seasonings and remainder of beer. Stir, then add the powdered cheese. Stir and thin with water or milk to desired consistency.

Soups   *Submitted by: Paul Gregg, Owner*

158 E. Main Street
Newark, DE 19711
Phone: 302-737-6100
Fax: 302-737-6199
Website: www.klondikekates.com

Located in the center of life on Main St. in Newark, Delaware, Klondike Kate's Restaurant & Saloon serves both local families and nearby University of Delaware students alike. The combination of Klondike Kate's historical charm with its modern business philosophy has helped to make Klondike Kate's a staple in the Newark community for over 30 years. One of the oldest buildings on Main Street, Kate's Victorian architecture mixed with the youthful energy of the staff and guests makes for a very desirable atmosphere and uniquely rich culture. At Kate's, you will find that it is a dedication to a customer-driven way of thinking and a commitment to extreme customer service that keeps the students and local residents coming back time and again.

Crab Bisque

1 c. sherry wine
2 c. chicken stock
2 c. crab stock
1 qt. half & half
1/4 c. Old Bay seasoning
2 c. blonde roux
1 lb. lump crab meat

Directions:
Reduce sherry wine over high heat by half. Add chicken stock and crab stock and bring to a boil. Add Old Bay seasoning. Add roux while stirring with a wire whisk. Soup will begin to thicken. Cook while whipping for ten minutes. Slowly add cream. Bring to a boil while continuing to whip. Turn heat down to a simmer and stir occasionally for ten minutes. Add the crab meat and adjust consistency of thickness if necessary. Season with salt and pepper.

Soups   *Submitted by: Executive Chef Peter Shade*

8 W. Main Street
(PO Box 448)
Sunburst, MT 59482
Phone: 406-937-2233
Fax: 406-937-2234

The Last Chance Cafe Cooperative was formed in May of 2009 as a means of re-opening a cafe in Sunburst, Montana, population 400. The cafe opened July 8th of 2009, and now provides employment for both adults and high school students within the community. We also have several co-op members who volunteer tirelessly baking homemade hamburger buns, cinnamon rolls, muffins, cookies, brownies and desserts...all local family recipes (they also wash dishes). Our soups are famous, and the clam chowder is a particular favorite of our customers, some driving as far as 110 miles every other Friday.

Clam Chowder

Base
- 1 c. chopped celery
- 1 c. chopped onion
- 1/2 c. butter
- 6 – 5 oz. cans of chopped clams (30 oz. total)
- 1/2 lb. bacon, chopped, fried and drained
- 2 - 4 oz. cans sliced mushrooms
- 3 lg. baking potatoes, washed and diced (leave skins on)
- 3 lg. carrots, shredded

Roux
- 1/2 c. butter
- 1 c. flour
- 4 c. milk
- 1/2 tsp. each - salt, pepper, garlic salt
- 1/2 tsp. each - Lawry's Seasoned Salt, Alpine Touch, Dried Rosemary (crushed) and Dried Dill

Directions:

Using a large soup pot, sauté celery and onions in butter until tender. Drain clams, saving juice. Set juice aside to settle. Wash the clams in cold water to get out any sand or grit. Add to the sauté mixture. Add the chopped, fried bacon and sliced mushrooms. While that is cooking prepare the potatoes and carrots and add them to the pot. Add the clear clam juice to the pot (throw away any sediment). If needed, add enough water to cover everything. Bring to a boil, cool and refrigerate overnight. If time allows, on the 2nd day, bring pot to a boil again, cool and refrigerate. OR, on the 2nd day, bring pot to a boil and then let simmer while preparing the roux. The more time you can use to make this chowder, the better the flavor. The Roux: Melt butter and add flour to make a paste. Add 1/2 of the milk (2 cups) and cook until thick, (be sure and stir regularly to keep from burning). Add remaining milk and continue to stir until thick. Add all the seasonings. Add roux to the clam base and bring to a boil. Take off heat immediately. Taste and add additional seasonings if necessary. Enjoy!

Soups

Submitted by: Peggy Tobin, Manager

Lewis And Clark Cafe

601 Main Avenue
Washburn, ND 58577
Phone: 701-462-3668

Imoved from New Jersey to North Dakota in the 70's. I was introduced to many different foods I have never heard of. This is a German dish that people in this area really like, and it is easy to make.

Knoephla Soup

4 stalks celery, diced
1 med. onion, diced
3 carrots, diced
3 Tbsp. chicken bouillon
Knoephla (see recipe)
4 qt. water
1 qt. milk
1 pt. heavy cream
Salt and pepper to taste

Knoephla Dough
4 c. flour
2 eggs
1 1/2 c. water

Directions:
In 4 quarts of water, boil all veggies and chicken bouillon until tender. Drop Knoephla in and boil until tender. Add milk and cream and season to taste.

Knoephla dough: Mix all ingredients together to form stiff dough. Take some of dough and roll between hand and hard surface to form into rope, about the thickness of a finger. Cut with knife into pieces, approx 1/2 inch.

Soups   *Submitted by: Trudy Shoemaker, Owner*

924 Main Street
Waterboro, ME 04087
Phone: 207-247-5222

Our story goes as follows: I'm Lois, and I'm Shelly, and we are two small town girls that just happened to meet and become friends. Lois is from Hollis, and Shelly is from Waterboro. We met while working for a local restaurant a few years back. Soon we discovered that between us, we could do just about anything in the kitchen. If one of us had never cooked a particular recipe, you could bank the other one had. And the rest is history.

Shelly's Roasted Tomato and Basil Soup

9 lb. Roma tomatoes	1 1/2 Tbsp. black pepper
1 lg. sweet onion	1/4 c. sugar
50 cloves garlic	2 Tbsp. dried basil
2 Tbsp. kosher salt	2 c. olive oil

Directions:

Use two 9x13 baking pans. Slice tomatoes and onion, put into large bowl, add garlic and remaining ingredients and toss well. Put into two 9x13 pans. Bake at 350° for 1 hour and 15 minutes. Let cool and puree in blender. Reheat when ready to serve. You may add 1-2 cups of cream to this before serving.

Soups

Submitted by: Lois Merrifield & Shelly Nelson, Co-owners

159 Main Street
Groton, MA 01450
Phone: 978-448-9634
Website: www.mainstreetcafegroton.com

The Main Street Cafe of Groton offers a homemade selection of Yankee and European cuisine, specializing in breakfasts, lunches, and our evening Acoustic Cafe dinners. Signature dishes include Parisian style sweet and savory crepes, omelets, eggs Benedict, homemade Quiche, specialty salads, sandwiches, wonderful soups and hearty stews and bisques. It is a community meeting place with free Wi-Fi, and jazz playing softly in the background. We host a weekly Author's Table where local authors meet and discuss their books. Our weekly Acoustic Cafe features talented local musicians. Our guests enjoy wonderful music, gourmet dinners and BYOB.

Creamy Mushroom Soup with the House Special Salad

Roux
- 1/2 c. extra virgin olive oil
- 1 c. chopped white onions
- 2 Tbsp. garlic powder
- 2/3 c. flour

Soup
- 3 c. water
- 2 c. milk
- 6 c. mushrooms
- 1 c. sour cream
- Salt and pepper to taste

House Special Salad
- Mixed greens
- Craisins
- Candied pecans
- Goat cheese
- Serve with Balsamic Vinaigrette

Directions:
In 5 quart pot, fry onions in oil until translucent and tan on edges; add flour and fry until roux is light tan in color. Add garlic and black pepper and stir. Quickly pour in cold water and stir, add mushrooms, stir, bring to boil on medium heat. As the soup thickens, add milk and heat to boil. Bring down heat and simmer 10 more minutes. Then add sour cream, salt to taste, stir and serve. It is nice with a garnish of fresh parsley, scallions or chives. For salad: Mix ingredients together in a salad bowl and serve dressing on the side.

Soups   *Submitted by: Carolyn & Bob Wright and Laurie & Alex Otto*

100 S. Main
Royal Oak, MI 48067
Phone: 248-543-4300
Fax: 248-543-3132

This Southern favorite is a hearty cross between a soup and a stew. No need to worry about a second course with this dish. Your family and friends will leave the table with full bellies and smiles on their faces. I know ours do!

Kentucky Burgoo

10 oz. tomato paste
10 oz. tomato puree
2 qt. chicken stock
2 qt. pork stock

8 oz. beef, pork, & chicken, cooked
10 oz. diced potatoes
1/2 c. chopped celery
1 c. diced onions
1 c. diced green peppers
2 c. corn
2 c. lima beans
2 c. peas
2 c. carrots
2 c. black-eyed peas

2 Tbsp. minced garlic
1 bay leaf
1 tsp. black pepper

Dash Tabasco
1/4 tsp. Worcestershire

Directions:
Add first four ingredients to the pot and mix well. Then add remaining ingredients and simmer 2-3 hours.

Soups   *Submitted by: Danielle Lehner, Manager*

19 S. Main Street
Churchville, NY 14428
Phone: 585-293-1111

The Johnson House is owned by Peggy Naughton since 1977. They serve dinner Tuesday-Saturday. This unique dining facility draws customers from all over the Greater Rochester Area. Cozy, intimate dining, open Hearth, and music at the Baby Grand Piano every Friday and Saturday.

Thai Curry Seafood Soup

1 c. chopped leeks
4 Tbsp. grated fresh ginger
1 Tbsp. curry powder
1 Tbsp. diced fresh jalapeno
2 cans coconut milk
1 lg. can clams in clam juice
1/2 c. rice
3 Tbsp. fresh lime juice
Seafood choice – Shrimp, Scallops, Crab, etc.

Directions:
Combine first 4 ingredients in a saucepan and sauté 5 minutes. Stir in the coconut milk, clams with juice and rice. Bring to a boil, and then simmer 15 minutes. Stir in lime juice. Add seafood and simmer 4 minutes.

Soups   *Submitted by: Peggy Naughton, Owner*

800 N. Main Street
Buffalo, WY 82834
Phone: 307-684-7172

Pistol Pete's has been a family owned and operated restaurant for 10 years and was voted "Best Breakfast" in 2008 and 2009. The waitresses are hard-working and friendly. The atmosphere is very "Wyoming" and inviting. There's a variety of western memorabilia on the walls to attract you while your food is prepared. For a bit of heaven, try the blueberry pancakes, stuffed with whole berries, along with the generous portions of eggs and bacon. The French toast and omelets are also great. For the money, you really can't go wrong with anything on the menu.

Pistol Pete's Chili

55.5 oz. kidney beans with juice
55.5 oz. pinto beans with juice
13 oz. can diced green chiles
51 oz. salsa style tomatoes with juice
4 heaping Tbsp. mild chili powder
2.5 lb. hamburger
1 lg. diced onion
Salt and pepper to taste

Directions:
Brown hamburger and drain off fat. Season with salt and pepper. In large pot add all ingredients plus cooked hamburger. Stir and bring to boil. Boil about one hour. Add cheese and enjoy! Serves about 18.

Soups   *Submitted by: Matt and Tina Erlenbusch, Owners*

R & H Cafe

509 Main Street
Gabbs, NV 89409
Phone: 775-285-4019
Fax: 775-285-2630

Gabbs, Nevada, population 400 came into existence as a defense plant during World War II, when magnesium was needed for the war effort. Magnesite was mined from the Paradise Mountains just east of the town-site. R & H Café was built in one of the old bunk houses moved off the mine site. Owners Ray and Hazel Dummar prepare their food with care. Portions are large and the price is right.

Soup "Tomato Mac"

50 oz. can tomato soup
16 oz. can V8 juice
1 lb. hamburger
1 med. onion, diced
4 ribs celery
2 Tbsp. Cajun seasoning
16 oz. can diced tomatoes
3 c. elbow macaroni
Salt and white pepper to taste

Directions:
Dice onion and celery, and sauté. Add hamburger and brown. Drain grease from the hamburger. Add remaining ingredients plus one half soup can of water. Bring to a boil. Add the macaroni and stir until macaroni is soft.

Soups

Submitted by: Hazel Dummar, Owner

23 N. Main Street
Enfield, CT 06082
Phone & Fax: 860-741- 6969
Website: www.silviasrestaurant.com

Owner Silvia Salvari, a native of Romania, came to this country in 1984. She worked in various restaurants in New York and New England, sharpening her cooking skills. Silvia brought with her from Romania knowledge of Eastern European cuisine. Her father was an Austrian baker and taught Silvia the art of making breads in his bakery. She is a five time gold medal winner in the National Chef's Tasting Competition; and was an invited guest of the White House Chefs. Silvia personally selects fresh, quality food ingredients for the menu items and dinner specials she prepares. She bakes her breads fresh daily from all natural ingredients.

Cabbage Soup

5 lbs cabbage, shredded
1 c. carrots, diced
1 c. thinly sliced onions
1 c. finely diced celery
2 c. dried red kidney beans
1/2 c. oil
1 c. chopped onions, sautéed until crispy
1 c. diced tomato, sautéed until soft

1 c. diced green or red peppers, sautéed until soft
1/2 c. lemon juice
2 Tbsp. salt (optional) or 2 chicken bouillon cubes
2 Tbsp. fresh dill
2 Tbsp. parsley
1 c. sour cream
1/2 c. water
1 egg yolk

Directions:
Boil first four ingredients in first pot containing about 8 cups (1/2 gal of water). Boil kidney beans until soft in a second pot containing about 6 cups of water. Change water at least twice while cooking (make sure to use hot water when changing water in pot). In third pot, sauté onions, tomato and peppers until soft. Remove and add to pot #1. Strain beans when done and add to pot #1. Add lemon juice, salt (or bouillon cubes), black pepper, dill and parsley to pot #1. Allow pot #1 to boil for another 10-15 minutes, then turn off heat and put aside to rest. In a separate bowl, mix together sour cream, 1/2 cup water and egg yolk. Put into soup in pot #1 and stir to mix well. Note: Can last up to one week in fridge or can be frozen.

Submitted by: Silvia Salvari, Owner/Executive Chef

416 S. Main Street
Montrose, PA 18801
Phone: 570-278-2000
Website: www.summerhousegrill.com

> Summerhouse Grill, a hip little bistro housed in a renovated 1920's carriage barn with a warm post and beam interior and a wood-fired oven, specializes in putting locally-farmed food on each and every plate.

Indian Red Lentil Soup

3/4 c. celery, finely chopped
3/4 c. carrots, finely chopped
1 1/2 c. onions, finely chopped
Canola oil or other light blend of oil
to sauté these vegetables
1 1/2 Tbsp. curry powder (high quality, like Madras)
1 1/2 Tbsp. fresh garlic, chopped
1 Tbsp. ginger, peeled and grated
1 1/2 c. white or sweet potatoes, diced
1 c. peppers or green beans, chopped (optional)
2 c. red lentils
1 14.5 oz. can whole peeled tomatoes (or 2 c. fresh)
10 c. water

1 Tbsp. Punch Phoran*
Salt and pepper to taste

* Punch Phoran is an Indian Five Spice Mix (cumin seed, fennel seed, mustard seed, fenugreek seed and black onion seed.) Available from Kalustyan's Spice Shop in Manhattan. www.kalustyans.com

Directions:
Heat canola oil in large soup pot. Add chopped celery, carrots, onions and begin to sauté, stirring occasionally. Add curry powder, garlic, ginger and potatoes. Cook for 10 minutes, and if desired, add green peppers or green beans. Add red lentils, tomatoes and water. Add less water for a thicker stew and more water for a thinner soup. **IMPORTANT! Do not add salt before lentils have cooked, or they will not absorb water properly.**

Soups

Recipe continued on next page

Recipe continued

Cook on medium heat, stirring occasionally, until the lentils burst. Then add salt and pepper. Heat a small amount of canola oil in a sauté pan and add the Punch Phoran. Heat, stirring or tossing frequently, until the first sesame seeds pop. This pan-toasting releases the flavors of the spices. Add toasted spices to the soup and stir. Purée soup with a wand blender (or in batches in a blender) until only mild chunks remain. Taste and adjust seasonings as needed. Serve with a dollop of *Mint Yogurt.*

Mint Yogurt

To a strained 16 oz. of Greek yogurt, add:
    1-2 Tbsp. fresh mint, chopped fine
    1-2 cloves garlic, minced
    (adjust amount to taste)
    Juice of 1 lemon
    1–1 1/2 Tbsp. canola oil
    Salt and pepper to taste

Not only is the food local, it is also sustainably-grown and humanely-raised by some really cool people. Every bite you take supports local families and promotes a healthy, local food economy. Delicious, fresh and very real.

good farms. good food. good friends.

Soups   *Submitted by: Rob Bognar, Chef & Kim Glemboski, Owner*

28 N. Main Street
Ambler, PA 19002
Phone: 215-643-6760
Fax: 215-643-6762
Website: www.sweetbytescafe.com

We invite you to visit us, not only to taste our delicious food, but also to become part of the Sweet Bytes family.

Below is a recipe that is not on our menu, but has been in our family for generations! This stewed shrimp is reminiscent of etouffee, but the art of making roux is not necessary! Enjoy!

Sweet Bytes Family Stewed Shrimp

2 lbs. fresh or frozen uncooked shrimp, peeled and deveined (16/20 or larger)
(Reserve the shells if you peel them yourself.)
1 med. bell pepper, chopped
1 sm. onion, chopped
1-2 cloves of garlic, minced
2 c. chicken stock
1/4 c. vegetable oil
1 c. flour
Lawry's Seasoned Salt to taste
Pepper to taste
Old Bay Seafood Seasoning to taste

Directions:

Peel and devein shrimp, saving the shells. Rinse shrimp and blot them on paper towels. Keep damp. Spread the shrimp on a long sheet of waxed paper. Season with seasoned salt, pepper, and Old Bay. In a saucepan, put in shells and 1 cup of water over medium heat. Boil shells until they turn orange. You will use this shrimp "stock" later. In a large skillet, heat the vegetable oil. When hot, add bell peppers and onions; sauté for about 5 minutes. Add garlic and sauté for about 2 minutes longer. Remove the vegetables to a bowl to return to pan later. In handful batches, toss the seasoned shrimp in flour until coated, place in hot skillet and fry in oil until light brown. DO NOT OVER COOK! Remove shrimp, place on plate, and repeat with another handful batch. Continue this process until all shrimp are lightly browned. Return all the shrimp and vegetables back to skillet and add shrimp stock and enough chicken stock to cover. Cover and simmer over low-medium heat, stirring occasionally to loosen the coating and create the stewing gravy. Check seasoning level and add salt, pepper and/or Old Bay to taste. Cook for about 20-25 minutes. Shrimp should be pink and tender. Serve over steamed rice or hominy grits. Makes 4 servings.

Soups   *Submitted by: Lorraine Cuffey & Donna Mitchell, Mother & Daughter Owners*

219 N. Main
Newton, KS 67114
Phone: 316-283-3811
Fax: 316-283-3650
Website: www.newtonbreadbasket.com

This recipe for Chicken Borscht has been a long time favorite here at the Breadbasket. We offer a wide variety of soups here, and the Borscht has been the best seller for many years. Hope you enjoy!

Chicken Borscht

2 lbs. cooked chicken, cubed
1.5 oz. chicken base (or 2 bouillon cubes)
Stock from cooked chicken (or 5 c. chicken broth)
1 – 12 oz. or 16 oz. can diced tomatoes
3 Tbsp. onion flakes
1/2 t. salt
1 tsp. dill weed
1 bay leaf
1/2 tsp. white pepper
1 1/2 lbs. cabbage, chopped
1 lb. diced potatoes

Directions:
Place all ingredients except potatoes in pot. Add enough water to just cover cabbage. Bring to boil for just a few minutes. Remove from heat. Peel and dice potatoes in approximately half inch cubes. Cook until al dente. Remove from heat and drain. Add to soup along with a splash of heavy cream and enjoy.

Soups
Submitted by: George Eason, Co-owner

207 S. Main Street
Akron, OH 44308
Phone: 330-252-5128
Website: www.thelockview.com

The Lockview is located in Downtown Akron, Ohio across from the historic Akron Civic Theatre. Known for our gourmet grilled cheese sandwiches and delicious homemade soups, we also boast a craft and import beer selection of over 140 varieties. Although, at times butternut squash can be difficult to work with, the finished product of this signature soup will more than make up for it. Best served with good beer and good friends.

Roasted Butternut Squash Sweet Potato Soup

2 lg. butternut squash, peeled and cut into 1 in. pieces
4 sweet potatoes, peeled, cut into 1 in. pieces
2 Idaho potatoes, peeled, cut into 1 in. pieces
1 lg. red onion, peeled, cut into 1 in. pieces
1 lg. carrot, peeled, cut into 1 in. pieces
6 garlic cloves, peeled
4 Tbsp. olive oil
1/2 qt. chicken or veggie stock
2 c. heavy cream or half and half
1/8 tsp. nutmeg
3 Tbsp. brown sugar
Salt & pepper

Photo: W. M. Tanner Young

Directions:
Mix all vegetables together in a large bowl with olive oil and a pinch each of salt and pepper. Layer mixture in a large sheet pan and roast in a 350° oven for approximately 1 hour, turning vegetables over half way through. When vegetables are soft, put into stock pot with stock, cream, nutmeg, brown sugar and a pinch each of salt and pepper. Bring to a boil, reduce to a simmer for 20 minutes. Blend to a creamy consistency with a stick blender or food processor. Serves 6-8.

Main St. Pub

113 W. Main Street
Monticello, IL 61856
Phone: 217-762-9414

Nice relaxed pub atmosphere with good food. Watch sports on any of our six televisions while trying one of our many appetizers.

Jambalaya

2 Tbsp. butter
1/2 c. (1 stalk) sliced celery
1/2 c. chopped green pepper
1/2 c. (1 med.) chopped onion
1/2 tsp. finely chopped fresh garlic
1/2 c. uncooked long grain rice
1 c. cubed 3/4 in. cooked chicken
1 c. water
16 oz. tomato sauce
1/2 lb. spicy sausage link, cut into 1/4 in. slices
1 1/2 tsp. instant chicken bouillon granules
1/2 tsp. paprika
1/8 tsp. dried thyme leaves
1/8 tsp. cayenne pepper
1 small bay leaf
1/2 lb. (10-12) fresh or frozen raw shrimp, shelled, deveined, rinsed
Hot pepper sauce

Directions:
In 3-quart saucepan melt butter; add celery, green pepper, onion and garlic. Cook over medium heat, stirring occasionally, until vegetables are tender (4-6 minutes). Add all remaining ingredients except shrimp and hot pepper sauce. Cook over high heat until mixture comes to a full boil (3-4 minutes). Cover and reduce heat to low. Continue cooking, stirring occasionally, until rice is fork tender (20-25 minutes). Add shrimp; continue cooking until shrimp turns pink (4-5 minutes). Remove bay leaf, stir with hot pepper sauce.

Soups   *Submitted by: Terri Norman, General Manager*

710 Main Street
Springfield, OR 97477
Phone: 541-726-0622
Fax: 541-746-1768

Welcome to the Pump Cafe. We've been open for business over 12 years in the same location. Please join Ray, Eva & Trudy 6 days a week for breakfast & lunch. We will be open for dinner Fridays starting May 9th for the Springfield Farmers Market. Please join us for a memorable dining experience with excellent food & service.

Chicken & Green Chili Soup

1 onion
1/2 stalk celery, diced
16 oz. mild or hot green chili
1 1/2 tsp. whole thyme
1 Tbsp. garlic
1/4 tsp. salt
1/2 tsp. pepper
2 c. chicken stock
2 c. diced chicken

Roux
2 qt. half and half cream
1 qt. heavy whipping cream

Directions:
Sauté the first seven ingredients until tender, then add chicken stock. Bring up temperature to almost a boil and add enough roux to slightly thicken. Add chicken and cream and simmer a few minutes. Serve and enjoy. (Roux: Cook flour and oil together until browned.)

Soups   *Submitted by: Trudy Logan, Owner*

1 S. Main Street
Waterbury, VT 05676
Phone: 802-244-7827
Website: www.waterburyreservoir.com

The Reservoir Restaurant & Tap Room is locally owned and operated since 2009. It is located in a historic 1934 Federal/Greek Revival building, one of the oldest in town. The restaurant is known for having the most draft beers in Vermont (currently 38 unique drafts) as well as some excellent locally focused pub fare. Some notable items are the Rezitarian, a homemade vegetarian burger, and the Truck Driver, a one pound burger stuffed with blue cheese and topped with bacon, cheddar and a fried egg.

Down East Fish Chowder

1 lb. fresh cod	3 lg. russet potatoes
1 lb. fresh haddock	1/2 lb. butter
1 qt. heavy cream	Fresh parsley
1 qt. whole milk	Salt and pepper
3 Spanish onions	Oyster crackers

Directions:
Chop onion into 1/2 to 3/4 inch pieces. Clean fish, cut into large hand-sized pieces. Sauté onion until translucent in 1/4 pound of butter, then salt and pepper it. Peel and dice the potatoes into 1/2 to 3/4 inch pieces. Add milk and cream over onions. Slowly bring to low boil. Add potatoes and simmer for 10 minutes. Turn off heat and add fish and rest of butter. Stir and season with salt and pepper. Cover and let cool overnight in pot. Reheat and lightly break fish into pieces. Garnish with fresh ground pepper, chopped parsley and oyster crackers.

Soups   *Submitted by: Mark Frier, Owner/operator*

37 Main Street
Westerly, RI 02891
Phone: 401-952-2770
Website: www.theuprivercafe.net

The Up River Café was born in October of 2001. Owner, Daniel King, served as general manager of several restaurants in San Francisco for the Real Restaurant Group, Mark Miller and for The Plumpjack Restaurant Group. The Up River Café represents his vision for a classic neighborhood bistro. It offers friendly and attentive service, fresh, locally grown ingredients, bartenders with an understanding of the nuances of classic cocktails, and a unique and ever-changing wine list highlighting boutique American wineries.

Heirloom Tomato Salad with Chilled Cucumber Soup

Heirloom Tomato Salad

4 oz feta cheese
1 lb. heirloom tomatoes
1 Tbsp. fresh oregano, chopped
1/2 of a med. size red onion, shaved
2 tsp. lemon juice
2 tsp. olive oil
Salt & pepper to taste
1/4 lb. Arugula

Chilled Cucumber Soup

2 cucumbers
2 oz. Greek yogurt
1 Tbsp. olive oil

1 Tbsp. fresh dill, chopped
2 tsp. lemon juice

1 Tbsp. local honey
1 tsp. salt

Recipe continued on next page

Recipe continued

Yogurt Buttermilk Vinaigrette

1/2 c. buttermilk
2 Tbsp. Greek yogurt
1 clove garlic, minced
1 Tbsp. mayo or Miracle Whip (Optional)
1 Tbsp. local honey
3 Tbsp. lemon juice
2 tsp. dill, chopped

Directions:

Chop the heirloom tomatoes into 1/4 inch cubes and put in bowl. Add chopped oregano, crumbled feta, lemon juice, olive oil, shaved red onion and season. Mix and set aside.

Peel and seed the cucumbers and chop. Place all soup ingredients in a blender, except dill, and puree until smooth. Add chopped dill and chill. Place buttermilk in a mixing bowl and whisk in yogurt then remaining ingredients. Chill four soup plates or salad bowls. Pour chilled cucumber soup in bottom, just to cover about 1/4 inch deep. Mix tomato salad with Arugula and place in the center of the soup. Top the tomato salad with a couple of dollops of the vinaigrette. Serves 4.

The Up River Café is situated on the banks of the Pawcatuck River in downtown Westerly. The Up River Café's Executive Chef Terrence Maul most recently hails from the American brasserie Red Stripe, Providence's "Best New Restaurant" as named by Rhode Island Monthly's readers' poll. Before Red Stripe, Terrence was the Executive Sous Chef under the James Beard Award Winner, honored Chef, and television personality, Ming Tsai, at Blue Ginger in Wellesley, Massachusetts. Terrence graduated from the prestigious Culinary Institute of America (Hyde Park, New York campus) in 1994.

THE UP RIVER CAFE
AND COCKTAIL BAR

Submitted by: Executive Chef Terrence Maul

Main Street, Stowe, VT 05672
Phone: 802-253-4400 ext. 615
Website: www.thewhip.com

The Whip Bar & Grill has been providing travelers respite and refreshment for generations. Dining here is a pleasure to be savored where delicious, flavorful food is creatively prepared with distinctive quality Vermont food products and the freshest ingredients our local farmers have to offer.

New England Corn Chowder

4 strips cooked bacon, chopped
1 c. butter
2 c. flour
1 onion, chopped
1 c. celery, chopped
1/4 c. fresh parsley
2 lg. cans creamed corn
2 lg. cans whole corn
1/2 qt. heavy cream
Salt & pepper to taste
6 drops of Tabasco
8 c. chicken or turkey stock
4 c. potatoes, cooked & diced

Directions:

Melt butter in large stockpot over medium high heat. Add celery and onions and cook until soft and translucent, stirring occasionally. Add flour, stir and continue to cook over medium heat for 5 minutes. Slowly add stock, stirring rapidly to avoid any lumps. When all the stock has been incorporated, add cream and corn. Bring to a simmer, stirring often to prevent scorching the thick chowder. Once simmering, add remaining ingredients and season with salt and pepper. Approximately 12 servings.

As a proud member of the Vermont Fresh Network www.greenmountaininn.com/vtfresh.html, The Whip features an extensive menu of perennial favorites and innovative selections showcasing the bounty and flavors of each season.

    Submitted by: Steven Truso, Executive Chef

Salads

Main Street

623 Main Street
Manchester, CT 06040
Phone: 860-432-7755

Corey Wry, co-owner, graduated from Johnson and Wales University, Providence, RI. With his degree in hand, Corey traveled for 10 years all over the country picking up experience in various resorts, restaurants and hotels. When he got back to his hometown, he, Jesse Russo, Brian Dowd, Rich Tyrol and Tyler Miller launched Corey's Catsup & Mustard in the heart of his beloved hometown.

Buried Under Cheeseburger Salad

2 heads Romaine lettuce hearts, washed & chopped
6 oz. real blue cheese dressing
1 sm. tomato, diced
2 oz. chopped bacon
1 sm. red onion, sliced thin
2 sesame seed buns, tops only, made into 3/4 inch cubes left out to stale
4 slices cheddar cheese
1 lb. ground beef, fat content is totally your choice
Salt and pepper to taste

Directions:
Prepare charcoal or propane grill on high. Using all the ground beef, divide into 4 equal patties and season to preference with salt and pepper. Cook on the grill to your liking. When the burger is about 1 minute away from being finished, top with a slice of cheddar. When the cheese has melted, place each burger in the center of its own plate. In a mixing bowl, mix romaine lettuce with the blue cheese dressing and sesame top cubes. Divide the mixture evenly onto 4 plates, trying to mound it as high as you can. Top lettuce with tomato, bacon and onion. Serves 4.

Salads   *Submitted by: Corey Wry, Owner*

Cultural Delight

208 Main Street
Beckley, WV 25801
Phone: 304-250-0371
Website: www.culturaldelight.com

Welcome to Cultural Delight. Join us for breakfast any time of the day, or stop in with friends for lunch or dinner. Of course no meal is complete without trying out our homemade pies, cake, or biscotti. We are also available to serve all your catering needs.

Chili Chicken Salad

2 lg. boneless skinless chicken breasts
1 lg. onion
1 lg. green pepper
1 can dark red kidney beans
1/4 c. chili powder, divided
1 Tbsp. garlic powder or 1 clove garlic, crushed
1 Tbsp. paprika
1 sm. can tomato paste or 2 lg. fresh tomatoes
1/2 c. chicken broth
1 Tbsp. sugar
1 1/2 heads romaine lettuce
2 Roma tomatoes
1 med. cucumber

Directions:

Cut chicken, onion and green pepper into stir fry size strips and sauté. Add salt and pepper. As chicken is cooking add your tomato paste, garlic, half of the chili powder and paprika; cook for about 10 minutes. Add chicken broth and simmer on medium heat for about 5 minutes; add remaining chili powder, kidney beans, and sugar; cook an additional 5 minutes. Prepare the lettuce, tomatoes, and cucumber for your salad. Top the salad with the chili chicken mixture. At Cultural Delight we like to top this all time favorite with sharp shredded cheese, salsa, and sour cream and finish it off with a large handful of tortilla rounds on the side. The dressing of our choice (if you must) is Ranch; it seems to really bring out the flavor. This is one of the cook's favorite salads and once you have tried it, we are sure you will agree. Enjoy!

Salads   *Submitted by: JJ & Angie Belinga, Owners*

6 N. Main Street
Chagrin Falls, OH 44022
Phone: 440-893-9599
Website: www.freshstartdiner.com

The Sunshine Salad is by far the favorite salad in our diner. One of our customers, Chuck, eats lunch here 5 to 6 times a week, and his standing order is the Sunshine Salad. You can also visit our other location in Twinsburg, Ohio.

Sunshine Salad

4 c. mixed greens
1/2 of a good sized apple, cut into wedges
2 oz. mandarin oranges
2 oz. dried cranberries
2 oz. walnut pieces
2 oz. crumbled blue cheese
3 oz. raspberry vinaigrette dressing on the side

Directions:
In a large salad bowl place the bed of mixed greens. Add evenly, the mandarin oranges, dried cranberries, walnuts and blue cheese. Place the apple wedges along the edge of the bowl pointing outward. Serve with the dressing in a dish and a dinner roll and butter.

Submitted by: Robert Wyman, U.P/Operator

701 Main Street
Rochester, IN 46975
Phone: 574-223-7101
Fax: 574-223-7162

Jarrety's Place is a family owned local café. We specialize in Gourmet sandwiches, soups, coffee drinks and salads. We opened our doors in December of 2006 and have loved every minute of it. This is my favorite salad on the menu. I hope you enjoy it as much as I do. The homemade dressing really makes this salad, but it is good with bottled dressings also. We serve it with our cranberry walnut bread on the side. Enjoy!

Cranberry Blue Salad

Mixed greens in your favorite salad bowl
2 Tbsp. dried cranberries
2 Tbsp. crumbled blue cheese

2 Tbsp. salted sunflower seeds
2 Tbsp. Parmesan Peppercorn dressing
(recipe follows)

Directions:
Serve as a side or sliced grilled chicken on top. Serves 1.

Peppercorn Parmesan Dressing
1 oz. grated Parmesan
1 Tbsp. pepper
3/4 tsp. Accent
1 Tbsp. lemon juice
1 generous dash of Tabasco

1 tsp. Worcestershire
1/3 c. plus 1 Tbsp. cider vinegar
1 Tbsp. grated onion
1 tsp. pureed garlic
1/3 c. cold water
1 qt. mayo

Directions:
Put all in mixer bowl and mix until smooth and creamy - do not over mix!

Salads   *Submitted by: Dawn Peterson, Owner*

Julia's
Home Cookin'

529 W. Main
Ottumwa, IA 52501
Phone: 641-683-6911

Julia's is a small "mom and pop" restaurant. We have been open for nearly 8 years, serving breakfast and lunch. Owners are Jim and Julia Leichty. We open at 6 am Monday thru Saturday. We believe in bringing our customers fresh food, rather than frozen or processed food. Our meatloaf to our catfish are made from scratch. We cut and tenderize our own tenderloins, no pork fritters here, bread them in egg and milk, mix and cracker meal and fry them. When you order your hash browns or fries, we cut fresh raw potatoes at that time. I will have peeled the apples before you get a piece of our homemade pie. Most of our cooking is done in front of the customer, allowing you to see what you are truly getting and interact with the chef, (Jim).

Broccoli Raisin Salad

1 head of broccoli
1 1/2 c. raisins
6 strips of crisp bacon, crumbled
2/3 c. mayo
2/3 c. sugar
3 Tbsp. vinegar

Directions:

Cut broccoli into bite size florets, add raisins and bacon, toss well. In a second bowl, stir together mayo, sugar, vinegar and whip together well. Pour over the broccoli mixture. Enjoy.

Salads

Submitted by: Julia Leichty, Owner

119 S. Main Street
Mackay, ID 83251
Phone: 208-589-4861

The "Mine Hill Grill" was named in honor of Mackay's mining heritage. We enjoy people stopping by en route to many area activities year round. The hill at the end of Main Street has been converted to a self guided tour of the old mines. Mackay is also at the base of Mount Borah – the highest peak in Idaho. Trail Creek Road connects us with Sun Valley and Copper Basin. Copper Basin is a hot spot for camping and snowmobiling. We currently have over 100 items on our menu from burgers, chicken, wraps, pizza, salads, ice cream and deep fried Twinkies. We are very well known for our Burnt Lemonade which is made by flame grilling lemons before squeezing the juice out of them. We are the place to stop for down home atmosphere and a great meal. Come and see us in the center of beautiful Mackay, Idaho just off Hwy 93.

Ranchero Salad or Wrap

8 oz. grilled meat (steak, chicken, or shrimp)
1/2 c. sliced mushrooms, sautéed in olive oil
4 onion rings, baked crispy and chopped in pieces
4 oz. Pico de Gallo* (see recipe)
6 oz. shredded jack/cheddar cheese
4 6 c. salad mix lettuce

Pico de Gallo

4 fresh diced tomatoes
1/4 c. fresh diced onions
1/4 c. diced jalapenos
1/4 tsp. salt and pepper
1/8 c. cilantro
1/4 c. vinegar or lemon juice

Directions for Ranchero Salad:
Mix all ingredients for the Pico de Gallo together and set aside. Put lettuce on two plates, layer on mushrooms, Pico de Gallo, cheese, meat, and onion rings. Serve with a side of BBQ sauce or favorite dressing. Serves 2.

Directions for Ranchero Wrap:
Use all above ingredients except lettuce with two 12 inch tortilla shells. Spread cheese down the center of each tortilla and warm in microwave for approximately 30 seconds. Immediately layer in meat, mushrooms, Pico de Gallo, onion rings, and 1 tablespoon of BBQ sauce, fold over sides and roll up. Serve with fresh salad or fruit. Serves 2.

Salads   *Submitted by: Marianne & Paul Lanier, Owners*

943 N. Main Avenue
Springfield, MO 65802
Phone: 417-866-8744

Pappy's Place has stood at this location since 1904. While now housing a bar/restaurant, the store first began as a family-owned shoe repair shop. Shortly after that, the owners opened a grocery store and kept it that way until the 1920s. New owners opened a cafe on the property in 1924. Following Prohibition, the cafe applied for a beer-by-the-drink license. This license, which is still held by Pappy's, is the oldest continuous license in Springfield. Pappy's Place may be old, and not very well-known, but it is a place of character. The people are friendly, the food is good and the beer is cold. A casual atmosphere makes for a laid-back time. For many people, it is a place of good memories.

Shrimp Salad

3 lbs. shrimp cooked, peeled and deveined
2 fresh jalapenos, seeded, deveined,
finely diced or cut into fine slivers
2 green onions, sliced on the diagonal
1 red bell pepper, seeded,
finely diced or cut into fine slivers
1/2 c. chopped cilantro
Juice of 2 limes
Drizzle of olive oil
1/2 tsp. sugar

Directions:
Mix all ingredients in a large bowl and add salt and pepper to taste. Chill!

Salads   *Submitted by: Chef Jack Rauhoff*

500 N. Main Street
P. O. Box 388
Roswell, NM 88201
Phone: 575-623-1700
Fax: 575-624-2308
Website: www.peppers-grill.com

Peppers Grill & Bar is a family owned restaurant located in the heart of the UFO capital of the world, Roswell, New Mexico. For 20 years, Peppers has been a local favorite offering authentic, made-from-scratch regional cuisine along with other traditional favorites.

Southwest Cobb Salad

10 chicken breast fillets
1 8 oz. bottle French dressing

Pico de Gallo
2 med. tomatoes
1/2 c. diced red onion
1 Tbsp. chopped cilantro
1 diced fresh jalapeno
Salt to taste

1 pkg. Roast Works frozen roasted corn blend
3 pkg. Pre-made salad mix
8 oz. pkg. shredded Mexican blend cheese
10 sliced boiled eggs
Favorite salad dressing

Directions:
Marinate chicken in French dressing at least one hour in refrigerator. Grill until cooked throughout & sliced into strips. Mix 5 ingredients for the Pico de Gallo and combine with the package of thawed roasted corn. Place salad mix on plate. In rows, spread shredded cheese, sliced egg, chicken breast strips, and corn blend. Top with favorite dressing and serve.

Salads   *Submitted by: Robert Johnston, Chef/VP*

Phood on main
A Hip & Creative Eaterie

3737 Main Street - Suite 100
Riverside, CA 95201
Phone: 951-276-7111
Fax: 951-276-7117
Website: www.phoodonmain.net

We used to always joke about working on your PhD in food when we taught classes. When we opened the restaurant, we decided to call ourselves PHOOD on Main and our catering is PHOOD for Thought. Our customers even call themselves "Phoodies" and our tagline came from one of them, "Phood so delicious it dances in your mouth."

Papaya Spinach Salad

Baby spinach
Papaya, peeled, seeded and sliced
Strawberries, quartered
Almonds, slivered and toasted
Croutons

Dressing
1/8 sweet Vidalia onion
1/2 c. papaya seeds
1/2 tsp. dry mustard
1 tsp. salt
2 c. salad oil
3/4 c. sugar
1/2 c. apple cider vinegar
1/2 c. seasoned rice wine vinegar

Directions:
Cover salad plate with spinach. Top with a generous amount of papaya, strawberries, almonds and croutons. For dressing: Place onion and papaya seeds in food processor and buzz until pureed. Add dry mustard, salt and canola oil. Buzz again. Add sugar and both vinegars. Remove and pour into container for pouring. Drizzle dressing on salad. Eat and then dance!

Salads   *Submitted by: Lyn Cloninger & Marla Cohen, Owners*

280 N. Main Street
Manchester, NH 03102
Phone: 603-668-4077
Fax: 603-668-1477

Rita Mae's is the best on the west side, with bragging rights for the largest filet of haddock in the city. We have the best and biggest breakfast in town, and you can enjoy it all day. We also offer unique appetizers, and wait until you taste our desserts. We have a full liquor license and plenty of on-street parking in addition to a parking lot across the street.

Northern Beauty Haddock Salad

1 c. all purpose batter
1 lg. haddock filet
2 c. lettuce, chopped large
1/4 c. diced tomatoes
1/4 c. diced peppers
2 Tbsp. olive oil
1 dash of sugar
1 Tbsp. vinegar
1 Tbsp. lemon pepper seasoning

Directions:
Toss all salad items in a bowl. Dip haddock filet into all purpose batter. Deep fry to golden brown. On large pasta bowl place salad, then top with fried haddock and serve. Yummy!

Salads   *Submitted by: Mary Lou Carter, Owner*

Sweet Surrender
Breads & Confections

339 Main Street
Ririe, ID 83443
Phone: 208-538-7226

Sweet Surrender has operated for 12 plus years in a small farming community located 15 miles from Idaho Falls, Idaho. The local customers, who have become like family, gather here for coffee, lunch, homemade donuts and lively conversations. We focus on home-style cooking from scratch, fast friendly service, and the best French fries around, made only from fresh cut Idaho Russet potatoes.

Penne Pasta Salad

8 oz. (1/2 box) penne pasta, cooked and drained
1/2 c. Italian dressing
1 c. mayonnaise
1/2 c. milk
2 Tbsp. sugar
1/2 tsp. garlic salt
1/2 can olives, sliced
1/8 tsp. ground celery seed
1/8 tsp. black pepper
2 med. tomatoes, diced 1/2 in.
1/2 cucumber, skin on, seeded and sliced
2 Tbsp. grated onion
1 tsp. salt free seasoning (Mrs. Dash)

Directions:
Combine cooked pasta and Italian dressing. In a small bowl, mix mayonnaise, garlic salt, celery seed, and pepper. Warm milk, add sugar and stir until dissolved. Whisk into mayonnaise. Add to pasta, toss to coat. Add remaining ingredients.

Salads   *Submitted by: Sheila Mathews, Owner/Chef*

246 Main Street
Longmont, CO 80501
Phone: 303-651-0630
Website: www.terroir-restaurant.com

Opened in 2007 in historic "Old Town" Longmont, Colorado, Terroir serves seasonal, modern American cuisine with Mediterranean influences. True to their namesake, Terroir draws its inspiration - in and out of the kitchen - from characteristics specific to Colorado. Ingredients are always sourced from local purveyors, and the shotgun alley space has been carefully preserved, reflecting its turn-of-the-century roots.

Beet Salad with Walnut Crusted Goat Cheese and Beet Vinaigrette

6 baby beets or 2 mature beets
4 c. salad greens
1/2 c. fresh goat cheese
1/2 c. walnuts

Vinaigrette
1/4 c. red wine vinegar
1/2 tsp. dry mustard
1 Tbsp. sugar
1/2 tsp. salt
1/2 tsp. pepper
1/3 c. cooked beets
1 c. vegetable oil

Directions:

Peel beets and cut into wedges half an inch thick. Place in sauce pan large enough to hold the beets and cover with enough cold water to cover the beets by 2 inches. Add one tablespoon of salt and cook until the beets can be cut with a fork. The time will vary depending on how mature your beets are. The more mature (or dense) your beets are, the longer it will take. Make sure your beets have enough water as they cook since some water may evaporate. If this occurs, add more water to cover the beets. Once the beets are finished, drain the beets (reserve some of the beet cooking liquid), and cool. In a food processor, add 1/3 cup of the beets, the vinegar, mustard powder, sugar, salt, and pepper. Turn food processor on and puree until the beets are pureed into a liquid. Add the oil in a slow steady stream until the oil is entirely incorporated into the puree. If the vinaigrette gets too thick, thin with the reserved beet cooking liquid. Taste and adjust with salt, pepper, or sugar to suit your tastes. Toast the walnuts in a sauté pan on medium heat on your stove top until they begin to brown and are fragrant. Place the walnuts on a plate to cool. In a food processor, pulse the walnuts until they are broken down into small pieces but not ground to fine powder. Form the goat cheese into small balls roughly 1 inch around. Flatten into thick disks and press into walnuts to crust on both sides. Place in your refrigerator. Toss the salad greens with 1/4 cup of the vinaigrette and place on serving plates. Heat the goat cheese cakes and beets until the cakes begin to soften slightly and the beets are warm. Arrange the beets on each salad and place a goat cheese cake on top of each salad. Finish the salad by drizzling more vinaigrette on top of each salad. Enjoy!!!

Salads   *Submitted by: Tim Payne & Melissa Newell, Owner/Chef*

201 Main Street S.E.
Minneapolis, MN 55414
Phone: 612-312-2000
Fax: 612-259-0191

This is not your average plain Jane house salad! With multiple flavors and textures in each bite, this will without a doubt please your family and friends' palates. Best served outdoors while on a patio or terrace.

House Salad with Mango-Pineapple Vinaigrette

2-3 bags mixed field greens
10 oz. Muenster cheese (1/2" diced)
10 oz. Havarti cheese (1/2" diced)
10 oz. Gouda cheese (shredded)
15 oz. assorted dried fruit
(cherries, blueberries, golden raisins,
cranberries, apricots, apples & mangos)

Plate Garnish:
1/2 fresh pineapple - cored & sliced
2 Roma tomatoes - sliced thin
1 head Romaine lettuce
Mango-Pineapple Vinaigrette (See recipe)

Directions:
On your chilled salad plates, place 2 slices pineapple, 2 Roma slices, and 2 Romaine leaves toward plate edge. In a large bowl, mix salad with dressing. Add Muenster, Havarti, and half of the shredded Gouda. Add half of the mixed fruit and lightly toss with tongs. Evenly place salad on garnished plates, then sprinkle remaining Gouda and fruit on top.

Mango-Pineapple Vinaigrette

3 c. diced mangos (fresh or frozen)
1/2 fresh pineapple (cored and diced)
1/2 c. apple cider vinegar
1/2 c. olive oil
1 tsp. coriander

1 tsp. garlic powder
2 Tbsp. brown sugar
1 tsp. ground mustard
1/2 c. white wine
1 tsp. kosher salt
Dash of cayenne pepper

Directions:
In your food processor, add mango and pineapple. Pulse until smooth. Add all of the seasonings. While machine is running slowly, add wine, oil and vinegar. Mix until smooth. Serves 10.

1237 Lower Main Street
Wailuku Maui, HI 96793
Phone: 808-244-8774, Fax: 808-244-7841
Website: www.akscafe.com

A K's Café is a locally owned family restaurant, where we love to serve healthy casual fare. Our food is enjoyed by our friends, family, and lots of repeat tourists that we look forward to seeing year after year. Our food is fresh and full of great flavor, and you'll never leave hungry. As our Motto says: EAT BETTER!!

Mushroom Veggie Wrap

1 zucchini, sliced
1 red bell pepper, quartered
1 cucumber, sliced
1 carrot, shredded
1 tomato, sliced
15 med. mushrooms
1 c. broccoli, cut into small pieces
3 c. romaine lettuce, chopped
4 Tbsp. parmesan cheese, shredded
1 small bottle balsamic vinaigrette
12 Tbsp. Caesar dressing
6 12 in. soft tortillas

Directions:
Place sliced zucchini, quartered red bell pepper, and whole mushrooms in a Ziploc bag. Pour the balsamic vinaigrette over the vegetables and marinate, about 30 minutes. Preheat the grill. When the grill is hot, grill the zucchini, red bell pepper, and mushrooms until cooked, about 5 minutes. Place 2 tablespoons of Caesar dressing on the tortilla, and spread it around the tortilla. Place 1/2 cup of lettuce on each tortilla, followed by 1/4 teaspoon of parmesan cheese, 2 slices of cucumber, 3 pieces of zucchini, 1 piece of bell pepper, 2 mushrooms, and 1/4 cup broccoli. Fold the sides of the tortilla inward, and gently roll the tortilla to form a burrito. Cut in half and serve immediately with your favorite green salad. Follow these same steps for the remaining 5 wraps. Enjoy!!! Serves 6.

Sandwiches   *Submitted by: Elaine Nakashima, Owner and Executive Chef*

Anoka's Premier Coffee Shop

215 E. Main Street
Anoka, MN 55303
Phone: 763-421-5036

Home of the "Anoka Mocha" • 763.421.5036

Avant Garden is Anoka's premiere coffee shop, celebrating 15 years as "the place" in Anoka to gather. We are owned and operated locally and represent the perfect local flavor in Anoka. Home of the Anoka Mocha, our atmosphere is addicting. We're a quaint, simple and soothing place to relax, read or gather with friends. We are well known for our lunches, offering delicious Panini sandwiches, fresh and healthy salad choices, hot soup or bakery items. Come and explore our secret garden, and enjoy our artistic atmosphere while sipping your favorite coffee, tea, or a variety of other beverages.

Grilled Mushroom Pesto Panini

1 8" round focaccia bread
3/4 c. prepared pesto
2 c. fresh sliced mushrooms
2 c. fresh spinach
1 c. sliced green olives
4 slices white cheddar cheese
2 tsp. fresh basil

Directions:
Slice focaccia bread in half so you have 2 rounds. Spread pesto evenly over bottom half. Press spinach into pesto and layer with the mushrooms and olives. Top with cheese and sprinkle the basil over the cheese. Then put top half of focaccia on. Lightly brush with olive oil and grill for 4-6 minutes on Panini grill. Slice into wedges. Serves 6.

Sandwiches   *Submitted by: Paddywac Sisters, Owners*

9 E. Main Street
Berryville, VA 22611
Phone: 540-955-4317

The Berryville Grille Restaurant opened in December of 2009. Brian, Heidi and Fred set out to create a new experience in Berryville to "Serve Good Food and Good Times" to the people of the community. Down Home affordable meals is what you are going to find at the Berryville Grille.

Asian Sliders

2 1/2 lbs. ground beef
3 Tbsp. fine chopped ginger
2 Tbsp. fine chopped garlic
2 Tbsp. fine chopped cilantro
2 green onions, chopped
1/3 c. soy sauce
1/3 c. sweet chili garlic sauce
18 sm. rolls (party dinner rolls work great)
Leaf lettuce
Chili Garlic Mayonnaise
1 c. mayonnaise
1 1/2 Tbsp. spicy chili garlic sauce (Sambal)

Directions:
Mix all burger ingredients and form into 9 - 2 ounce patties. Cook to desired doneness. Mix the "spicy" chili sauce in the mayonnaise. Toast the buns on a griddle or in a pan if desired. Place a small piece of lettuce on the bottom bun. Place burger on top of lettuce and spoon a small amount of spicy mayonnaise on top of the burger, then place the top bun. Enjoy!!! This recipe serves 6 people three sliders each.

Sandwiches   *Submitted by: Heidi Grubb-McClemens, Owner*

192 Main Street
Somersworth, NH 03878
Phone: 603-692-4811

Back in the 1940's the building located on Main Street was an auto repair shop, but they shut down in the 60's. "Mill Side Grill" came in the early 80's. Then in the late 80's, they opened "My Brothers Place." Cindi worked part-time at both restaurants as a bartender. In 1996 it was bought by Mark Gauthier. He re-opened it in 1997 as "Loud Pipes Saloon." Cindi worked there during the 10 years he owned it and got married on the patio in 2002. He closed in 2007. A couple leased the place, remodeled it, opened in January 2008 and closed June 30, 2009. Mark and Cindi did a purchase and sales agreement, and Mark helped her get all her licenses and trade name. As of February 2010, Cindi bought the building. Cindi says, "I feel I'm part of the history of the building."

Daisy Burger

6 oz. ground beef patty
1 slice American cheese
2 slices cooked bacon
1 thin slice red onion

Leaf lettuce
1 slice tomato
2 thin slices honey ham
2 thin slices smoked turkey breast

We are open 7 days a week, serving breakfast, lunch and dinner with a full liquor license. We serve fresh seafood on the weekends. The patio will be open Memorial Day until fall to enjoy the outside.

Directions:
Cook beef patty with salt and pepper, then assemble on a Kaiser roll the remaining ingredients.

Sandwiches

Submitted by: Cindi Arseneault, Owner

623 Main Street N.
Kimberly, ID 83341
Phone: 208-423-4322
Website: Facebook

Our Hoagie Street Deli is locally-family owned by Greg and Darla Griggs since 1995. We offer over 50 specialty hoagies and breadless hoagie salads. Our salads are high protein, low carb meals and are ideal for personal diabetic and gluten needs. We do not use a grill or deep fry our foods. Our daily fresh-sliced meats and veggies, offer a welcome healthy choice on the street, for individuals who are looking for food choices without preservatives, fats, or grease.

Italian Combo Hoagie

1 pkg. hoagie buns:
(6) wheat or sour dough
2 slices pastrami
2 slices ham
3 slices Genoa Salami (4")
4 slices pepperoni
4 slices dry salami
3 slices lg. tomato
Red onion rings

1/4 c. chopped pepperoncini
Chopped romaine or green leaf
2 slices swiss cheese
2 slices mild provolone
Fresh parmesan cheese
Italian seasoning
Basil
Vinegar and Oil
Dijon Mustard

Pesto Spread
1/4 c. black olives
1/4 c. green olives
4 slices dill pickle
2 tsp. roasted garlic
Chop small in processor
Makes 6 hoagies

Directions:

Combine ingredients for Pesto Spread in food processor and chop very small. Makes enough spread for 6 hoagies. Above ingredients make 1 hoagie. Squeeze mustard on top and bottom bun. Alternate pastrami and ham onto wax paper. Spread pesto onto top bun and sprinkle onto the meat. Cover meat with one slice of each cheese. Micro for 2 minutes or heat in oven until edges become slightly red, curled and crispy. Sprinkle both seasonings and parmesan onto hot meat and cheese. Place 3 onion rings, pepperoncini, 3 Genoa Salami, 3 onion rings, pepperoncini, 1 slice of each cheese, 4 pepperoni (heat 25 sec), parmesan, sprinkle pesto, 3 onion rings, pepperoncini, 4 dry salami, 3 slices tomato, lettuce, vinegar and oil, sprinkle both seasonings, finish with heavy parmesan. Repeat the process for each hoagie.

Sandwiches   *Submitted by: Greg Griggs, Owner*

101 S. Main Street
Nicholasville, KY 40356
Phone: 859-885-7511
Website: www.mainandmaplecoffeehouse.com

Welcome to Main and Maple Coffeehouse, located in downtown Nicholasville, Kentucky! We strive to be a safe, welcoming place where people from all walks of life can gather to enjoy wholesome food, drinks, and fun. We always offer Free Wireless! At a time when everyone is looking to save $ - we wanted to remind people that we have a reputation for not sweating the small stuff. After all, "life is too short to be difficult!"

The Chicken "Quesa-nini"

1 lg. herb garlic wrap
3 oz. diced grilled seasoned chicken breast
2-3 oz. mild banana peppers
2-3 oz. sliced red onion
2 slices provolone cheese
1 slice pepper jack cheese

Directions:
Place 2 pieces of provolone cheese on half of the herb garlic wrap, then top with the diced chicken, onion, peppers and cheese. Fold the wrap in half, and place on a Panini grill for 4-5 minutes, until wrap is crispy and cheese is melted. Slice into 3 pie shaped wedges and serve with Vidalia onion dressing or a dip of your choice.

Sandwiches   *Submitted by: Michelle Kovach, Manager*

Main & Water Street
Wiscasset, ME 04578
Phone: 207-882-6128

Red's Eats has been in operation since 1938. Now owned and operated by Debbie Gagnon-Cronk, Cindy Gagnon-Collamore, David Gagnon & Joseph Gagnon, our famous signature sandwich is our Lobster Roll which has been featured in numerous publications and television shows including Food Network, CBS Sunday Morning, USA Today, and even Nippon Television in Japan. Our fresh Maine seafood and 70 other delicious menu items continue to delight guests from all over the world.

Lobster Roll

2 fresh Maine lobsters
Top split roll, buttered and grilled
Extra heavy mayonnaise, if desired
Drawn butter, if desired

Directions:
Boil salted water, cook lobsters for 15 minutes and then shut off heat, leaving covered for another 5 minutes. Pick out lobster meat and devein both tails. Pull tails into 2 sections each. Tear meat by hand...do not use utensils. Butter and grill roll until golden brown. Fill roll with torn body meat, knuckle and tail meat. Put one claw on each side of roll. Top with whole split tail. Serve with hot drawn butter and / or mayonnaise on the side.

Sandwiches   *Submitted by:* Debbie Gagnon-Cronk

611 E. Main Street
Boise City, OK 73933
Phone: 580-544-2844
Fax: 580-549-2868

The Rockin' A Cafe was established in February 2010, by the Axtell Family: Mark, Cindy, Heather, Remington and Colt. The cafe is operated daily by our family. The restaurant walls illustrate life in our community with framed photos of local people and places. The many signs hanging in our restaurant express local attitudes, such as, "A friend is someone who knows all about you but likes you anyway," and "You can't fix stupid." Our home-cooked fare and family setting bring many travelers back again and again.

Mexican Hamburger

We created this recipe to provide our customers with all the things they loved in one tortilla wrap. It has since become one of our top sellers in the cafe.

Hamburger patties
Favorite southwest seasoning
Whole green chiles, peeled
12 in. flour tortillas

Cheese Sauce:
2 cans aged cheddar cheese sauce
1 lb. Velveeta, shredded
1 lb. pepper jack, shredded
5 jalapenos, finely diced
1 red bell pepper, finely diced
1/2 pkg. fajita seasoning
1/4 c. lime juice

Green Chile Sauce:
1 can green chiles, diced   1 can cream of chicken soup
2 jalapenos   1 Tbsp. crushed red pepper

Directions:
Combine ingredients in Cheese Sauce and melt. For Green Chili Sauce, blend green chiles and jalapenos until smooth. Add cream of chicken soup and red pepper, and mix well. Heat and thicken with cornstarch. Fry hamburger patties which have been seasoned with your favorite southwest seasoning. Place some cheese sauce in the center of a tortilla. Place the cooked hamburger patty on top, then place one whole green chile on top of the patty. Fold the tortilla over all this, then cover with Green Chile sauce.

Sandwiches   *Submitted by: The Axtell Family, Owners*

216 S. Main
Burnet, TX 78611
Phone: 512-756-7636
Fax: 512-715-9074

Tea-Licious, locally owned and operated by Sam and Vicki McLeod since 1996, is located on the charming historic Burnet Square and known for its quality food and service, artistic tables, beautiful quilts, specialty gifts, catering and of course our famous peach tea and gourmet sweet pickles.

Cilantro Grilled Chicken Wrap

Grilled chicken
Romaine lettuce
Sliced tomato
Monterrey Jack cheese
Tomato basil tortilla wrap
Cilantro Sour Cream Sauce (recipe below)

Directions:
Spread a generous helping of cilantro sauce on your tomato basil wrap, then starting about one inch from one side spread the rest of the ingredients across in a straight line (romaine, sliced tomato, grilled chicken and cheese). Leave approximately an inch on the other side. Fold up the wrap "burrito style," bringing in the sides and roll tightly. You will get a better roll with a room temperature wrap. Grill the wrap on either an open countertop grill with a brick press or use a Panini grill. Serve with your favorite side.

Cilantro Sour Cream Sauce Recipe

2 c. sour cream
1 bunch fresh cilantro
2 oz. fresh squeezed lime juice
1 Tbsp. fresh minced garlic

4 oz. May Ploy Sweet Chili Sauce
4 oz. water
1 tsp. kosher salt
1 tsp. white pepper

Directions:
Blend well and puree in a blender till smooth. Place in a squirt bottle for easy serving and refrigerate. Recipe may be cut in half for smaller serving.

Sandwiches   *Submitted by: The Dedicated Kitchen Staff of Tea-Licious*

236 W. Main Street
Danville, KY 40422
Phone: 859-936-0001
Website: www.thehubcoffeehousencafe.com

Welcome to The Hub where people from all walks of life can enjoy great food, fellowship, and fun! We are proud to offer free wireless, made-to-order breakfast, lunch and dinner, and a friendly and welcome attitude that reflects our philosophy that "life is too short to be difficult."

"The Triple T"

Title Town Turkey

1 Ciabatta roll
1-2 Tbsp. whipped cream cheese
1-2 Tbsp. basil pesto
3-4 slices Roma tomatoes
2-3 slices smoked turkey breast

Directions:
Slice a Ciabatta roll in half. Spread the whipped cream cheese on the top half of the roll. On the bottom section spread the pesto, then top with the tomato slices and turkey. Place both sections together and grill on a Panini for 3-5 minutes or until the roll is crispy. Slice in half, serve and enjoy!

Sandwiches   *Submitted by: Jim Davis, Owner*

210 W. Main Street
Cavalier, ND 58220
Phone: 701-265-4848
Fax: 701-265-3304

Thompson's Cafe was established in 1979 and is owned and operated by Daryl and Kelley Thompson. It is open 7 days a week from 6 a.m. to 9 p.m. Thompson's Cafe offers a variety of services including: catering, senior meal programs, and in-town delivery. It specializes in homemade pizza, burgers, and traditional family style dinners, such as roast turkey, ribs, and walleye.

Santa Fe Wrap

2 chicken breasts, sliced or diced
1 pkg. fajita seasoning
1 Tbsp. diced tomatoes
1 Tbsp. diced onions

6 10 in. flour tortillas
2 oz. Blended Colby & Monterey cheese
5 oz. Homemade Chili (recipe below)

Directions:
Sauté chicken with fajita seasoning, diced tomatoes, and onions until golden brown. Wrap the chicken, cheese, and veggies in a 10 inch flour tortilla. Smother the wrap with the Homemade Chili and a nice handful of cheese. Side it with lettuce and cheese and enjoy this Thompson's Cafe Classic!!

Homemade Chili
10 lb. hamburger
2 c. diced onions
1 c. diced green peppers
1/2 c. diced jalapeño pepper
Pepper

Garlic salt
2 46 oz. cans tomato soup
1 6 lb. 6 oz. can diced tomatoes
1 6 lb. 14 oz. can chili beans
1 c. chili powder

Directions:
Brown hamburger with onions, green peppers, jalapeño peppers, and season with pepper and garlic salt. When the hamburger is browned, drain off the grease. Put the cooked hamburger back on the heat. Add the cans of tomato soup, diced tomatoes, chili beans, and cup of chili powder. Mix well and let simmer for about 45 minutes, stirring occasionally. Serves 50.

Sandwiches   *Submitted by: Kelley Thompson, Manager*

2637 Main Street
Lawrenceville, NJ 08648
Phone: 609-895-9885
Website: www.acaciacuisine.com

As executive chef, Joseph Immordino brings a wealth of knowledge and experience into the kitchen, and his creations have been winning praise for over a decade. From romantic meals to your next corporate event, Acacia brings innovative new approaches to fine dining and is breathing new life into the Lawrenceville restaurant scene. As always, Acacia features more than just your typical "fine dining" experience. We offer wine tastings, art and food exhibits, live music and other informal dining ventures. We are proud to meet any culinary challenge fathomable, and invite you to pull a chair up to our table and sample everything Acacia has to offer.

Barbecued Squab with Black Trumpet Mushrooms

2 Tbsp. honey
1/4 c. balsamic vinegar
1 c. extra virgin olive oil
Fresh sage
Fresh thyme
Fresh rosemary
1 lg. red onion, thinly sliced

2 whole squabs, cavity and backbones removed
Kosher salt and coarse black pepper
Chioggia beets
2 oz. black trumpet mushrooms
3 Tbsp. Dijon mustard
1 Tbsp. Worcestershire

Directions:
In a 2 inch pan, fit all the squab in one layer. Combine the honey, Dijon mustard, vinegar, olive oil, fresh herbs, and onion and mix well. Pour over the squab, making sure it is completely drenched in the marinade. Cover and refrigerate for 4 hours. Preheat oven to 375º. Remove squab from marinade and season with salt and pepper. Heat oil in pan and sear squab on both sides. Place cooked squab in baking dish, using any leftover marinade to coat before placing in oven. Add pre-sautéed roasted beets and mushrooms. Broil for 8 minutes or until medium rare.

Entrees   *Submitted by: Joseph Immordino, Chef*

2607 Main Street
Irvine, CA 92614
Phone: 949-387-8887
Website: www.andreisrestaurant.com

At Andrei's we believe in sustainability, which means buying from our local farms, using only seasonal ingredients and giving back to our community. We showcase the freshest local and organically-grown produce, as well as naturally raised meats and sustainable seafood in our "Conscious Cuisine." We incorporate only the finest ingredients into our recipes, utilizing seasonal fresh fruits and vegetables to provide unparalleled flavor and nutrition. Our culinary style incorporates the cultural diversity of California cuisine, emphasizing Mediterranean flavors and principles of the "Slow Food" movement.

Alaskan Halibut Wrapped in Basil & Pancetta Ham with Mediterranean Hummus, Fava Beans & Baby Fennel

4   6 oz. Alaskan halibut filet
4   1 oz. large pancetta ham slice
4 lg. basil leaves
12 oz. hummus
12 oz. blanched baby fennel
12 oz. fava beans, blanched, no skin
4 Tbsp. Greek yogurt
   (Drain overnight to remove any milk from the yogurt)
3 Tbsp. extra virgin olive oil
2 Tbsp. chopped mint
4 Tbsp. pomegranate molasses
4 Tbsp. any green herbs mix with dill & cilantro, parsley, tarragon

Kosher salt to taste
White ground pepper to taste
1/4 tsp. ground cumin

Directions:

Season the halibut with salt, pepper and cumin on both sides. On a cutting board, wrap the halibut with a basil leaf and then with a slice of pancetta ham. In a saucepan, cook the halibut over a medium flame with olive oil for 3 minutes each side. In a bowl, mix the Greek yogurt and chopped mint. Sauté the fennel and fava beans in olive oil until they have light coloration. Season. Display hummus on a plate, place the fava beans next to the hummus in circular fashion around the edge of the dish. Place the fennel over the hummus, then the halibut on top of all. Garnish the halibut with mint yogurt and herb salad. Drizzle pomegranate molasses around edge of plate. Serves 4.

Entrees   *Submitted by: Rick Boller, General Manager*

672 Main Street
East Haven, CT 06512
Phone: 203-469-2386
Fax: 203-488-4963
Website: www.antonios-672main.com

Welcome to Antonio's Ristorante in East Haven, Connecticut. Owned and operated by the Colavolpe family, Antonio's specializes in serving Old World Neopolitan fare with modern twists. At Antonio's, Chef Gina Colavolpe-DiLegge, previously the Executive Chef at Il Pranzo in Branford, Connecticut has re-created many favorite Italian dishes and also offers her patrons a variety of personal specialties. Antonio's boasts a quaint dining atmosphere with a casual, yet elegant flare. It is the perfect spot for all your dining needs - from casual family dinners to large parties.

Shrimp Scamponi

18 whole raw shrimp, peeled & cleaned
1 can straw mushrooms (or shittake)
3-4 garlic cloves (smashed, leave somewhat whole)
1 garlic clove, chopped
1/4 c. capers
1 peeled shallot
1/8 c. extra virgin olive oil
1 c. clam juice

1/4 c. cream sherry (cooking wine)
1 bag baby spinach
1/3 c. flour, seasoned to dust shrimp
1 sm. can whole tomatoes
Basil, chopped (to taste)
Parsley, chopped (to taste)
Salt and pepper to taste

Directions:
Put oil (lightly coat) into large sauté pan. Coat shrimp with flour; dust off excess. Let sit (do not move). Let cook about 2 minutes on each side. Remove from pan and set aside. If needed, add a little more oil. Add shallots and smashed garlic cloves and let cook a little; add mushrooms, capers, 1-2 tomatoes from can (break them up). Let cook. Deglaze with cream sherry and clam juice. Let simmer. Add basil and parsley and let simmer about 5 minutes. When ready, add shrimp and cook another 5 minutes. Turn heat off. In another sauté pan, heat oil (lightly coated) and add chopped garlic and spinach. Season with salt and pepper. Cook just until spinach starts to wilt. Put spinach in the middle of a platter or divide and individually plate. Top with shrimp and spoon sauce over. ENJOY! Serves 6-8.

Entrees   *Submitted by: Geri Colavolpe, Owner*

7618 Main Street
Sykesville, MD 21784
Phone: 410-795-1041
Website: www.baldwinsstation.com

Pan Seared Chilean Sea Bass with Butter Poached Snap Peas and Strawberry Poppy Emulsion

Strawberry Poppy Seed Emulsion

1 pt. fresh cleaned strawberries
1/4 c. poppy seeds
1 c. smooth Dijon mustard
1/2 c. brown sugar
10 oz. rice wine vinegar
1/2 gal. vegetable oil or blended oil of your choice
Honey to taste
Salt & Pepper to taste

Directions:

Strawberry Poppy Seed Emulsion:

Add mustard, 7 ounces of vinegar and brown sugar into mixing bowl. Mix ingredients, add blended oil slowly and consistently until all oil is incorporated. Add the rest of the vinegar if you wish to have a thinner emulsion. Add honey, strawberries, salt and pepper. At this point, mix until all ingredients are fully incorporated into emulsion.

Entrees

Recipe continued on next page

Baldwin's Station Restaurant
Historic 1883 Train Station
Overlooking the Patapsco River
Fine Dining • Rehearsal Diners • Receptions
Indoor or Outdoor Areas Available
Seating 2-200 People
Award Winning Chef
Eclectic Collection of Entrees

Dearie's ingenious and creative approach to the restaurant industry has turned Baldwin's into much more than a one-of-a-kind destination providing exceptional food and outstanding service. He features live concerts of nationally known Jazz, Folk, and Bluegrass artists and offers Children's Theatre performances as well. He is able to blend the visual, the audible and the edible and continues to win new fans with the Station's antique setting, contemporary cuisine, and fascinating entertainment.

Recipe continued

Pan Seared Chilean Sea Bass

   8 oz. Chilean sea bass filet
   2 oz. blended oil
   Salt & pepper

Butter Poached Snap Peas

   3 oz. fresh snap peas
   4 oz. unsalted butter
   Salt & pepper

Directions:

Pan Seared Chilean Sea Bass:
Pat dry sea bass filet and season with salt and pepper. Add 2 ounces of oil to sauté pan; heat until a faint trail of vapor appears to be rising from the oil. At this point add the sea bass and sear for several minutes on each side until a nice golden brown crust forms. Finish fish in the oven, for 6-10 minutes at 400°.

Butter Poached Snap Peas:
Heat butter in pan to 165°. Season snap peas and add to butter; let poach until al dente. Remove from butter, adjust seasoning and serve immediately.

Garnish:
Tomato *concasay, small diced and sprinkled around the plate with mixed mescaline greens in citrus bowl and crispy tortilla strips. (*Tomato concasay is peeled, seeded and diced.)

Entrees   *Submitted by: Darrick Granai, Executive Chef*

721 Main Street
Shelbyville, KY 40065
Phone: 502-437-5678
Fax: 502-437-5677
Website: www.BellHouseRestaurant.com

Bell House Restaurant is a locally owned and operated family business that opened in June of 2009. Nestled in the heart of Downtown Shelbyville, they are located in a renovated home that is more than 100 years old.

Pasta Primavera with Grilled Chicken

Chicken breast
Pesto
Garlic powder to taste
Salt and pepper to taste
2 Tbsp. canola oil
3/4 c. broccoli florets, steamed
1/3 c. baby carrot,
sliced and steamed
2 Tbsp. minced garlic
1/2 c. red bell peppers, diced
4 oz. cavatappi pasta, cooked and drained
1 Tbsp. pesto sauce
1/4 c. chicken broth

1/3 c. Roma tomatoes, diced
1/4 c. parmesan cheese, shredded
2 Tbsp. chopped parsley

Our chef John Lewis was trained at the French Culinary Institute in New York City and was the Executive Sous Chef at Tavern on the Green. Our cuisine is Italian & French - American for dinner, and for lunch we serve a variety of soups, salads, and sandwiches. We use fresh herbs and vegetables for the best flavor.

Directions:

Cover top of one chicken breast with pesto, garlic, salt, and pepper. Bake in oven at 365° for 13 minutes (ovens may vary). When done cooking, place on cutting board and slice into 4 or 5 strips. Heat canola oil in a skillet. Sauté broccoli, carrots, garlic, and red bell pepper until warmed (3-4 minutes). Add cavatappi pasta, pesto sauce, and chicken broth. Heat through. Transfer pasta and vegetables from skillet to a plate. Lay strips of chicken vertically on pasta, to make a mountain top. Garnish with diced Roma tomatoes, parmesan cheese, and parsley. "Voila!!!"

Entrees   *Submitted by: Mary Andriot Miller, Administrator*

35 S. Main Street
Cohasset, MA 02025
Phone: 781-383-0464
Website: www.biabistro.com

Bia is a labor of love for Chef/owner Brian Houlihan. He has fashioned a gem in historic Cohasset Village, MA. Combining city-level quality with suburban charm, he sprinkles magnificent Southern French–New Italian fare with thoughtful touches. But it's the service - carefully timed and discrete - that ultimately sets the stage for an enchanting evening. While his roots are in Ireland, Chef Brian Houlihan has made a home for himself on the South Shore with his New Celtic Cuisine - a fine blend of European Cooking Techniques and the use of abundant local product. Chef Houlihan's 'Love for Food' is apparent by tasting any one of his numerous award-winning dishes.

Crisp Duck Confit with Roasted Sweet Potatoes

Duck Confit
   2 c. kosher coarse grain salt
   1 c. sugar
   1 tsp. coriander
   2 tsp. cumin
   8-10 Frenched duck legs
   1 pt. duck fat

Roasted Sweet Potatoes
   2 1/2 lb. sweet potatoes, peeled and diced
   2 oz. duck fat
   Salt and pepper
   1 Tbsp. rosemary

Directions:

Duck Confit: Mix all dry ingredients to make a curing salt. Pat curing salt on dry, washed duck legs, and allow to cure for 24 hours in a refrigerated, air-tight container. Remove from refrigerator; wash and pat dry. Cook in a casserole dish with duck fat in a 350° oven for 2 hours. Remove from oven and place each duck leg, skin side down, in a skillet to brown. Roasted Sweet Potatoes: Toss diced sweet potatoes with duck fat, rosemary, salt and pepper and roast for 45 minutes at 350°. Top Roasted Sweet Potatoes with Crisp Duck Confit Leg and serve with local grilled, organic vegetables.

Entrees   *Submitted by: Chef Brian Houlihan*

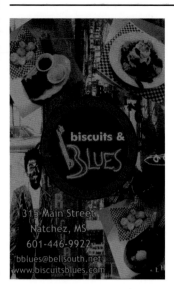

315 Main Street
Natchez, MS 39120
Phone: 601-446-9922
Fax: 601-445-7777
Website: www.biscuitsblues.com

Biscuits & Blues was founded by my sister Regina Charboneau in 1995 in San Francisco. I opened Biscuits & Blues in 1998 on Main Street in Natchez, MS using the family recipes. This dish is best served with a white wine.

Grilled Shrimp with Penne Pasta

Penne sauce
1/2 lb. butter
2 Tbsp. white wine
2 minced garlic cloves
16 oz. cream cheese
1 Tbsp. Tony's Creole seasoning
1/2 c. chopped green onions
2 Tbsp. flour
1 qt. half & half cream
2/3 c. parmesan cheese

Directions:

Melt butter. Add white wine, Tony's Creole seasoning, minced garlic and green onions. Sauté for 3-4 minutes. Stir in flour smoothly; add cream cheese and half and half cream, mix well. Blend in parmesan cheese. Boil penne noodles and drain. Grill 6 shrimp, peeled, no tails. Put pasta on plate, cover with penne sauce. Top with grilled shrimp. Serve with a small dinner salad and bread.

Entrees

Submitted by: Peter Trosclair, Owner

...Mount Horeb's downtown cornerstone

101 E. Main Street
Mount Horeb, WI 53572
Phone: 608-437-9463
Fax: 608-437-9465
Website: www.hoffbistro101.com

Bistro 101 brings the best of the Midwest and Mediterranean to the Madison area in a gorgeous atmosphere. Serving a seasonally changing menu, guests dine on fresh fish and seafood, flavorful steaks, pasta as if you were in Italy, Mediterranean-influenced appetizers, undeniably the best burger around and so much more. House-made desserts vary weekly, but often include Mocha Crème Brûlée and Flourless Chocolate Cake.

Greek Chicken

8 10-12 oz. bone-in, skin-on chicken breasts

Marinade

1 Tbsp. dried oregano
1 Tbsp. dried thyme leaves
1/2 tsp. kosher salt
1/2 tsp. cracked black pepper
1/4 c. olive oil
3/4 c. canola or vegetable oil

Filling

1 lb. feta cheese
Zest of 2 lemons
1 Tbsp. dried oregano
1 1/2 tsp. granulated garlic
1 Tbsp. dried thyme leaves
1/2 tsp. cracked black pepper

Directions:
Pre-heat oven to 350°. Marinade: Whisk all marinade ingredients together in a large container.
Filling: In food processor, blend all filling ingredients until they form a smooth paste. Make a 1 inch long slit in each chicken breast and gently move knife around to make a pocket for stuffing. Using a small spoon, stuff each chicken breast with the feta filling and secure closed with two toothpicks. Place all chicken breasts into marinade and refrigerate for 3-4 hours.

Entrees

Recipe continued on next page

The custom-made bar boasts a variety of Wisconsin beers along with the best Margaritas for miles. And, if you're searching for a great glass of wine, search no more. The humble, but growing wine list features offerings from California, Oregon, Spain, France, Italy, Australia, Chile and more.

Recipe continued:

Garlic cream sauce

    1 qt. heavy whipping cream
    15 garlic cloves
    1/4 c. olive oil
    1/4 tsp. kosher salt
    1/4 tsp. cracked black pepper

Directions:

Picture courtesy of: Heather H. Gallina

Garlic cream sauce:
Place peeled garlic cloves and olive oil in oven-proof pan; cover with foil and roast in 350° oven for 50-55 minutes. Remove the garlic cloves from the oil; they should be soft, golden & tender. In a large sauté pan, pour in the heavy whipping cream and add the garlic cloves, salt and pepper. Stirring occasionally, reduce the sauce by half over medium to medium high heat. Using the back of a wooden spoon, mash the garlic cloves to release their flavor.

Roasting the chicken:
Remove chicken breasts from the marinade and place them skin-side down on a roasting pan that has been heating up in a 425° oven. After 15-20 minutes, turn the chicken breasts skin-side up and cook until all juices run clear. (Bone-in chicken is considered completely cooked at 180°.) Serve with the Greek Chicken and Garlic Cream Sauce, mashed potatoes and sautéed seasonal vegetables.

Entrees   *Submitted by: Lisa Boté, Owner & Kevin Reible, Chef*

32/34 Main Street
Warrenton, VA 20186
Phone: 540-428-1005
Fax: 540-428-1006

Chef Todd and his wife Liz don't believe that their guests should have to dress up or pay high dollar for quality, fresh, locally grown, gourmet food. The Bistro is a casual pub featuring Virginia beers on tap, local wines and a menu utilizing as much fresh, seasonal and local ingredients as possible.

Summer Time Flank with 3 Pepper Salsa

2 flank steaks (grass fed)
Salt and pepper to taste

3 Pepper Salsa

1 bottle your favorite ale
1/2 c. soy sauce
1/2 c fresh cilantro
5 jalapenos, fresh
5 poblano peppers, fresh
10 serrano peppers, fresh
2 heirloom tomatoes
1 red onion

1 tsp. fresh rosemary
1 tsp. cumin
1 tsp. fresh oregano
2 tsp. garlic
1/4 c. red wine vinegar
1 c. tomato juice
1/4 c. olive oil

Directions:

Season flank steak with salt and pepper. For salsa: Mix together ale, soy sauce and 1/4 cup cilantro. Pour mix over steaks and marinate at least one hour. Deseed all peppers, and thinly slice. Place in mixing bowl. Dice tomatoes and red onion; add to bowl. Chop all herbs and garlic; add to bowl. Add rest of ingredients and mix well. Refrigerate 1 hour, season with salt and pepper. Grill flank to desired temperature; thinly slice. This can be served a variety of ways: in a tortilla, fanned around a warm potato salad, or on a garden salad. Top it with your 3 pepper salsa and enjoy these fresh summer flavors!

5 Main Street
Bristol, VT 05443
Phone: 802-453-3311
Website: www.bobcatcafe.com

The Bobcat Cafe and Brewery is a community supported restaurant and brewery that serves creative comfort food and a dozen house brewed beers seven nights a week. Our venison and chorizo meatloaf has remained a local favorite even as the rest of our menu changes with the seasons.

Vermont Venison and Chorizo Meatloaf

2 onions, diced small
1 green pepper, diced small
1 red pepper, diced small
3 stalks celery, diced small

10 cloves garlic, minced
2 Tbsp. fresh thyme, minced
2 Tbsp. fresh oregano, minced
2 Tbsp. fennel seed
1 Tbsp. chili flake

2 lb. ground local venison
2 lb. ground pork

4 links chorizo, medium diced
1 c. ketchup
1/2 c. balsamic vinegar
1/2 c. Worcestershire
1/2 c. soy sauce
1/4 c. kosher salt
4 eggs
8 c. Panko bread crumbs

1/2 can chipotle peppers in adobo, pureed
1 c. ketchup

Directions:

Sauté onions, peppers, and celery until soft. Add garlic, herbs, fennel seed and chili flake. Sauté until fragrant. Cool vegetable mixture and add to remaining ingredients. Mix thoroughly. Bake in 8 ounce soup cups for 8 individual loaves. Bake at 350° for about 45 minutes. To serve, remove from cups and top with pureed chipotles mixed with remaining ketchup. Bake until the chipotle ketchup turns slightly brown.

Entrees   *Submitted by: Erin Chamoff and Sanderson Wheeler, Co-Chefs*

519 Main Street
Covington, KY 41011
Phone: 859-491-7777
Website: www.bouquetrestaurant.com

Bouquet Restaurant and Wine Bar, located in the heart of Mainstrasse Village in Covington, Kentucky offers an extensive wine list and a seasonal menu of contemporary American cuisine which features locally grown ingredients. This recipe in particular embodies the style of one of our featured entrees.

Filet with Orange Madeira Sauce

2 – 8 oz. filets
1 lb. quartered red skin potatoes
1/2 lb. trimmed green beans
1/2 lb. quartered button mushrooms
1 clove of black garlic, sliced

Chopped rosemary and parsley to finish
Salt and pepper to taste
1 c. Madeira wine
1 c. orange juice

Directions:
Bake potatoes and mushrooms at 350° for 15-20 minutes, until golden brown. Combine Madeira and orange juice in a non-reactive pan and reduce by 2/3 or until the consistency of a thick soup. Pan sear or grill mark filets on both sides, then cook filets for 6-8 minutes at 400° until desired temperature is reached. In a hot skillet coated with olive oil, sauté green beans, potatoes, and salt and pepper to taste. Drizzle Madeira sauce over filet, top filet with black garlic, and enjoy!

Entrees   *Submitted by: Stephen Williams, Chef/Owner*

Downtown

614 W. Main Street
Louisville, KY 40202
Phone: 502-582-1995
Fax: 502-582-3536
Website: www.bristolbarandgrille.com

The Bristol Bar & Grille is locally owned and operated since 1977. Our first location in the Highlands of Louisville was the kickoff to what is now known as "restaurant row." The Bristol now operates five full-service restaurant locations and a full-service catering/commissary operation. Known for many of our menu items, our staples are the Famous Green Chili Wontons and The Bristol Burger, both of which have been recognized in publications such as Southern Living, Food & Dining and Louisville Magazines.

Paella Valenciana

3 oz. extra virgin olive oil
2 oz. minced yellow onion
1 tsp. chopped garlic
1 oz. thin sliced green pepper
2 oz. thin sliced red pepper
2 oz. diced raw chicken
2 oz. monk fish or any other firm fish, such as lobster pieces
2 oz. chorizo

2 c. white rice
1 pinch saffron
1 Tbsp. crushed tomato
3 1/2 c. chicken stock
1 tsp. cracked black pepper
1 tsp. salt
6 large shrimp
3 oz. calamari, cut in rings
8 fresh mussels
1 1/2 oz. green peas

Directions:

In Paella dish or 12 inch iron skillet, sauté onion, garlic, peppers, diced chicken, monk fish, or lobster pieces, and chorizo; cook until tender. Add rice, saffron, crushed tomatoes and stir together on medium to low heat. Add chicken stock and cracked black pepper. Cook for 6 minutes on top of stove, occasionally stirring. When done, arrange the remaining seafood and place on top; then cover with foil and cook 12 minutes in oven at 400°. Remove from oven and let sit for 5 additional minutes. Serves: 2 People.

Entrees

Submitted by: Chef Ramon Forcelledo

1804 E. Main Street
Russellville, AR 72801
Phone: 479-968-3360

Brown's Catfish, locally owned since 1988, operates in its original location on Main Street in the center of the beautiful Ozark Mountains of Arkansas. Brown's is an "All you can eat" buffet featuring the "Best Southern Fried Catfish Around" with all the trimmings. In addition to the variety of seafood items on our buffet, we have served banquets and caterings all over the Arkansas River Valley. The following recipe is one of the most requested of those offerings.

Chicken Marsala Ozark Style

2 lb. chicken tenders
1 red bell pepper
1 yellow bell pepper
1 green bell pepper
1/2 med. onion
4 oz. sun dried tomatoes

1 sm. can mushrooms
(stems and pieces)
4 oz. shredded carrots
1 garlic clove, crushed
1 c. chicken broth
1 c. Marsala wine
1 c. seasoned flour

Directions:
Sauté garlic in butter slowly till clear. Wash and prepare tenders, dredge in seasoned flour. Remove chicken and deglaze pan with wine, then add chicken broth. Add peppers, onion, tomatoes and carrots to pan and simmer 3-5 minutes. Add mushrooms and reintroduce chicken to the pan, season to taste. Cover and place in 325° oven for 20-25 minutes. Serve over wild rice or Linguini noodles. (Can be made ahead and placed in the oven on warm.)

Entrees   *Submitted by: Al Brown, Owner*

599 W. Main
P O Box 750149
Torrey, UT 84775
Phone: 435-425-3070
Website: www.cafediablo.net

Cafe Diablo is nestled along Utah's Scenic Highway 24, near the entrance to Capitol Reef National Park, in the tiny western hamlet of Torrey, Utah. Located just four hours south of Salt Lake City, Cafe Diablo is open for dinner seven days a week, from 5:00 to 10:00 p.m., mid-April to mid-October.

Pumpkin Seed-Crusted Trout

4 (6-8 oz.) trout fillets
1/2 c. flour
1/2 c. egg wash
1 c. unsalted green pumpkin seeds, slightly crushed
2 Tbsp. oil

Lime Butter Sauce

1/2 c. white wine
Juice of 2 limes
1 oz. chopped cilantro
6 Tbsp. butter
Salt to taste

Cafe Diablo opened in June of 1994 and specializes in innovative Southwest cuisine. It provides an excellent selection of Southwestern entrees, small plates, and unique specialties of the house. The Cafe also features local products and organically grown fruits and vegetables. Groups, private parties, and catering are also available.

Directions:

For the trout, coat the meaty side of the trout fillets with flour. Dip in the egg wash and then in the pumpkin seeds. Heat the olive oil in a 10-inch sauté pan and add the fillets seed side down. Sauté over medium heat for 5 minutes or until the seeds are brown. Turn the trout and sauté for 5 minutes longer. Bake at 325° for 5 minutes. Remove to serving plates. For the sauce, add the wine and lime juice to the sauté pan. Bring to a boil over high heat and reduce the heat. Simmer for 2 minutes. Add the cilantro, butter and salt. Cook over high heat until thickened and creamy, whisking to mix well. Spoon over the fish. Serves Four.

Entrees

Submitted by: Gary Pankow, Owner/Chef

CAFE LEBANON
RESTAURANT & CATERING

1390 Main Street
Springfield, MA 01103
Phone: 413-737-7373
Website: www.cafelebanon.com

At Cafe Lebanon we are dedicated to providing you with outstanding Middle Eastern style food and top quality service in an elegant, yet relaxed atmosphere. We cordially invite you to Cafe Lebanon to experience all that we have to offer. Locally owned and operated in Springfield and East Longmeadow, Massachusetts, we are conveniently located close to US 91 in downtown Springfield on Main Street and in East Longmeadow on Shaker Road. We hope that our superior wait staff and fine Middle Eastern cuisine will encourage you to become one of our many repeat customers!

Simmered Chicken Over Hashwee' Rice Topped With Roasted Pine Nuts, Almonds and Gravy

3-4 lb. chicken
2 c. rice
1 tsp. black pepper
1 tsp. allspice
1 1/2 tsp. ground cinnamon

1/2 lb. ground beef (80-20)
1/4 c. pine nuts
1/4 c. sliced almonds
2 cinnamon sticks
2 bay leaves

Directions:
Boil chicken with 2 cinnamon sticks and 2 bay leaves till tender (approximately 1/2 hour). Take out of water and drain broth. You'll need 3 cups of broth. Cook ground beef in pot with all spices. Do not drain grease. Add rice and broth and let cook on low flame approximately 12-15 minutes. While rice is cooking, separate meat from bone and set aside. Sauté pine nuts and almonds with a little oil. When done, set on paper napkins to drain. Serve chicken over rice and top with pine nuts, almonds, and gravy.

Our specialty food combines both Eastern and Western culinary influences. These influences include French, Mediterranean, North African, and traditional Middle Eastern cuisine. Lebanon's cuisine is a "melting pot" of flavors which provide a tantalizing feast for not only the stomach, but also for the eyes. Lebanese food is dominated by healthy grains, vegetables, light oils, and low fat grilled meats. Vegetarians will find more palatable options at Cafe Lebanon than at other area restaurants.

831 Main Street
Winchester, MA 01890
Phone: 781-838-6092

It started with a dream and ended with reality for 24 year old Alessandra Siniscalco who started the business at the age of 18. Beginning in a basement Cafe with only 4 seats, decorated with Old Italian traditions from the closets and attics of her grandparents, Alessandra started with imported Italian gelato and pastries and a real Italian espresso bar. Alessandra slowly started introducing food to her young establishment. Now, five years later her little cafe has flourished and is now a full Italian Trattoria with cathedral height Italian architecture and four season gazebo, seating nearly 60 people.

Clam, Shrimp, and Lobster Habanero

1 whole large lobster, boiled and pulled
20 littleneck clams
10 jumbo shrimp, peeled and deveined
1 sm. habanero pepper, seeds removed and chopped
1 c. white wine
(Preferably Fianno Di Avellino, Mastroberardino)

2 c. vine ripe tomato sauce,
(or any basic tomato sauce recipe from home)
Extra virgin olive oil (high quality)
2 cloves garlic, hand minced
2 stalks scallion

Directions:
Lightly coat a 14 inch sauté pan with the olive oil. Add garlic and heat until garlic just starts to lightly brown. Toss in clams, and stir to lift any garlic from the bottom of the pan. Add the wine, habanero, and one chopped scallion stalk. After the clams start to pop open and 1/4 of the wine has burnt off, add two cups of vine ripe tomato sauce, *(we make a sauce from fresh vine ripe tomatoes, onion, and white wine with basil and sea salt and it's a stock that slowly cooks all day and is one of our favorite entrees as well as a basic tomato sauce to use in almost any recipe).*
Stir well to see the colors of the vine ripe tomato sauce start to become lightened by the wine and the clams' stock. Add the shrimp and cover. Once the shrimp and clams have been cooked, lower heat and add the pulled fresh lobster meat and stir just to warm the meat without over cooking it. You may add the legs of the lobster for added flavor and garnish. In a separate pot boil linguini or bucantini pasta (or any of your favorite spaghetti-like pastas). Plate the pasta first and pour the broth with the seafood on top. Slice the remaining stalk of scallion the long way and lay them on top for garnish. Serves 2.

Entrees   *Submitted by: Alessandra Siniscalco, Owner*

265 S. Main Street
Yuma, AZ 85364
Phone: 928-782-0499
Website: www.Carlarenees.com

Carla Renee` is locally owned by Carla Renee` and Dick Gravley and located in Historical Downtown Yuma, AZ. For locals and visitors alike, Carla Renee` has become a regular spot for lunch, pre-theatre drinks and a nice evening out. Carla Renee` and Executive Chef Kyle Splawn regularly introduce new recipes to delight their guests and they take pride in their homemade creations. They find inspiration from family recipes (such as Paprika Pork Chops) and American standards, while adding their own contemporary twists. Favorites from their menu include Kobe Sliders, Steamed Shrimp Wontons with a Creamy Chili Sauce, Lamb with a Blackberry Port Sauce and Fresh Fish Daily.

Paprika Pork Chops

8-10 bone-in pork chops (about 1/2 in. thick)
1/2 c. all purpose flour
4 tsp. salt
1/2 tsp. freshly ground pepper
3 tsp. paprika
6 Tbsp. butter
4 c. heavy cream

Directions:
Combine all dry ingredients in a large Ziploc bag. Put a few pork chops in the bag at a time to fully coat each one and then set aside. Heat the butter in a large skillet, brown both sides of the pork chops and then remove to a warm plate on the side. When all pork chops have been lightly browned on both sides, whisk remaining flour mixture into the skillet. Whisk until flour has combined with the butter, about 2 minutes. Then slowly stir in the heavy cream and return the pork chops to the skillet with the cream sauce. Cover and simmer for 1 hour. Serve on a bed of rice with sauce over the top. Fabulous! Serves 8.

Entrees   *Submitted by: Carla Renee', Owner and Kyle Splawn, Chef*

108 W. Main Street
Newark, DE 19711
Phone: 302-369-9414
Fax: 302-369-9567
Website: www.deerparktavern.com

The Deer Park Tavern has been a landmark in Newark since 1851. After the original St. Patrick's Inn burnt to the ground, the present building was erected using materials found locally in the Newark area. The Deer Park, once considered one of the finest hotels on the East Coast, has also housed a barbershop and a ballroom, been used as a woman's seminary, a political meeting place, and a polling location. One thing that has never changed is the welcoming atmosphere and the tradition of serving great food and drinks with good fellowship and cheer.

Lemon Rosemary Roasted Chicken

Whole Chicken
Salt
Pepper
1 Lemon Rind
Rosemary
Lemon Juice
Olive Oil
Bread Crumbs

Directions:
To prep, chop off the ends of the chicken legs just above the ankle. Cut the skin and tendon just above the elbow. Pull off forearm leaving just raw bone on elbow. This is called Frenching. Remove back bone. Stuff the inside of the chicken with salt, pepper, one lemon rind, and rosemary. Tie the outside of the chicken together with butcher's twine to keep the legs in close to the breast to ensure even cooking. This is called trussing. Season the skin of the chicken with chopped rosemary, salt, pepper, lemon juice, olive oil and bread crumbs. Cook the chicken, breast up, on 375°, until internal temperature of 165° degrees. Allow 10 minutes to rest before cutting. Remove string carefully and garnish with grilled lemons.

Entrees   *Submitted by: Chef Brian Ashby*

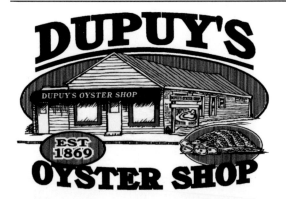

108 S. Main Street
Abbeville, LA 70512
Phone: 337-893-2336
Fax: 337-898-3188
Website: www.dupuysoystershop.com

Jody and Tonya Hebert have owned this restaurant since 1998. The restaurant was established in 1869 at this same location. This recipe was created by Jody Hebert, Chef/Owner.

Eggplant Dupuy

(Fried eggplant topped with shrimp and tossed with herb cream sauce)

2 whole eggplants
5 c. bread crumbs
1 pt. buttermilk
1 qt. heavy cream
2 c. diced Tasso
1 Tbsp. dry basil
1/4 c. chopped green onions
1 Tbsp. minced garlic

1 Tbsp. chopped parsley
1/2 c. margarine (melted)
1 c. flour
1 lb. baby shrimp (peeled)
1 tsp. salt or to taste
1 tsp. black pepper or to taste
1 qt. vegetable oil

Directions:

Peel eggplant, slice in 1/4 inch thick medallions. Dip eggplant in buttermilk, then in bread crumbs; repeat twice. Set aside eggplant until later. In a medium saucepan, pour heavy cream, Tasso, basil, green onions, minced garlic and parsley. Cook for 15 minutes on medium heat, stirring occasionally. In a small bowl, mix melted margarine and flour to make a white roux until thick paste forms. Add small amounts of roux to cream mixture until slightly thick. Add shrimp, salt and pepper. Cook until shrimp are done. Fry eggplant in vegetable oil until golden brown. Place eggplant on plate, add shrimp and Tasso herb cream sauce on top of eggplant. Excellent appetizer for 8 or entrée for 4. (Recommend serving with pasta.)

Entrees   *Submitted by: Jody Hebert, Chef/Owner*

925 N. Main Avenue
Choteau, MT 59422
Phone: 406-466-3311
Website: www.elkcountrygrill.com

We don't live close to the ocean, but we can still come up with some wonderful seafood ideas that are so delicious and easy to do. It's a nice surprise to those passing through our town, and also for the locals, to come up with something everyone will like.

Crab Alfredo

3-4 oz. crab meat per person
1 Tbsp. of Pinot Grigio wine
1/4 c. butter
1 c. heavy cream
2/3 c. freshly grated parmesan cheese
Salt and pepper to taste
12 oz. linguini pasta

Directions:

Melt the butter in a large pan or skillet. Add the cream and bring it to a boil. Simmer for 5 minutes, stirring, and then add the parmesan with salt and pepper. Turn off the heat under pan.

Bring a large pan of salted water to a boil. Drop in all pasta and bring back to boil, stirring occasionally. Cook according to directions on package, or a little less to have them al dente. Drain well. Sauté crab in butter and Pinot Grigio, to warm up meat. Turn heat back on low under the sauce and add in pasta noodles; toss noodles until coated. Place on plate, then add crab meat. To garnish, add fresh parsley and fresh grated parmesan cheese. Serves 4 people.

975 Main Street
West Warwick, RI 02893
Phone: 401-821-8FEN (8336)
Website: www.FensExpress.com

Fen came from Shanghai in May 1981, and she started Fen's Express in May 2009 so she could bring authentic Chinese food to Rhode Island. Her tasty signature dishes make your mouth water, offering items from many well-known cuisines. Fen's serves authentic Chinese cuisine with exciting dishes and unique ambiance. At Fen's, every dish is created using only the freshest and finest ingredients. She uses choice meats and seafood, Jasmine rice, and vegetables that are fresh from the market. Fen's authentic menu and cooking create a truly enjoyable meal.

Black Pepper Shrimp

12 lg. shrimp
1/8 c. salad oil
1 Tbsp. salad oil
1/2 tsp. sesame oil
2/3 c. green & red pepper, triangular cut
1/3 c. zucchini, .3 x 1 in. cut
1/3 c. onion, triangular cut
1/8 c. green scallion
3/4 tsp. garlic salt
1 1/2 tsp. ground black pepper

Directions:
Heat clean pot or wok for 10 seconds. Pour 1/8 cup salad oil into pot or wok and heat to 250-300ºF. Add Shrimp into pot or wok and stir quickly for 30 seconds, then remove from pot or wok. Reheat the pot or wok for 5 seconds. Then add 1 Tablespoon of salad oil. Stir garlic salt and black pepper into the chopped vegetables, then place in pot or wok over high heat and stir fry for 60 seconds. Add 1/2 teaspoon of sesame oil and stir for 10 seconds. Place finished product into serving dish.

Entrees   *Submitted by: Hua Fen Wang, Owner*

203 Main Street
Hamilton, MT 59840
Phone: 406-363-4567

The Filling Station Grille is located in beautiful downtown Hamilton, Montana. Known for our authentic New Mexican Cuisine and hometown hospitality, the Filling Station features fresh Hatch green chili to create our homemade dishes. Voted the most hospitable restaurant, and best soup in the Bitterroot Valley. While dining our patrons enjoy the fun and nostalgic atmosphere of an old time gas station.

Chicken Stuffed Sopapillas

(A Filling Station Favorite)

4 c. flour
1 Tbsp. baking powder
2 tsp. sugar
1 1/2 tsp. salt
1/4 c. lard

1 1/4 c. water, or more if needed
4 c. cooked shredded chicken
2 c. shredded sharp cheddar cheese
Green chili sauce

Directions:
Sift dry ingredients together. Cut in lard until crumbly. Slowly add water and mix until dough holds together. Knead 10-15 times or until dough forms a smooth ball. Cover and let set for 20 minutes. Divide dough into two parts. On a lightly floured board, roll dough to 1/8" thickness. Cut the dough into 5 inch triangles. Do not allow the dough to dry. Be sure to cover the dough waiting to be fried. When ready to fry, turn upside down so that the surface on bottom while resting is on top when frying. Fry in 4 inches hot oil until golden brown, turning once. Add only a few at a time to maintain proper temperature. Allow sopapillas to cool just enough to slice. To fill the sopapilla, gently cut a slit around two edges of the sopapilla. Using a spoon, fill the sopapilla with shredded chicken and top it with green chile sauce and shredded cheese. Serve with a side of Spanish rice and pinto beans. Garnish with lettuce and tomatoes.

Entrees

Submitted by: Raina Young, Owner/Chef

350 E. Main Street
Marlborough, MA 01752
Phone: 508-357-8883
Fax: 508-357-8884
Website: www.fireflysbbq.com

Walk into one of our restaurants, and in addition to receiving a warm welcome with Southern-style hospitality, you'll be greeted by the mouthwatering aromas of authentic American bar-b-que. We smoke our meats for up to 12 hours, blending apple, cherry and hickory woods to create the signature red smoke ring that identifies the genuine low-fire, slow-cooking process of true bar-b-que.

Grilled Cider-Brined Pork & Apricot Pizza

6 oz. apricot preserves
1 1/2 tsp. Dijon mustard
1 1/2 tsp. parsley, chopped

1 (12-16 oz.) pizza dough, fresh
6-8 oz. smoked mozzarella cheese, shredded

8-10 slices Vidalia onion, 1/2 in. thick
Olive oil
Salt to taste
Black pepper, fresh cracked to taste

1 (12-16 oz.) pork tenderloin, cider brined
1 oz. scallions, shredded

Directions:
Combine the apricot preserves and Dijon mustard in a small saucepan. Constantly whisking, heat over a medium heat for 6-8 minutes and continue whisking until smooth. Add parsley and remove from heat. Drizzle onions with olive oil and sprinkle with salt and pepper. Place onions on grill for 3–5 minutes, carefully turning halfway through. Roll out pizza dough on a lightly flour dusted surface. Brush the dough with olive oil and place on grill until cooked, 3 to 4 minutes on each side. Remove dough from grill and brush with apricot preserve mixture. Take pizza dough and spread the grilled Vidalia onions over the preserves. Sprinkle the mozzarella cheese over the top and set aside.

Entrees

Recipe continued on next page

Recipe continued:

<u>Place cider brined pork tenderloin</u> on a medium hot grill and cook until desired doneness. Remove the tenderloin from the grill and place on plate to rest. Place pizza on low grill heat and cover until the cheese is melted or can be finished in a 350° oven, heating until the cheese is completely melted. Slice the pork tenderloin on the bias and place on top of the cheese. Sprinkle with scallions. Cut pizza and serve immediately. Yield: 1 pizza.

Cider Brine

    16 oz. apple cider
    16 oz. water
    1/4 c. salt
    1/4 c. brown sugar
    4 1/2 tsp. black pepper, cracked
    1 tsp. sage, ground
    1/2 tsp. cinnamon
    1/8 tsp. nutmeg
    1/8 tsp. mace

Directions For Brine:
Blend ingredients well. Place meat in brine for a suggested time of 2 to 24 hours before grilling. Yield: 2 quarts.

We offer two different styles of ribs and mop sauces from around the South including North Carolina, Tennessee and Texas. In addition to bar-b-cue, you'll find many other Southern specialties on our menu including Cracklin' Bread, Fried Chicken, Red Beans 'n Rice, Sweet Potato Pecan Puddin' and more!

Entrees

Submitted by: Steve Uliss, Owner/Chef

401 N. Main
Hendersonville, NC 28792
Phone: 828-694-1030
Website: www.flightwoodgrill.com

Your total dining experience begins the moment you walk in the door of Flight, from the stunning flowers in the vestibule to the pleasant greeting from the hostess. The original 1920s bank building is softened with retro-modern décor. A mobile of three hundred handmade birds glides overhead. Contemporary and colorful artwork adorns the walls while hand-blown glass graces the niches along the wall. Notice the leafy wrought iron balcony railing. Soft jazz plays in the background while the apple wood grill sizzles with everything from salmon to filet mignon.

Grilled Grouper with Sautéed Spinach, Pecans and Bacon

4 pieces of grouper - 6-8 oz. each   8 oz. toasted pecans
1-2 lb. spinach   1 lb. bacon

Directions:

Grill grouper until firm. Fry the bacon and reserve oil for cooking spinach. Place spinach in sauté pan and cook until tender. Place cooked fish on plate and top with spinach first then pecans and bacon. Would be great with mashed potatoes served family style or a nice rice pilaf and some rosemary biscuits and honey butter.
Serves 4.

Flight offers several distinct dining options: On the main floor, there is the hustle and bustle of friends and families gathering together. The bar is a convivial place for those dining alone to meet friends yet unmet or for those who want a quick bite. On the balcony level, the booths and small tables, some overlooking Main Street, offer more privacy and an opportunity for romance. The Vault, so named because it once housed the bank's safety deposit boxes, is now home to selected bottles of fine wine. It is available for private parties. Flight is the only restaurant in Hendersonville, NC to offer such an extensive wine list and 40 wines by the glass. The premiere restaurant of Hendersonville, NC!

Entrees   *Submitted by: Rob Keener, Executive Chef*

901 N. Main Street
Cottonwood, AZ 86326
Phone: 928 634-3829
Website: www.fstopfood.com

We are Old Town Cottonwood's inspired dining spot. We are a casual lunch venue using only the best ingredients from specialty suppliers, and we offer a variety of items. For dinner we offer Chef Rick's delicious creations. Our specialty pizza is another dinner offering. Stop in soon, whether it's for a sandwich at lunch or a take-out order.

Veal Braciole

2 tsp. garlic, chopped

3 Tbsp. scallions, chopped

3 Tbsp. basil, chopped

3 Tbsp. Italian parsley, chopped

1/4 c. canola/olive oil blend

Salt and pepper to taste

2 1/4 lb. veal shoulder

(cut into six 6-oz. portions)

1/4 c. whole currants

1/4 c. toasted hazelnuts

5 Tbsp. olive oil

2 oz. smoked bacon, chopped

1 c. of dry red wine

Tomato Sauce (Recipe next page)

1 1/2 c. grated Pecorino Romano cheese

Directions:

Lay the veal shoulder on a work surface. Using a mallet, gently pound each veal slice to approximately 1/4 inch thickness. Combine the first 6 ingredients in a medium mixing bowl, and spread evenly onto the veal. Using a food processor, coarsely mix hazelnuts and currants. Add mixture to the center of each veal slice, leaving 1/2 inch on each side. Roll up each piece to enclose the filling completely. Using butcher's twine, tie the veal roll to secure. In a cast iron pan, heat 4 tablespoons of olive oil over high heat until almost smoking. Sauté veal rolls for approximately 4 minutes or until all sides are golden brown. Wipe out pan. Add remaining tablespoon of olive oil to cast iron pan and sauté smoked bacon. Set aside for garnish. Pour wine into a large pot and bring to a boil. Add tomato sauce and reduce to a low flame. Add veal, cover tightly and simmer for approximately 1 hour. Remove from heat and set aside for 10 minutes. Spoon sauce over veal, and sprinkle with bacon and grated cheese. Serves 6.

Entrees

Recipe continued on next page

Recipe continued

Tomato Sauce

1/2 c. extra-virgin olive oil
1 sm. onion, chopped
3 cloves garlic, chopped
2 Tbsp. thyme
2 Tbsp. oregano
4 basil leaves
2 dry bay leaves
2 (32-oz.) cans of whole tomatoes
Salt and fresh ground pepper
1/4 c. tomato paste

For Tomato Sauce:
In a large pot, heat oil over medium-high heat. Add onion and garlic and sauté until soft and translucent, about 2 minutes. Add thyme and oregano, and season with salt and pepper. Mash whole tomatoes, and add them to the pot with basil and bay leaves. Reduce to simmer. Add tomato paste. Cover the pot and simmer for 1 hour or until thick. Remove bay leaves and taste for seasoning. Yield: 6 cups

You will enjoy the food and our courteous staff. We also offer a special menu for canine visitors! Dine with Your Dog on our patio!

Entrees   *Submitted by: Chef Rick Cohen, Owner*

Granny's Frying Pan

407 N. Main Street
Havana, FL 32333
Phone: 850-539-4726
Website: www.grannysfryingpan.com

We opened our restaurant to honor our mother, Yvonne Owens Cardwell, in December 2008. We cook down-home meals and serve down-home portions at a very reasonable price. Our slogan is "Everybody loves Granny's," and we do our best to make sure that everybody does.

Meatloaf

3 lb. ground turkey or beef
1 c. bread crumbs (4-5 slices toasted)
3 lg. eggs, beaten
3/4 c. ketchup
1 Tbsp. salt or to taste
2 Tbsp. minced garlic
1 lg. onion, minced
1 tsp. black pepper or to taste
1 can Rotel (diced tomatoes with chilies)

Directions:

In a large bowl beat eggs with spices and onions and garlic. Add ketchup and Rotel and mix well. Add meat and breadcrumbs and combine. Put mixture into 2 loaf pans or a 1/2 hotel pan and cover with foil. Bake in a 375° oven for 45 minutes. Remove from oven and drain liquid; return to oven without foil for 30 minutes or until brown. Serve with mashed potatoes and gravy.

Entrees   *Submitted by: Amanda Higgins, Co-owner*

134 Main Street
Nyack, NY 10960
Phone: 845-353-1355
Fax: 845-353-1459
Website: www.hudsonhousenyack.com

New York City Trained Executive Chef Christopher Dunn & Baker/Owner Matt Hudson have combined their creative talents to provide an ongoing, benchmark experience of Refined American Cuisine at the Hudson House of Nyack. Halibut has positioned itself as a staple on the specials board. Customers find satisfaction in its many select platings. Since opening in 1990 Matt's homestyle desserts have been a cornerstone and perfect finish to any meal.

Halibut Filet with French Beans, Potatoes & Truffled Creamed Leeks

6 - 8 oz. halibut filets
3 large leeks
2 c. heavy cream
4 Tbsp. white or black truffle oil
3/4 lb. haricots verts (French green beans)
3/4 lb. Yukon gold potatoes
4 oz. unsalted butter
1 1/2 c. whole milk
8 Tbsp. canola oil

Directions:

Warm 3 tablespoons of oil in medium sauté pan, add cleaned leeks, and season with salt and pepper. "Sweat" leeks till translucent; do not brown. Add cream and simmer for 5 minutes. Remove from heat and add truffle oil. Hold warm till served. Blanch haricots verts. Hold chilled. Boil potatoes with well salted water. Pass potatoes through ricer and add milk and butter. Salt and pepper fish filets. Sear seasoned fish in large sauté pan with 4 tablespoons of oil over medium heat (best in cast iron pan). Allow fish to brown, then turn. Cook through and remove fish. Sauté haricots verts in same pan as fish. Spoon whipped potatoes into center of plate. Place haricots verts over potatoes. Place fish over haricots verts. To finish, spoon creamed leeks over fish.

Entrees   *Submitted by: Executive Chef Christopher Dunn*

80 N. Main Street
Hudson, OH 44236
Phone: 330-650-1955
Fax: 330-650-6867
Website: www.hudsonsrestaurant.com

Hudson's Restaurant on the Green is a "finer casual" dining experience serving fresh, chef prepared food at moderate prices. The restaurant opened in 2006 by the 3 Foodies, John Altomare, a veteran of over 30 years in the restaurant industry and his two sons, J.J. and Kevin, who are both graduates of the Culinary Institute of America.

Garlic Scape Pesto Pasta

Garlic Scape Pesto
    6 oz. Garlic Scape Pesto (recipe next page)
    24 oz. Cream Sauce (recipe next page)
    30 oz. penne pasta
    18 oz. fresh Italian sausage links
    3 Tbsp. olive oil
    2 ripe tomatoes, diced
    6 oz. parmesan cheese

Directions:
Fill a pasta pot half full of water. Salt the water generously. Bring water to a roaring boil and add pasta. Cook until al dente. Slice the sausage link into 1/2 inch segments. Sear in sauté pan over medium heat with olive oil. Once the sausage is cooked, add the garlic scape pesto into the sauté pan and begin to heat. Add the cream sauce into the pan and fully incorporate with the pesto. Remove pasta from water and add to the sauce. Toss to cover pasta. Serve in a pasta bowl and garnish with diced tomatoes and parmesan cheese.

Recipe continued:

P assion for fresh ingredients and flavorful food comes to life in this seasonal pasta special that is one of our guests' favorite dishes!

Garlic Scape Pesto

30 garlic scapes
1 bunch parsley
1 tsp. crushed red pepper
1 Tbsp. kosher salt

1/2 tsp. black pepper
2 oz. fresh squeezed lemon juice
1/2 c. walnuts
1 1/2 c. olive oil

Directions:

Cut garlic scapes into 1-inch segments. Cut parsley off stems, place garlic scapes and parsley in food processor. Pulse until minced. Add crushed red pepper, salt, black pepper, lemon juice and walnuts into food processor; begin to pulverize until fully incorporated while slowly drizzling olive oil into the food processor. Pesto should be almost smooth. Yield: 6 servings.

Hudson's Cream Sauce

1 qt. heavy cream
2 c. half and half
1 tsp. salt
1 tsp. pepper

4 oz. parmesan cheese
4 oz. butter
4 oz. flour

Directions:

Heat heavy cream and half and half over medium heat in a medium sauce pot. Add salt and pepper. Melt butter in a sauté pan, slowly add flour and fully incorporate. Place roux (butter and flour mixture) in 300° oven until blond in color. Add roux to cream mixture and whisk until completely dissolved. Continue to simmer until sauce begins to thicken. Once thick, remove from heat, add parmesan cheese and stir well.

Entrees   *Submitted by: The 3 Foodies, Chefs/Owners*

4015 E. Main Street
Danville, IL 61834
Phone: 217-446-2120
Fax: 217-446-3866
Website:
www.iandistatelinetavern.com

The I & I State Line Tavern is locally owned and operated. It has been known as The I & I for over 75 years because it is situated on the Indiana/Illinois state line. Our staples are catfish, organic bison, elk, ostrich, and seasonal produce. We also serve fresh beef, chicken, and pork. We have outdoor dining, live music every weekend, and are open 7 days a week.

Organic Bison Filet Feast

1 organic 8 oz. bison filet
1 slice organic uncured bacon
2 Tbsp. organic grape seed oil
1/2 tsp. cracked pepper
1/2 tsp. sea salt
1/2 c. demi-glace, prepared
1 ea. organic Portobello, shitake mushroom
1 organic garlic clove, crushed
2 Tbsp. organic butter
2 tsp. fresh organic parsley
2 tsp. organic red wine
2 organic asparagus spears
1 organic parsnip, cut into strips
1/2 organic sweet potato, cut into strips
1 sprig fresh organic rosemary
3 Tbsp. organic olive oil

Directions:
Wrap thawed bison filet with bacon and rub the grape seed oil, sea salt, and cracked pepper on the filet. Let stand at room temperature while preparing mushrooms. In saucepan, melt butter. Add crushed garlic, sliced Portobello and shitake mushrooms. Sauté 2 minutes and add parsley and red wine. Simmer on low until reduced. Cook filet on high heat to charbroil, 2 1/2 – 3 minutes per side depending on preference. This dish pairs well with organic grilled asparagus, organic parsnips, and organic sweet potato strips. Drizzle vegetables with organic olive oil, sea salt, and fresh organic rosemary. Grill until tender. Plate filet and cover with demi-glace and mushroom mixture. Serve with grilled organic vegetables on the side.

130 N. Main Street
Logan, UT 84321
Phone: 435-787-1757
Fax: 435-787-4011
Website: www.indianovenutah.com

The Indian Oven, located in the heart of historic downtown Logan, Utah, specializes in delicious and reasonably priced cuisine, including house specialties and customer favorites. Our cuisine entrees are served in a relaxed and welcoming setting that friends and family are sure to enjoy. Some of our specialties include our award-winning Chicken Tikka Masala, flavorful Shrimp Biryani, and the familiar Lamb Curry. The Indian Oven has won multiple awards and accolades; it's a great place to come for an adventure and experience the aroma of spices! This recipe is an excellent outdoor dish. No Tandoor, no problem! A charcoal grill will work just fine.

Mixed Tandoori Grill

1 doz. jumbo shrimp, peeled and deveined
2 lb. lamb leg, boned, cubed 1"
2 lb. chicken breast, cubed 1"
5 leg quarters, halved
1 1/2 c. yogurt
4-6 drops yellow food coloring
1 Tbsp. salt
2 Tbsp. garam masala

1/2 c. lemon juice
3 green bell peppers, julienned
3 lg. onions, julienned
4 Tbsp. oil
2 Tbsp. tomato puree
2 Tbsp. curry powder
Cilantro and lime wedges for garnish

Directions:
Mix yogurt, lemon juice, salt, food coloring, and garam masala. Divide marinade into 3 separate containers (the shrimp will require less marinade) and marinate meats separately for 2 hours. Cook all meats (except shrimp) on preheated charcoal grill for 25 minutes. Cook shrimp for 6 minutes only. Place in large decorative bowl. Keep shrimp separate to add later. Sauté onions and bell peppers in large pan with oil until light brown. Stir in tomato puree and curry powder. Remove from heat. Pour onions and bell pepper mixture over meat and stir. Salt to taste. Place shrimp decoratively on top. Garnish with cilantro and lime wedges. Best served with Basmati rice. Serves 10 people.

Entrees   *Submitted by: Ash Oberoi, Chef/Owner*

Joseph's Pizza

7316 N. Main Street
Jacksonville, FL 32208
Phone: 904-765-0335
Fax: 904-766-0310
Website: www.josephspizza.com

Joseph's Pizza has been a family owned Jacksonville landmark since opening in 1956. Our entire family is an integral part of Joseph's Pizza. Mama Rose, Susie, Sandra and Sabrina are all still actively involved in the daily operations. Our love for Italian cooking was brought out by our father Joseph, who was always in the kitchen. We still use only the freshest ingredients with absolutely NO preservatives in everything at Joseph's. We raise our heads and wine glasses high with pride to say, "Everything at Joseph's is homemade." Please visit our additional location at 30 Ocean Blvd., Atlantic Beach, FL 32233, Phone: (904) 270-1122.

Chicken Marsala

2 - 4 oz. boneless, skinless chicken breasts

Marinade
1 oz. olive oil
Dash of black pepper
Dash of salt
1/2 tsp. allspice
1/2 tsp. nutmeg
1/2 tsp. granulated garlic
1 Tbsp. lemon

Marsala
1 c. fresh mushroom
4 oz. dry Marsala wine
2 oz. heavy cream
6 oz. chicken broth
1/2 tsp. beef base
2 Tbsp. butter

Directions:

For best results, tenderize chicken and marinate overnight. Dredge chicken in flour and sauté in butter for 3 minutes at medium–high heat on each side until lightly seared. Add mushrooms, chicken broth and beef base and simmer at medium heat for 3 minutes. Add heavy cream and let simmer at low heat for 8-10 minutes. Serve over pasta.

Entrees   *Submitted by: Susie and Sandra, Owners*

Kathy's PASTA

329 S. Main Avenue
Bolivar, MO 65613
Phone: 417-326-4100

The charm of Kathy's Pasta dates back to the grand opening on March 23, 1994. Originally located on Springfield Street in Bolivar, Missouri, in April of 1997, Kathy and her husband, Larry, purchased the present location on Main Street in Bolivar.

Kathy's has expanded to add a stylish banquet room including a deck for dining outside. Patrons can also dine around the fountain out front. With seating for 97, a full-selection menu and catering services, Kathy's Pasta is proud to offer the Bolivar area a unique Italian dining experience, while maintaining the quiet charm of the early days. We look forward to seeing you!

Polenta with Beef and Sausage Stew

3 Tbsp. olive oil	2 garlic cloves	1/4 c. minced carrots
1/4 c. butter	1/4 tsp. pepper	1 c. diced tomatoes (can or fresh)
1/4 lb. onions, diced	1/4 tsp. salt	1/2 lb. fresh mushrooms, diced
1 1/2 lb. lean beef, cut in cubes	1/2 c. white wine	Pinch of nutmeg
3/4 lb. Italian sausage, ground	1/4 c. minced celery	

Directions:

Combine olive oil and butter, then add onions and sauté until golden. Add beef and sausage and brown. Add garlic, pepper and salt, cook for 10 minutes. Add wine, celery, carrots, tomatoes, mushrooms and nutmeg. Cover and simmer for 40 minutes or until beef is tender.

Polenta

1/2 tsp. salt	2 1/2 c. chicken broth
2 c. water	1 1/4 c. cornmeal

Directions:

Put first three ingredients in large, deep saucepan. Turn on heat, then stir in cornmeal. Bring to a boil, stirring with wire whisk for five minutes. Remove from heat and pour in greased shallow glass dish. Allow to firm for 1 hour and slice. May be baked or fried. Serve with Beef and Sausage Stew.

105 E. Main Street
Endicott, NY 13760
Phone: 607-748-5200

Chef Kyle

Lampy's Mediterranean Grill is a relatively small fine dining establishment in Endicott, just outside the city of Binghamton, NY. It seats about 70 guests, with a somewhat casual, yet respectable Mediterranean ambiance. It is the "little sister" restaurant to the Number 5 in Binghamton, both owned by James McCoy, and each considered the quintessential fine dining establishments in their respective areas. The menu includes Italian classics like Veal Parmigiana, Linguini Fra Diavolo, and Rigatoni alla Vodka, as well as contemporary dishes like Pepper Crusted Ahi Tuna and a variety of high quality steaks and chops. Lampy's Scampi is a signature of Lampy's Mediterranean Grill and one of its best sellers, crisp fried gulf shrimp tossed in a sweet rosemary Marsala sauce with sautéed mushrooms.

Lampy's Scampi

14 U-15 Gulf shrimp, peeled and deveined, tails removed (about 1 lb.)
1 c. all purpose flour
3 eggs, beaten
Vegetable oil, for deep frying
4 Tbsp. butter, salted
1/2 lb. baby button mushrooms or sliced white mushrooms

1/2 tsp. salt
1/2 tsp. black pepper, freshly ground
1 tsp. fresh rosemary, finely chopped
1 c. Marsala wine
1/2 c. chicken or vegetable stock
1 tsp. fresh parsley, finely chopped

Directions:
Heat oil in a large heavy bottomed saucepan to 350°. Place flour and eggs in separate containers. Toss shrimp in flour, coating evenly. Shake gently to remove excess, and place in egg mixture. Coat evenly and repeat, dredging again in flour then in egg. Transfer shrimp to oil and fry until golden brown and crispy. Remove to a paper towel to drain. Meanwhile, heat half of the butter in a sauté pan over medium high heat. Add mushrooms and sauté 1 minute or until tender. Season to taste with salt and pepper. Add rosemary and toss to combine. Remove pan from heat and carefully pour in Marsala. Return to heat, add stock and simmer 1-2 minutes to reduce liquid by about 25%. Add remaining butter and fresh parsley. Whisk until butter melts into sauce. Add shrimp to pan and toss to coat. Arrange 7 shrimp in a circle on each plate, and pour mushrooms and sauce into the center. Serves 2 people.

Submitted by: Kyle Maurer, Executive Chef

101 E. Main
Spartanburg, SC 29302
Phone: 864-542-2171
Website: www.Limeleaf101.com

Welcome to Lime Leaf Thai Cuisine of Spartanburg, South Carolina. Since 2005 Lime Leaf has become a favorite restaurant of many families and friends throughout downtown Spartanburg. Owned and operated by the Lam couple, Kanas, who manages and upkeeps the restaurant floor full time, and David, the chef. Visit their additional location at 342 E. Main St., Hendersonville, NC.

Lime Leaf has been voted best Thai Restaurant by The Beat and recognized through many major events of Hub City including Creative Taste and The Spring Fling.

Chun lamb

Basil Lamb

12 New Zealand lamb chops
1/2 c. freshly chopped basil
1 tsp. white pepper
2 tsp. curry paste
1/2 tsp. curry powder
3 tsp. Lime Leaf brown sauce

Directions
Combine ingredients and marinate for 2 hours. Grill lamb chops on medium heat for 3 minutes per side. Best served with brown rice! Serves 4.

Entrees

Submitted by: David Cheng, Chef

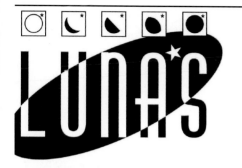

200 Main Street, Hunt Tower
Gainesville, GA 30501
Phone: 770-531-0848
Fax: 770-532-4120
Website: www.lunas.com

Luna's Restaurant, located on Main Street in Gainesville, Georgia, has been a local favorite since 1997. Chef Albert Luna is a graduate from Johnston and Wales and has been Executive Chef for Luna's since 2000. Chef Albert brings a gourmet twist to classic continental fare. Luna's also boasts private dining facilities and an eclectic piano lounge.

Grilled Shrimp and Scallops with Vegetable and Rice Stir-fry

40 shrimp (16/20) peeled and deveined
40 scallops, dry pack
20 cloves garlic, divided & minced
10 tsp. vegetable oil
10 tsp. sesame oil
10 tsp. soy sauce

5 c. Savoy cabbage julienne
5 c. purple cabbage julienne
2 1/2 c. carrots, julienne
2 1/2 c. red peppers, julienne
5 c. cooked rice
Scallions for garnish

Directions:

Rub shrimp and scallops with garlic and vegetable oil and grill. Be sure to not overcook the seafood. Set aside. Stir-fry the garlic in sesame oil; add all vegetables for approximately one minute. Add rice for approximately one minute. Drizzle with soy sauce and stir all ingredients together. Remove from heat. Serve rice to your plate and top dish with shrimp and scallops. Add scallions for garnish. Yield: 10 Servings.

Entrees

Submitted by: Albert Luna, Executive Chef

1411 Main Street
Hilton Head Island, SC 29926
Phone: 843-689-3999
Website:
www.hiltonheadcafe.com

In November of 1999, two brothers-in-law had an idea that Hilton Head Island needed a friendly, unassuming neighborhood restaurant that served good food at reasonable prices. So, John Roppelt and Chef Aaron Glugover opened the Main Street Café & Pub in Main Street Village.

Our comfortable and laid back café on Main Street has become a favorite of local residents on Hilton Head Island, not to mention the savvy tourists that have inquired as to where the "locals" eat. Specializing in Southern seafood and family favorites, our restaurant serves "Pub fair with a creative flair." When your appetite calls for real food, creatively prepared and fairly priced in an unpretentious atmosphere, stroll on in to Main Street Café & Pub and prepare to be delighted! Come in and let our family treat your family to an unforgettable evening.

Blackened Shrimp and Gruyere Cheese Grits

2 lb. (21-25) peeled & deveined shrimp
8 c. lobster stock
8 c. water
2 pats butter
1 Tbsp. fresh garlic
1 Tbsp. six pepper blend
4 c. stone ground grits
1/2 c. heavy cream (40%)
1 c. diced gruyere cheese
Salt to taste

Directions:
Bring lobster stock and water to a boil with butter, garlic and six pepper blend. Add grits and whisk occasionally. When at desired consistency (about 30 minutes) maintain a low heat and add heavy cream. Stir. Add diced cheese and stir until fully melted. Dust shrimp with preferred blackening seasoning. Sear on medium heat for 90 seconds each side. Top grits with shrimp. Serves 10-12.

Submitted by: Chef Aaron Glogover

153A E. Main Street
Orange, VA 22960
Phone: 540-672-3344
Website: www.marios-in-orange.com

Mario's brings true Sicilian inflection to the menu and uses nothing but pure, cold pressed, extra virgin Italian olive oil, an expensive Italian mozzarella, USDA top sirloin, and an envious tomato sauce made from choice, crushed tomatoes. Their attention toward, and expense of quality ingredients, while not readily seen, is evident when you dine at the restaurant.

Sicilian Style Shrimp over Penne Rigate

1/4 c. extra virgin olive oil
3 cloves garlic, chopped
1/4 c. sun-dried tomatoes, julienne-style
3 lg. white mushrooms, thick sliced
2 tsp. nonpareil capers
(capers should be lightly washed
to remove excess salt)
Garlic seasoning (garlic salt, fresh ground
black pepper), to taste
4 fresh basil leaves, torn
6-8 shrimp,
(peeled and deveined,
washed in cold water and patted dry)
Penne Rigate
Romano cheese
1/2 tsp. crushed chiles, optional

Recipe continued:

Directions:

Warm olive oil in skillet to sauté temperature and add the chopped garlic, sun-dried tomatoes, sliced mushrooms and capers.

Sauté all ingredients until golden brown; add garlic seasoning to taste. Add coarsely chopped basil and the shrimp and additional olive oil to coat all ingredients, folding occasionally to blend.

Cover and allow to simmer until shrimp show a light orange color, being careful not to overcook as they will get tough.

Remove from heat, fold. Toss into Penne Rigate, cooked to preference although al dente is suggested.

Lightly sprinkle with grated Romano cheese and serve with your favorite Merlot and garlic bread.
Serving for 1.

Mario's is a family owned, family run business. "We came to Virginia looking for a town that wanted our true Italian-culture restaurant. We are happy to say we found that and more here in Orange. Thanks to the Lord and the people here, our authentically prepared meals have succeeded. We use only the finest quality ingredients in all our dishes and pizzas. I come from Sicily and with pride I bring to you that originality in our dishes."

Submitted by: Chef Ignazio & Janet Abbene, Owners

MERMAID CAFE
OLDINLET BOOKSHOP AND B&B

HOMER, ALASKA

3487 Main Street
Homer, AK 99603
Phone: 907-235-7649
Website: www.mermaidcafe.net

The Alaskan White King has a delicious taste, milder than a normal king with a distinct flavor all its own and rarity that makes it one of Alaska's most sought-after delicacies. Although it is hard to get and a bit pricey, get it if you can. No worries though, as the recipe will work for any salmon.

Alaska White King Salmon with Gai Lan and Asparagus Salad

1 king salmon steak or fillet
2 Tbsp. sesame oil
1 Tbsp. ginger
1 bunch gai lan* or other hearty green
1 daikon radish
3 stalks asparagus
1 tangerine
2 tsp. rice vinegar

Directions:
Preheat oven to 425º. Pat dry and salt and pepper the salmon on one side. To sear the Salmon I prefer a cast iron skillet, but any sturdy heavy bottom pan will do. Heat 1 tablespoon of the sesame oil to just below the smoking point. Drop salmon in oil, salt and pepper side down. Sear for about 2 minutes, then without turning place into the oven. The salmon should be done in about 5 minutes; this will depend on the thickness of the steak. A great method is to leave the skin on and when it pulls away easily, the fish should be just about perfect.

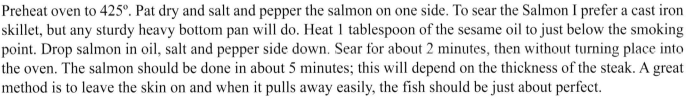

✱ Gai Lan is an Asian green also known as Chinese broccoli. Although any good hearty green will do, this is just what I had on hand today. The local farmers bring all sorts of cultivars, and all are wonderful. No special preparation is necessary. Simplicity is the key. Pour a bit of olive or sesame oil and some ginger and garlic in a hot pan, and then just sauté away to your liking.

309 N. Main Street
Carlsbad, NM 88220
Phone: 575-628-1339

Mi Casita is family owned and has a friendly, efficient staff. Our clean, colorful dining area creates a wonderful atmosphere for our guests. Our food is fresh and homemade, and our specials keep our regulars coming back again and again.

Green Chile Posole with Shrimp

10-15 New Mexico long green chiles
Olive oil
3 slices thick cut bacon, cubed
2 smoked ham hocks
32 oz. chicken stock
32 oz. beef stock
1/4 c. clam juice
6 lb. can of hominy
14.5 oz. can diced tomatoes
(fire roasted preferred)
2 c. water
2 tsp. kosher salt
2 tsp. garlic powder
2 tsp. dried oregano
2 lb. med. raw shrimp (60-70 count)

Garnishes
1 yellow Spanish onion
1 bunch fresh cilantro

4-6 limes, cut into wedges
3-4 avocados, cubed

Serve with: 1 box saltine crackers

Entrees

Recipe continued on next page

Recipe continued:

Directions:

<u>Prepare the chiles:</u>
On a large cookie sheet, place the New Mexico green chiles and drizzle them liberally with olive oil. Place under the broiler until the skins are charred (they will look as though they are burnt). Remove chiles and place them in a Ziploc bag and let stand for 10 to 15 minutes with bag closed. Take the chiles from the bag and remove the charred skins. Once all chiles are peeled, chop them up and set aside.

In a large pot (10 to 13 quarts) place 3 tablespoons of olive oil and the cubed bacon. Cook on medium to high heat until the bacon is crisp. Remove the crisp bacon and set aside. In the same pot place both ham hocks and let fry for 3 minutes on each side or until brown. Once ham hocks are finished (do not remove them) add the chicken stock, beef stock, and clam juice. Open and drain the juice from the can of hominy and add to the pot. Then add the entire can of tomatoes and the chopped green chiles. Now add 2 cups of water and stir.

To season the mixture add the salt, garlic powder, and oregano and bring to boil. Once the posole comes to a boil turn the heat down, cover, and let simmer for an hour and a half stirring occasionally. While posole is simmering, prep the garnishes for serving.

Dice the onions, finely chop the cilantro, wedge the limes, and cube the avocados. Place all the garnishes in separate bowls and set them aside.

After posole has simmered for an hour and 15 minutes, remove the ham hocks. Remove the meat from the ham hock and chop it into cubes. Add the cubed ham hock meat, crisped bacon (made earlier), and the peeled raw shrimp. Stir and continue to simmer for another 10 to 15 minutes.

Before serving, taste the posole for flavor and add more seasoning if necessary. Place the bowls of garnish out so guests can access them along with one box of saltine crackers. Ladle posole into bowls and allow the guests to add garnish to their preference.

Entrees   *Submitted by: Mary and Jeremy Molinar*

419 Main Street
Cedar Falls, IA 50613
Phone: 319-266-9920
Website: www.my-verona.com

Owner, Russ Wasendorf envisioned bringing fresh and northern Italian flair to Cedar Falls, Iowa, which inspired myVerona Ristorante Italiano. In the fall of 2008, myVerona opened on the Cedar Falls Parkade, serving hand-cut pastas, breads made daily from scratch, homemade desserts, soups and more!

Verona Scallops with Gnocchi, Spinach and Sun-Dried Tomato Drizzled with a Truffle Beaurre Blanc

For Beurre Blanc

1 shallot, diced
1 sprig fresh thyme
1 sprig fresh oregano
1 sprig fresh sage
10 black peppercorns
4 bay leaves
2 c. white wine
8 Tbsp. cold butter
1 lemon
1 Tbsp. black truffle paste
Salt and pepper to taste

Recipe continued on next page

Recipe continued:

For Scallop and Sauté

16 U10 dry scallops
3 Tbsp. extra virgin olive oil
1 Tbsp. butter
12 oz. potato gnocchi
6 sliced sun-dried tomatoes
1 bag of spinach
3 cloves garlic, minced
Salt and white pepper to taste

Offering an impressive wine list, myVerona also has fresh seafood and other northern Italian specialties for all to enjoy!

Directions:

<u>Begin by making the Beurre Blanc.</u> Add first seven ingredients into a small pot and bring to a boil. Boil until the white wine is almost gone and then add the cream. Cook the cream at a simmer and let reduce until thick. While still hot, whisk in cold butter in stages; be careful not to get the mix cold. Add lemon juice, salt and sugar at the end to taste and strain the mix in a fine mesh strainer. Fold truffle paste into the mixture and set aside.

<u>To prepare the scallops:</u> In a large sauté pan or two medium pans, bring two tablespoons of olive oil and one tablespoon of butter to a bubble. Salt and pepper the scallops on both sides and place flat face of the scallop in the pan. Cook the scallops 90% on one side and flip over. Cook to desired temperature. In a separate sauté pan, add gnocchi, 1 tablespoon of olive oil, sun-dried tomatoes and garlic. Sauté for one to two minutes or until the gnocchi is hot and then add the spinach. Season with salt and pepper. Place this mix in the center of the plate. Drizzle the truffle Beurre Blanc around the plate and serve the scallops right on top of the spinach and gnocchi mixture.

myVerona
RISTORANTE ITALIANO

943 N. Main Avenue
Springfield, MO 65802
Phone: 417-866-8744

Pappy's Place has stood at this location since 1904. While now housing a bar/restaurant, the store was a family-owned shoe repair shop and a grocery store. New owners opened a cafe on the property in 1924. The people are friendly, the food is good and the beer is cold. A casual atmosphere makes for a laid-back time. For many people, it is a place of good memories.

Vegan Tamales

10 corn husks

Dough
2 c. Masa Harina
1/8 c. olive oil
Dash of salt
1 ½ c. warm water or vegetable stock

Filling
4 oz. crumbled veggie burger
1/2 onion, chopped
1/2 c. fresh corn, scraped from a cob (or use frozen corn)
Add a dash of olive oil, chili powder, cumin and oregano

Directions:
To prepare Husks: Submerge 10 husks in a pan of hot water for 30 minutes. Separate husks and rinse to wash away brown silks. Combine dough ingredients and mix well to form dough. If it is too dry add more liquid. Vegan Filling: Sauté onions for a few minutes to soften them. Next add crumbled veggie burger and corn. Stir while cooking for a few minutes and set aside to cool.
To Assemble: Place a husk in front of you with the narrow end toward you. Take a piece of dough and spread it using your finger by pressing it to the sides and about 3 inches from both ends. Put a small spoonful of filling at the center of the tamale. Take the narrow end of husk and fold it toward the top to sandwich the filling in the center of the husk. (It only takes a few tries to become confident!) Next, take the sides of the tamale (there may only be an inch or two) and fold them inwards. Fold the husk a little bit more toward the top. Take a husk and tear a long strip from it. Tie the tamale around the center, or take two strips and tie it for an even more dramatic effect. Steam Tamales in a streamer or improvise. (I use a Chinese wok and a small vegetable steam tray.) Cover for 1 hour. Arrange wrapped tamales on a plate and serve with your favorite Mexican side dish. Serves 4. Enjoy!

Entrees   *Submitted by: Chef Jack Rauhoff*

2500 Main Street
Ft. Myers Beach, FL 33931
Phone: 239-463-3257
Fax: 239-463-2415
Website: www.myparrotkcy.com

A slice of Key West tucked in the Matanzas Harbor. Decorated with colorful Parrots, a fantastic view and Fresh "Flaribbean Flavor."

Grouper Mediterranean

8 oz. fresh grouper

4 oz. Kalmata olives

4 oz. grape tomatoes

1 oz. chopped garlic

1 oz. lemon juice

2 oz. white wine

4 oz. unsalted butter

Salt & pepper to taste

1 oz. flour

1 oz. olive oil

Directions:

Dredge grouper in flour and shake off excess. In hot sauté pan, sauté grouper in olive oil 6-8 minutes or until brown. Remove from pan; add garlic, olives and tomatoes. When tender, add lemon juice, white wine. Reduce till half, then add butter to finish. Finish grouper in oven until cooked. Plate grouper with sauce napped on top.

Entrees   *Submitted by: Jon Venuto, Chef/Partner*

601 Main Street
Bayard, NE 69334
Phone: 308-586-1125

We at R&S have a lot of things besides food. One of our customers made a sign that says it all. The recipe we have for you today is meatloaf.

Sharon's Meatloaf

4 lb. lean hamburger
1 box dry onion soup mix
1 can Rotel diced chilies and tomatoes
2 oz. Heinz 57 sauce
1 sm. diced onion, or fresh chives (about 1/4 c.)
2 oz. Worcestershire sauce
1 box saltine crackers
3 eggs, beaten
1/2 c. chopped bell peppers
3 strip bacon
Ketchup

Directions:
Mix by hand the meat, soup mix, green chilies, tomatoes, onion, 57 sauce, Worcestershire sauce, crackers, eggs and bell peppers. Shape into a loaf and put into roasting pan. Put ketchup on top and then lay the bacon on top of the ketchup. Bake for 1 1/2 hours on 350°. Take out of oven and let set for 10 minutes before serving. No other seasonings are needed.

Entrees   *Submitted by: Sharon Orosz, Owner*

RATTLESNAKE RANCH

559 E. Main Street
Denville, NJ 07834
Phone: 973-586-3800
Fax: 973-586-2098
Website: www.rattlesnakeranchcafe.com

The Rattlesnake Ranch has been serving its award winning Southwestern cuisine in Northern New Jersey since 1994. The restaurant is owned and operated by John Cahillane. Our jambalaya is a local favorite and is best served with your favorite Mexican beer.

Alligator and Chicken Jambalaya

3 lg. boneless chicken breasts
1 lb. alligator tenderloin (available at local fish market)
1 lb. chorizo sausage
1 med. Spanish onion
2 green bell peppers
2 red bell peppers
1 lg. tomato

3 ribs celery
2 – 12 oz. cans of V-8 juice
12 oz. chicken broth
3 Tbsp. Cajun seasoning
Salt & pepper to taste
3 oz. olive oil
Precook 8 servings of favorite rice

Directions:
Cut chicken, sausage and alligator into thin strips. Cut all vegetables into inch squares. In a medium stock pot, heat olive oil. Add sausage, chicken and alligator. Cook until lightly browned (8-10 minutes). Add V-8 and simmer for another 10 minutes. Add rice, salt, pepper and Cajun seasoning. Simmer for 5 minutes. All liquid should be gone. Serves 8-10 people.

Entrees   *Submitted by: John Cahillone, Owner/Chef*

600 E. Main Street
Allen, TX 75002
Phone: 972-396-5000

The Reel Thing Catfish Cafe has been serving up the best seafood and BBQ west of the Mississippi since 2000. "Where Friends and Families Meet to Eat."

Shrimp Etoufee

1/2 stick butter
2 Tbsp. flour
1 c. chopped onions
1/3 c. chopped bell peppers
1/2 c. chopped celery
1 clove (large) garlic, mashed
1 Tbsp. Worcestershire sauce
1 Tbsp. minced parsley
1 tsp. salt
1/8 tsp. cayenne pepper
1 c. water
1 1/2 lb. shrimp, peeled and deveined
Hot cooked rice

Directions:

In a heavy two quart saucepan, melt better. Add flour and cook over low heat, stirring constantly to make a light brown roux. Add onion, celery, bell pepper and garlic. Cook until vegetables are soft. Add remaining ingredients except shrimp. Simmer for 15 minutes, stirring occasionally. Add shrimp and cook until done, three to five minutes. Turn off heat and let cool. Flavor is enhanced if refrigerated overnight and reheated. Serve over hot rice.

Entrees   *Submitted by: Jim Brevard, VP*

Main Street
East Burke Village, VT 05832
Phone: 802-626-3514

Nick and I as owners of a small, causal, fine dining restaurant, take pride in everything being fresh and homemade. We make all of the desserts, ice creams and sorbets. We make all of our sauces to order. We also make all of our salad dressings, our most popular dressings are the Poppy Seed and Maple Balsamic Vinaigrette made with local Vermont maple syrup.

Chicken Marsala

4 chicken breasts
1/4 c. Marsala wine
1/2 c. heavy cream
2 tsp. chopped garlic
4 oz. mushrooms
Salt and pepper
2 tsp. canola oil enough to cover bottom of pan

Directions:

Heat large sauté pan over medium heat and add oil. Slice chicken breasts in half, dredge in flour, shake off excess. Sauté chicken breasts for 3 minutes, then flip. Add Marsala wine and cook until alcohol is evaporated, about 2 to 4 minutes. Add garlic and mushrooms and let cook for 2 minutes; add cream and let simmer until sauce coats the back of the spoon (add a little more Marsala and cream if you want more sauce. Season with salt and pepper to taste. Best served with linguine or rice pilaf and green beans or asparagus.

Entrees   *Submitted by: Travis Chapman, Head Chef*

540 Main Street
Park City, UT 84098
Phone: 435-649-3536
Website: www.riverhorsegroup.com

Since opening its doors in the winter of 1987, the Riverhorse on Main has been highly regarded by both diners and restaurant critics alike. After receiving the coveted Mobile Travel 4-star award in 2000 and the DiRONA Award, the Riverhorse has continued to provide diners with a memorable dining experience. The eclectic American Cuisine is sure to intrigue any diner whether they join us during the peak of ski season or the beautiful summers of Park City.

Pistachio Crusted Red Trout Pomegranate-Fennel Salsa & Lemon Emulsion

4 ea. 6 oz. trout filets
Buttermilk (as needed)
Olive Oil (as needed)

For the Breading

1 c. pistachio nuts, ground
1 c. Panko bread crumbs
1 Tbsp. salt
1/2 Tbsp. pepper

For the Sauce

1/4 c. shallots, chopped
1 oz. olive oil
1/2 c. lemon juice

1 lb. butter, unsalted- softened
Salt and white pepper (as needed)
Cayenne pepper

Entrees

Recipe continued on next page

Recipe continued:

For the Salsa

    1 c. pomegranate seeds
    1 c. fennel, minced
    1 c. rice wine vinegar
    1/2 c. extra virgin olive oil
    3 Tbsp. honey
    1 bunch cilantro, chopped
    1 tsp. salt
    1/2 tsp. pepper

Directions:

Pre-heat oven to 425°. In a food processor, blend the nuts until they resemble coarse corn meal. Then add the bread crumbs, salt and pepper. Set Aside. Place the trout filet in buttermilk, then crust with breading.

<u>For the Sauce:</u> In a sauce pan, heat the oil until almost smoking; add the shallots and sauté for 1 minute, stirring constantly without letting it get brown. Then add the lemon juice and reduce heat. Simmer the lemon juice until it is almost dry. Turn off the heat. Then divide the butter into 6 equal portions. Using a whisk, slowly whisk in the softened butter one portion at a time. Try to keep the sauce at the same temperature. Do not boil. Season the mixture with salt, white pepper and cayenne to taste. Strain the sauce through a double mesh.

<u>For the salsa:</u> Mix all of the ingredients together and chill.

<u>For the service:</u>
In a sauté pan, heat olive oil, place fish flesh side down; sear until brown, flip the fish and finish in the oven, about 3-4 minutes. Top with lemon sauce and pomegranate salsa. Serve with rice and fresh vegetables.

Entrees   *Submitted by: Seth Adams, Chef*

260 W. Main Street
PO Box 553
West Brookfield, MA 01585
Phone: 508-867-2345
Website: www.salemcrossinn.com

Perhaps one of the most unique and flavorful offerings at Salem Cross Inn is the famous fireplace roasted prime rib. Prepared on the only known, working 17th century roasting jack, the farm raised beef is hand rubbed with a seasonal blend of herbs and spices, then slowly roasted in front of a roaring fire for nearly 3 hours. Served with herbed red potatoes and seasonal vegetables, this is truly a "one of a kind" experience!

1700 Style Roasted Prime Rib

15-18 lb. rib roast, bone in
1 Tbsp. chopped garlic
10 lg. bay leaves
2 Tbsp. chopped fresh basil
2 tsp. kosher salt
2 Tbsp. chopped fresh oregano
1 Tbsp. fresh ground black pepper
2 Tbsp. chopped fresh parsley
4 Tbsp. olive oil
2 Tbsp. chopped fresh rosemary

Directions:

Mix garlic, herbs, salt and pepper in a blender on high speed until well pulverized. Reduce speed to low and slowly add olive oil until well incorporated. Remove mixture from blender and rub entire surface of the roast with a generous amount.

Entrees   **Recipe continued on next page**

Recipe continued:

Put the roast in a roasting pan, bone side down, then place in preheated 325 ° oven. Cook for 2 1/2 - 3 hours. The internal temperature of the roast should reach 130° for medium – medium rare. Once meat is cooked to desired doneness, remove from oven and let rest for 20 minutes before carving.

* If you have leftover herb rub, store it in an airtight container in the refrigerator for up to 2 weeks.

Helpful hint: Put bone in a stock pot with 8 cups of water, 1 large chopped onion, 2 cloves chopped garlic, 2 large chopped celery stalks, 2 large chopped carrots, 1/2 teaspoon kosher salt, 1/2 teaspoon ground pepper and 1 tablespoon of chopped parsley. Let come to a rapid boil for 5 minutes and reduce heat to simmer for 20 minutes. Strain broth from ingredients, put broth up into 2-cup freezer containers and store in freezer. Fresh beef stock is best used within 6 months and is a great base for soups, stews and gravies.

23 N. Main Street
Enfield, CT 06082
Phone & Fax: 860-741- 6969
Website: www.silviasrestaurant.com

Owner Silvia Salvari, a native of Romania, came to this country in 1984. She worked in various restaurants in New York and New England, sharpening her cooking skills. Silvia brought with her from Romania knowledge of Eastern European cuisine. Her father was an Austrian baker and taught Silvia the art of making breads in his bakery. She is a five time gold medal winner in the National Chef's Tasting Competition; and was an invited guest of the White House Chefs. Silvia personally selects fresh, quality food ingredients for the menu items and dinner specials she prepares. She bakes her breads fresh daily from all natural ingredients.

Salmon

2 pieces salmon fillet
1 tsp. ea. black pepper, salt, fresh parsley & dill
2 lb. crabmeat, shrimp, scallops or lobster, any combination chopped
2 sm. onions, diced and sautéed in a pan
2 tomatoes, sautéed with onions
2 c. breadcrumbs & crackers mixture
Juice of 1 lemon
1/2 c. heavy cream
Butter
Egg Wash

Directions:
Preheat oven to 350°. Pound salmon fillets thin and put first piece onto greased pan. Mix together stuffing, crabmeat or combination, onions, tomatoes, black pepper, salt, parsley and dill, breadcrumb/cracker mixture, lemon juice and heavy cream. Spread stuffing on first piece of salmon. Put second piece of salmon on top of stuffing. Sprinkle fish with salt, pepper and lemon juice. Dot with butter and brush with egg wash before cooking. Cook at 350° for about 45 minutes.

Entrees   *Submitted by: Silvia Salvari, Owner/Executive Chef*

1618 N. Main
Opelousas, LA 70570
Phone: 337-942-2985
Fax: 337-942-1830

Founded in 1937, Clarence Soileau opened Soileau's Dinner Club for business in Opelousas, Louisiana when Main Street was only a dirt road. After all these years, it is still located on Main Street. Now into our third generation of the Soileau family, Scott, Beth and Josh invite you to enjoy the finest in Cajun Cuisine. "Acadiana's finest serving Acadiana's finest."

Soileau's Shrimp Creole

5 lb. peeled gulf shrimp, drained and seasoned (40-50 count is preferred)
2 sticks butter
2 sticks margarine
3 lg. yellow onions, diced
2 med. bell peppers, diced
4 Tbsp. garlic, chopped
4 – 10 oz. cans diced Rotel tomatoes undrained (diced tomatoes with green chilis)
4 oz. premium tomato sauce
V-8 vegetable juice (in place of adding water)
2 Tbsp. cornstarch mixed with 1/3 c. cool water

Directions:

Sauté diced onion and bell pepper on medium heat in melted butter and margarine until soft and translucent (do not brown), add chopped garlic. Add Rotel and tomato sauce and cook on medium heat for 45-60 minutes. The longer it cooks, the better the sauce will be. Add small amount of V-8 juice when needed to thin the sauce. The sauce will thicken as it cooks down. Do not add water. Add seasoned shrimp and mix thoroughly. Cook at medium heat with slight bubble in sauce. The shrimp will begin to lose its water and thin the sauce. Continue cooking until the shrimp are tender (about 45 minutes). Add a little cornstarch mixture to the sauce to thicken as needed. Sauce will be light pink in color and shrimp should be plump and slightly firm. Garnish with cut green onion tops and serve over hot fluffy white rice. We complete this meal with French bread and a garden salad. Serves 10-12 hungry people.

Entrees   *Submitted by: Scott Soileau, Owner*

29 N. Main Street
Tooele, UT 84074
Phone: 435-882-4922

Red Pesto Gnocchi with Tempura Prawns

Roasted Tomato Pesto

1 c. yellow sun roasted tomatoes
1 Tbsp. fresh minced garlic
1/2 c. shelled pine nuts
1 oz. fresh basil leaves
4 oz. fresh grated Parmesan cheese
3 oz. Pomace olive oil
Salt & black pepper to taste

Directions:

First prepare the Roasted Tomato Pesto by placing the garlic, pine nuts, basil and tomatoes in a food processor and pureeing. Slowly drizzle the olive oil into the mixture until it becomes smooth. Add the Parmesan and pulse until fully incorporated. Finish with salt and pepper to taste. Refrigerate until ready to begin sautéing.

Entrees   **Recipe continued on next page**

Recipe continued:

Tempura Prawns

    24 ea. U-12 shrimp tail on, peeled and deveined
    1 c. tempura batter

"We select only the finest ingredients and creatively prepare every dish to make your dining experience memorable. Enjoy our freshly-made lunches and dinners, and appreciate loved ones and the gifts of each day. It is our greatest pleasure to serve you." - Spiros Makris - Owner

Gnocchi Pasta

    24 oz. potato gnocchi, blanched
    2 oz. Pomace olive oil
    2 tsp. fresh minced garlic
    9 ea. artichoke hearts, unmarinated & halved
    8 oz. red sun roasted tomatoes
    4 oz. white wine
    6 oz. Roasted Tomato Pesto
    3 oz. baby spinach leaves
    6 oz. heavy cream
    Salt & black pepper to taste

Directions continued:

Prepare a small deep-frying pan with peanut or canola oil at 350°. Pat the shrimp with paper towels to dry then dip in cold tempura batter and fry in the oil until batter is off white in color (approximately 1-2 minutes) then place on paper towels in a baking dish and hold in a warm place.

For the pasta heat 2 ounces of olive oil in a large sauté pan then add garlic, artichokes and red tomatoes. When hot, add white wine and reduce for 1 minute, then add Pesto, heavy cream, spinach and blanched gnocchi. Toss together and season with salt and pepper to taste. To assemble dish, place equal portions of the pasta in four bowls and then place four prawns on top of each pasta portion with the tails standing up. Garnish with fresh rosemary sprigs in the center of each dish. Yield: Four 16 ounce portions.

Entrees

Submitted by: Steven J. Berzansky Head Chef

111 E. Main Street
Carrboro, NC 27510
Phone: 919-933-1117
www.thespotteddogrestaurant.com.

Since 1998, the 103 year-old, peculiar wedge-shaped building in downtown Carrboro has been home to the Spotted Dog, a casual eatery with a personality as friendly as its name and as eccentric. The menu features an eclectic mix of vegetarian and non-vegetarian fare. Under whimsical headings such as Kibbles 'n Bits (appetizers) and Fetch 'n Catch (seafood), the offering covers the spectrum from burgers (beef or veggie) to house specialties such as black-eyed pea cakes and veggie "soy" BBQ.

Black-Eyed Pea Cakes with Chipotle Sauce

Pea Cakes:
- 4 13.5 oz. cans black-eyed peas
- 4 Tbsp. fresh garlic
- 1 c. chopped cilantro
- 1 1/2 tsp. salt
- 2 Tbsp. cumin
- 1 c. red peppers, minced
- 1 c. celery, minced
- 1/2 c. jalapeños, minced
- 1/3 c. lime juice
- 1 egg
- 3 1/2 c. breadcrumbs

Chipotle Sauce
- 1 Tbsp. chipotle in adobo sauce
- 1 c. sour cream
- 1 c. mayo

Flash-Fried Cilantro
- Fresh cilantro

Directions:

Pea Cakes: Drain peas and coarsely mash. Place in large mixing bowl. Add next 7 ingredients, thru jalapeños. Stir in lime juice and egg; mix well. Add bread crumbs, 1 cup at a time until all mixed in. Final mixture should be tacky to the touch. Heat a greased skillet. Scoop out and hand patty the cakes (about 2 inch cakes). Place in hot skillet, cook until golden brown and slightly crispy. Chipotle Sauce: Place chipotle mixture in food processor and purée. Transfer to bowl; add sour cream and mayonnaise. Mix well with a whisk. Flash-Fried Cilantro: Heat oil in skillet to 350º. Carefully drop in cilantro and fry just until crispy. Drain on cloth; set aside. To serve: Place 2-3 cakes on a plate, garnish with a dollop of chipotle sauce on each cake, a small wedge of tomato, and the flash-fried cilantro. We suggest serving with a side of organic mesclun spring mix.
Makes 17-18 cakes; serves 6-8.

Entrees   *Submitted by: Linda Bourne & Karin Mills, Co-owners*

525 N. Main Street
Washington, LA 70589
Phone: 337-826-7227
Fax: 337-826-7877
Website: www.steamboatwarehouse.com

The Steamboat Restaurant is the last of seven warehouses built on Bayou Courtableau during the 1800s. It was built circa 1819 and was the largest stop for the steamboats traveling from New Orleans to St. Louis, Missouri.

Soft Shell Crab Vermillion

4 Cypremort Point soft shell crabs
1/2 c. peanut oil
1/4 c. Worcestershire sauce
1/4 c. lemon juice
2 c. all purpose flour
4 eggs
2 c. whole milk
All purpose seasoning

Chef Jason Huguet started working at Steamboat Warehouse Restaurant in 1994 as a busboy and has moved up over the years to become the owner. Jason is a Bachelor of Science graduate from the Chef John Folse Culinary Institute at Nichols State University.

Directions:
Season the flour and set aside. Beat the eggs, add the milk and seasoning, then set aside. Heat the oil in a large skillet, season the soft shell crabs then add to the pan. Do not overload the pan; you may have to cook in two batches. Pan fry the crabs on a medium flame about 2-3 minutes on each side or until golden. When the crabs are done, mix the Worcestershire sauce and lemon juice together and add about 2-3 tablespoons to the pan. Remove the crabs and place on a paper towel to remove excess oil.

Entrees **Recipe continued on next page**

Recipe continued:

Champagne Sauce

1 celery rib (finely diced)
2 green onions (finely sliced)
5 button mushrooms (thinly sliced)
2 Tbsp. minced garlic
1/2 c. olive oil
1/4 bottle extra dry champagne
2 c. heavy whipping cream
Salt and white pepper, to taste
1 lb. fresh all lump crabmeat
1/2 c. green onion (thinly sliced)

Directions:

Heat the oil in sauté pan then add the first three ingredients. Sauté until wilted, about 5 minutes. Add salt and pepper. De-glaze the pan with the champagne and let reduce to a third. Add the whipping cream and reduce to desired thickness. Feel through the crabmeat and remove any remaining shells that may be present. Add the crabmeat and the remaining green onions to the sauce. Taste for seasoning and adjust accordingly. Place the soft shell crabs over your favorite type of pasta and finish with the champagne sauce. Garnish with chopped parsley and/or sliced green onion. Feeds about 4-5 people.

Submitted by: Jason Huguet, Chef/Owner

Stellina
RESTAURANT

47 Main Street
Watertown, MA 02472
Phone: 617-924-9475
Fax: 617-924-7048
Website: www.stellinarestaurant.com

Stellina Restaurant has been serving regional Italian food in Watertown Square for over twenty years. Taking inspiration from all corners of Italy, our menu changes frequently in tune with the seasons. Throughout the year you can almost always find long-time customer favorites -- like our award winning Warm Tomato Salad -- along with new, fresh culinary interpretations.

Jumbo Shrimp Aranciata

10 jumbo shrimp, peeled, tail on
1 1/2 Tbsp. minced garlic
3 Tbsp. extra virgin olive oil
2 Tbsp. parsley
Salt & black pepper to taste
2 c. orange juice

1 lg. seedless orange
2 Tbsp. unsalted butter
1/2 tsp. red pepper flakes
1 c. shredded radichio
5-6 oz. orange liqueur
2 lemon wedges

✱ Cooking tips: Shrimp listed as U8-U12 are the perfect size. For extra flavor leave the shells on. We recommend either Grand Marnier or Grand Gala liqueur. This dish can be served with rice pilaf or a sweet corn risotto.

Directions:
Marinate the shrimp with 1/2 tablespoon garlic, 1 tablespoon oil, 1 tablespoon parsley, salt and pepper. Cover and refrigerate for 30 minutes. Reduce the orange juice in a saucepan to 1/2 cup; set aside. Peel the orange and cut into 6-8 round slices. Preheat oven to 450°. Combine the shrimp and butter in an oven-proof 12 inch skillet over high heat. Once the butter sizzles, add the remaining garlic and olive oil, along with pepper flakes, radichio and pinch of salt. Cover the pan and place in the oven for 4-5 minutes, until the shrimp are just cooked through. Add the reduced orange juice, orange slices and liqueur and reduce by half over high heat. Serve immediately with pan juices drizzled on top, garnished with chopped parsley and lemon. Serves two.

Entrees   *Submitted by: Virginia Curcio, Owner*

1167 Main Street
Blowing Rock, NC 28605
Phone: 828-295-7075
Website: www.storiestreetgrille.com

Storie Street Grille, located in the heart of downtown Blowing Rock, North Carolina, is a contemporary American bistro, serving memorable dishes in warm, comfortable surroundings. Our menu offers an eclectic selection of regional flavors, with an emphasis on local meats and seasonal produce. Our Blowing Rock restaurant offers a full bar and covered patio seating. Come experience why we've been a neighborhood favorite since 2000.

Pasta Inferno

1 Tbsp. cooking oil
16 oz. mild Italian sausage links, sliced
10-12 jarred pepperoncini peppers,
stems and seeds removed
2 c. liquid from pepperoncinis
1 Tbsp. blackening seasoning
1/2 c. shallots, diced small
2 c. high quality marinara sauce
1 qt. heavy whipping cream
1/2 c. sliced green onions
1 lb. penne pasta, cooked
4 Tbsp. shredded Asiago cheese
2 lb. 16/20 shrimp, peeled and deveined

Blackening Spice
6 Tbsp. smoked paprika
4 tsp. dried thyme
3 Tbsp. finely ground black pepper
4 tsp. dried oregano
2 Tbsp. kosher salt
4 tsp. dried basil
4 tsp. granulated garlic
1 Tbsp. cayenne pepper
1 Tbsp. granulated onion
Mix all ingredients well.

Directions:

Heat oil over high heat in large saucepan. Add sausage, peppers, shallots, and blackening spices to pot, stirring until brown, about 2 minutes. Add pepperoncini juice, marinara, and heavy cream to pot, along with shrimp. Continue cooking on high heat until liquid is reduced by about half, or until it coats the back of a spoon. Add cooked pasta, 1/4 cup of sliced green onions and 2 tablespoons of shredded Asiago. Mix well; continue stirring until pasta is heated through. Plate and garnish with remaining green onions and Asiago cheese.

Entrees   *Submitted by: Andrew A. Long, General Manager/Chef de Cuisine*

206 N. Main St.
Gunnison, CO 81230
Phone: 970-641-4990
Fax: 970-641-1820
Website: www.sugahscafe.com

Sugah's Cafe is a Southern Bistro in the heart of the beautiful Gunnison Country on the Western Slope of the Rocky Mountains. We are serving Creole, Southern Soul Food, and Low Country cuisine to a friendly small mountain town. This is fine dining with a Southern accent.

Lamb Osso Bucco with Orzo

12 Lamb shanks
Salt and pepper
4 onions, sliced thick
30 garlic cloves
6 carrots, peeled and cut in 2" pieces
6 celery stalks, cut in 2" pieces
1 can tomato paste

Spices

1 Tbsp. marjoram
1 coriander, ground
2 Tbsp. olive oil
10 whole cloves
2 tsp. cinnamon
1 tsp. turmeric
2 Tbsp. cumin
1 tsp. ground chipotle
1 Tbsp. cracked black pepper
2 Tbsp. thyme

Entrees

Recipe continued on next page

Recipe continued:

4 c. red wine   6 c chicken stock
1 tsp. ground chipotle   1 Tbsp. cracked black pepper

Directions:

Sprinkle shanks with salt and pepper and brown them on all sides (5-7 minutes). Remove shanks and set aside. In same pan using the rendered fat, add onions, garlic, carrots, celery, tomato paste and 1/3 of spices, and a sprinkle of salt. Sauté vegetables to soften about 5 minutes. Add wine, then stock, stirring to loosen bits from bottom of pan. Bring to simmer; transfer vegetables and liquid to deep braising pan big enough to hold shanks in single layer. Add shanks and sprinkle with remaining spices. Cover pan and transfer to a 350° oven. Braise for 2-3 hours. Uncover and continue braising about 30 minutes or until tops are brown. Turn and braise until other side is brown and shanks are tender. Serve with Mediterranean Orzo.

Mediterranean Orzo

2 lb. Orzo   1 1/2 c. diced tomato
2 gal. water   1 c. diced red bell peppers
6 Tbsp. mint   2 c. calamata olives
4 Tbsp. fresh basil   2 c. black olives
                                     Salt and pepper to taste

Directions:

Boil pasta al dente. Mix in large bowl.

540 S. Main Street
Memphis, TN 38103
Phone: 901-526-5757
Website: www.arcaderestaurant.com

The Arcade has the honor of being Memphis' oldest restaurant. Speros Zepatos founded the diner in 1919 after emigrating from Cephalonia, Greece. A marker outside of the front door lists the Arcade Restaurant as a historic landmark. It's like a trip back in time! It is this nostalgic feeling that has attracted photographers, artists, writers, and movie makers from around the world. Scenes from many well known movies have all been filmed in the restaurant. Many of the celebrities from the movies have eaten the same foods you will eat today. At one time, even Elvis was a regular.

Greek Chicken & Potatoes

1 whole chicken
1 clove garlic, minced
1/2 onion
Salt & pepper to taste
2-4 baking potatoes
Juice of three lemons
1 Tbsp. oregano
1/2 c. butter
1/2 c. cup virgin olive oil

Third generation owners Harry and Karan Zepatos can now be found running the day to day operations of the Arcade. Although many changes have been made over the years, great care has been taken to preserve the old-time charm. So while the glowing neon signs and the 1920s architecture may transport you to the past, the pesto, feta, and walnut pizza will bring your taste buds to the present. The South Main Historic District, the whistle of the trolley, and the Arcade Restaurant... it doesn't get any more Memphis than this!

Directions:
Wash and cut chicken into quarters or single pieces. Season with salt and pepper. Peel potatoes and cut into bite size cubes. Combine all other ingredients in oven safe dish. Add chicken and potatoes. Cut the leftover lemon into slices and place over chicken. Bake at 325° for about two hours or until tender. Baste often. Most excellent with a Greek Salad. Enjoy!

Entrees

Submitted by: Harry & Karan Zepatos, Owners

649 N. Main Street
Bishop, CA 93514
Phone: 760-873-5777

The Back Alley Grill & Bar is located in the heart of the Eastern Sierras in the Owens Valley. Our lunch menu features fresh ground American beef burgers in variations you've only dreamed of while our dinner fare features dishes from Lobster Tail, Prime Rib, and Steak Oscar to freshly tossed Caesar Salad. Steak Imperial is a simple yet very popular entree. Many enjoy the combination of fresh asparagus and steak brought together by the shrimp scampi.

Steak Imperial

10 oz. flat iron steak
3 trimmed, cooked asparagus spears
3 lg. shrimp, peeled and deveined
1 Tbsp. olive oil
Pinch of salt

Scampi Butter
3 fresh chopped garlic cloves
1 tsp. parsley
Zest of one lemon
1/2 c. butter, softened

Directions:

Two hours before meal preparation, prepare the scampi butter by folding ingredients into softened butter until all ingredients are well mixed. Then cover and refrigerate for two hours.

Begin by charbroiling the flat iron. Remove from heat. Lightly sauté shrimp in olive oil. Add scampi butter to pan and continue to simmer on low heat for 2 minutes. Place cooked steak on plate, top with the asparagus spears and the shrimp. Lightly drizzle with half the remaining butter in pan. Serve.

Entrees   *Submitted by: Dee Taylor, General Manager & Chef Jake C.*

1324 S. Main
Tulsa, OK 74119
Phone: 918-582-1964
Fax: 918-382-6013

Pistachio and Basil Encrusted Rack of Lamb

Celery Root Mash

8 med. size celery roots
8 Yukon gold potatoes
1 qt. heavy cream
1/2 lb. butter
Salt & white pepper
4 16 oz. portions of rack of lamb

The Chalkboard Restaurant, nestled in the basement of the historic Hotel Ambassador, is a Tulsa favorite for pre-theater and concert dining and the perfect place to celebrate special occasions and impress out of town guests, for breakfast, lunch, or dinner, 365 days a year. Owner Ayhan Ozaras and Chef Cameron Werry focus on blending European and Continental Cuisine and unparalled customer service.

Pistachio and Basil Crust

1 lb. fresh arugula
1 lb. fresh basil
1/2 c. grated asiago cheese
1 c. toasted pistachios
3 c. olive oil
2 c. Panko bread crumbs

Balsamic Hollandaise

6 egg yolks
1 oz. balsamic vinegar reduction
2 c. clarified butter

3/4 c. water
Salt and pepper to taste

Directions:

For Celery root mash: Boil peeled celery root in lightly salted water till fork tender. Strain half of liquid, then blend in food processor till very smooth, about 5 minutes. Boil peeled potatoes in lightly salted water till fork tender, strain off all liquid, add heavy whipping cream and butter and mash with a heavy duty whisk till smooth. Combine 4 cups of potato mixture and 2 cups of celery puree with salt and pepper to taste.

Pistachio and basil crust: Combine arugula, basil, Asiago cheese, toasted pistachio, and olive oil in food processor to a paste-like consistency. Place in bowl and mix in Panko bread crumbs.

Balsamic Hollandaise: In steel bowl, whisk 6 egg yolks, 3/4 cups of water and 1 ounce of balsamic reduction to a custard-like consistency. In a small saucepan, over low heat, warm clarified butter. Place egg mixture in blender on medium speed; slowly add clarified butter. You may add warm water if necessary to thin out sauce. Add salt and pepper to taste.

Lamb prep: Trim off excess fat, and cut racks in half. Coat skillet with olive oil. On high heat, pan sear lamb 1 minute per side or until golden brown. Remove from pan, drizzle with more olive oil, and coat lamb with crust mixture. Place in new pan and bake in oven at 400º about 6-8 minutes. Let rest 5 minutes before cutting into. Serve over celery root mash and drizzle with hollandaise.

Entrees   *Submitted by: Dori Joffe, Manager*

Home Cooking Away From Home

167 N. Main Street
Decatur, AR 72722
Phone: 479-752-8300
Fax: 479-752-3799

We had to trade 6 secret recipes for salad dressings to a Native American grandmother for her recipe for Indian Tacos. WE got the better end of the deal.

Indian Taco

8 c. self rising flour
2 3/4 c. hot water

Chili*
Shredded cheese
Lettuce
Tomatoes
Chopped onions
Jalapenos
Sour cream
Salsa

Directions:
Mix self rising flour and hot water just until moistened. Do Not Over mix! Cover and let stand for at least 2 hours. Take a large spoonful of dough the size of a tennis ball and pat out almost flat in a pan of dry flour. The size of the flat dough should be the size of a salad plate. Drop carefully into a deep fryer at 350°. Fry until golden brown and flip over. Remove when both sides are golden brown. Cover with chili, shredded cheese, lettuce, tomatoes, chopped onions, jalapenos, sour cream and salsa.

*Chili recipe available on page 57

Entrees   *Submitted by: Stacy Brooks, Owner*

61 E. Main Street
White Sulphur Springs, WV 24986
Phone: 304-536-5001
Website: www.masonjarwv.com

Located in downtown White Sulphur Springs, West Virginia, the Mason Jar is home to a fine variety of steaks, seafood, and more. Check out our excellent menu, and whether it be for your next lunch, dinner, or catered meal, let the Mason Jar take care of you!

Braised Brisket

Good as a main entree or can be served for sandwiches.

8-10 lb. brisket (Sam's Club)

Season Blend
Onion powder
Salt
Garlic powder
Course black pepper

Directions:
Preheat Oven to 400°. Prepare season blend. Trim some fat from the brisket, leaving some for flavor. Generously season entire body of meat with season blend. In Roasting pan, with fatty side up, cook till brown (about 1 hour). Remove from oven and wrap in aluminum foil. Fill roasting pan half full of water. Return beef to pan and bake for 8 hours at 250° temperature. Allow beef to rest at least one hour before slicing to serve. Save juices from roasting pan to serve as an Au Jus sauce.

Entrees   *Submitted by: Adam Sydenstricker, Chef*

41 Main Street, Bradford, PA 16701
Phone: 814-368-4780
Fax: 814-368-4349
Website: www.theoptionhouserestaurant.com

The newly restored Option House Restaurant and Lounge is one of Bradford's historic landmarks. The establishment's history dates back to the early 1900's when oil speculators negotiated oil (five million barrels daily) "option" contracts here. The Option House features two restaurants for fine dining. The first floor "Trading Room Lounge" has a rustic, European, pub-like atmosphere. The upstairs restaurant, "Peacock Parlor," is a formal room for individual diners and for banquets and special events. Its elegance is unsurpassed in the region. The most common comment heard from guests entering The Option House is, "WOW!" The Option House introduced the tapas dining concept to the Bradford area and also offers a different ethnic cuisine each month, as well as a full menu.

Portabella Mignon a la Option

4 oz. beef tenderloin
1 lg. portabella mushroom cap
Balsamic vinaigrette for basting
Salt and pepper to taste
Butter
2 oz. fresh spinach (de-stemmed)
2 oz. Gorgonzola, crumbled
3 oz. Bordelaise sauce

Directions:

To prepare portabella cap, first baste with white balsamic vinaigrette, or vinaigrette of your choice, and bake at 350° for approximately 25 minutes or until tender. Remove and cool. Season tenderloin with salt and pepper and grill until medium rare. Concurrently, warm the portabella by placing on the grill. Lightly cover bottom of skillet or frying pan with clarified butter. Heat, add spinach and sauté until completely soft and wilted. To plate, first ladle bordelaise sauce into a pool in middle of plate. Place mushroom cap, upside down, in middle of pooled sauce. Thinly slice tenderloin and shingle on top of mushroom. Top with crumbled gorgonzola and caramelize with a torch, or under broiler. Top with spinach and serve immediately. Makes one serving.

Entrees   *Submitted by: Sam Sylvester, Owner*

19391 Main Street
Buchanan, VA 24066
Phone: 540-254-2455
Website: www.therheinriverinn.com

Set just off the Blue Ridge Parkway in Virginia, The Rhein River Inn has served hungry outdoorsman, Civil War enthusiasts and locals since 2007. The restaurant and B&B is the creation of owners John and Maggi George, who lovingly restored this 1840's country mansion to house their business. Offering German Specialties as well as lamb and salmon dishes, diners can enjoy the elegance of the dining room or the serenity of the outdoor Biergarten set among the flowers and fountains. Of all the German dishes on the menu including Rouladen, Sausages, Schnitzels and more, the most popular dish is Oma's Sauerbraten - just like grandmom used to make! Serve this dish with sauerkraut, red cabbage, potato salad and noodles with mushroom gravy for a winning combination along with a nice cold German beer!

Oma's Sauerbraten

5 lb. bottom round roast

Marinade

2 c. water	1 tsp. ground mustard
1 c. white vinegar	4-5 whole bay leaves
1 c. red wine vinegar	1 tsp. celery seed
1 tsp. whole cloves	1 tsp. salt
1/2 tsp. nutmeg	1/2 tsp. black pepper

Directions:

Mix marinade ingredients together in a large bowl. Slice the roast down the middle, long ways to expose more of the meat to the marinade. Place the meat in a sealable container large enough to hold the meat and the marinade. Pour the marinade over the meat, being sure all the meat is drizzled with the marinade. Cover or close the container and place it in the refrigerator for 2-3 days, being sure to baste the meat with the marinade a few times daily. Unlike all the other Sauerbraten recipes I've known, mine differs here because when you are ready to roast, place the meat in a heavy, deep roasting pan with a lid and use all the marinade as a liquid in which to cook the meat instead of removing the meat from the marinade and throwing the marinade away. By cooking in the marinade you will achieve a much deeper infusion of the spices - especially the nutmeg and cloves, thus adding to the rich flavor of this Sauerbraten! Cook at 350° for 1 1/2 to 2 hours. Remove the roast and slice in 1/2 inch thick slices replacing them into the baking dish stacked at an angle on top of each other in the marinade bath so they will continue to bake in the juice for another 1 1/2 hours. Serves up to 10.

Entrees   *Submitted by: Maggi George, Proprietor & Head Cook*

SILVER GRILLE
Cafe & Wines

206 E. Main Street
Silverton, OR 97381
Phone: 503-873-8000
Website: www.silvergrille.com

Owners Jeff and Naomi Nizlek serve "Willamette Valley Cuisine," using locally grown products to produce unique, crafted ever-changing cuisine for a memorable dining experience. The following recipe is from a fall dinner menu featuring local lamb and organic goat cheese.

Slow Roasted Lamb Shoulder with Fairview Farms Cynthian Goat Cheese Gratin and Glazed Baby Turnips

1 Sudan Farms lamb shoulder, boneless
1 head garlic, leave 4 cloves unpeeled and peel the rest
1 onion, peeled and diced 1/2"
2 carrots, peeled and diced 1/2"

2 c. red wine
1/2 c. olive oil
Kosher salt
White pepper

Directions:

For the Lamb Shoulder - Use a boneless lamb shoulder, which will come in a webbing to hold the meat together. Rinse and clean thoroughly and dry on clean towels to remove all moisture. Coat liberally with salt and white pepper. Heat oven to 275º. Place carrots, onions, and garlic on bed of roasting pan and place lamb shoulder in center. Brush on olive oil or rub with fingers to coat the lamb shoulder, and then cover lamb with aluminum foil, forming a tent. Place lamb in oven and roast for three hours, checking every 30 minutes. After 3 hours, remove lamb from the oven, and place the lamb on a rack over another pan and return, uncovered to the oven. Raise temperature to 300º and add the Goat Cheese/Potato Gratin (recipe on next page.) Place the roasting pan over high heat and add the red wine, reducing it to a glaze. Add the lamb or veal stock and return to a boil. Reduce heat to a simmer and cook until reduced by half. Strain contents through a fine mesh strainer into a new pot. Return to heat and reduce until sauce coats the back of a spoon. Remove lamb from oven and allow meat to rest for 15 minutes. Place in the center of a platter, straining the cooking juices into the sauce. Surround the meat with the turnips (recipe on next page) and serve with the Goat Cheese Gratin and Sauce separately. Serves 8.

Entrees   **Recipe continued on next page**

SILVER GRILLE
Cafe & Wines

Recipe continued

Fairview Farms Goat Cheese Gratin

1 qt. cream	1 sprig thyme	8 oz. Fairview Farms Goat Cheese
2 c. milk	1 sprig rosemary	(Cynthian here, but others can be used)
1 clove garlic	Kosher salt & white pepper	3 lb. Yukon Gold potatoes

Directions:
Bring cream and milk to a boil with a garlic clove, sprig of thyme and rosemary, and salt and white pepper; remove and allow to infuse. Using a peeler, shave the cheese into a bowl. Using a 13 x 9 inch baking pan, brush the inside with a clove of minced garlic. Peel and thinly slice the potatoes and blot with paper towel to remove moisture. Ladle 2 ounces of cream into pan and place a layer of potatoes in the bottom of pan. Ladle more cream over the potatoes, covering in a complete layer. Sprinkle goat cheese over the cream, and repeat process until potatoes are used. Layer cream and cheese to cover, and bake in oven for 1 to 1 1/2 hours, until deep brown crust forms and sides are bubbling. Check doneness with toothpick; remove from oven and let rest 15 minutes before serving.

Glazed Turnips

1 lb. baby turnips	Kosher salt	1 Tbsp. butter
1 Tbsp. olive oil	White pepper	Veal, lamb or vegetable stock

Directions:
Trim turnips and wash thoroughly, drying well on paper towels. Place heavy bottomed pan over medium high heat and add 1 tablespoon of olive oil. When pan is hot, add turnips to pan and season with salt and white pepper. Add 1 tablespoon of butter to the pan. Allow it to brown, shaking the pan to redistribute turnips into an even layer. When the butter has just caramelized, deglaze with 2-3 ounces of lamb stock or vegetable stock and allow to reduce. Check turnips and repeat process until done. Serve at once.

Entrees   *Submitted by: Jeff Nizlek, Owner/Chef*

707 Main Street
Norwell, MA 02061
Phone: 781-561-7361
Website: www.thetinkersson.com

Chefs: Brian Houlihan & Melinda Lynch

The Tinker's Son is an Authentic Irish Pub in the center of Historic Norwell, Massachusetts. The rustic interior, with large beams and hardwood floors, is reminiscent of the pubs in Dublin. The Tinker's Son prides itself on using organic, locally grown produce in its made-from-scratch Kitchen. At the Bar, built from reclaimed wood, you are sure to find inviting conversation alongside your favorite pint or specialty cocktail.

Guinness Braised Short Ribs with Blue Cheese Whipped Potatoes

Short Ribs
- 4 lb. bone-in beef short ribs
- 5 Tbsp. vegetable oil
- Salt and pepper
- 1 1/2 pt. chicken stock
- 8 oz. Guinness
- 3 oz. Port
- 1/2 lb. wild mushrooms, sautéed
- 1/2 lb. Spanish onions, sautéed
- 4 oz. butter

Blue Cheese Whipped Potatoes
- 2 1/2 lbs. peeled potatoes
- 10 oz. heavy cream
- Salt and pepper
- 3 Tbsp. butter
- 4 oz. blue cheese

Directions:

Brown Short Ribs on all sides in vegetable oil using a heavy pot. Remove Short Ribs from pan and deglaze with Port and Guinness. Return to pan with chicken stock and let simmer a few minutes. Braise in 450° oven for 2-3 hours or until fork-tender. Remove from oven, skim fat from top and remove Short Ribs. Add Sautéed Mushrooms and Onions and reduce by half. Finish with salt, pepper and butter. Pour over Short Ribs. For Whipped Potatoes: Boil peeled potatoes until fork-tender. Simmer heavy cream and butter then incorporate hot, diced potatoes, and blue cheese. Salt and pepper to taste. Top blue cheese whipped potatoes with Short Ribs and mushroom and onion glaze. Serve with local, grilled, organic vegetables.

Entrees   *Submitted by: Chef Brian Houlihan*

136 N. Main Street
Sellersville, PA 18960
Phone: 215-257-3000
Fax: 215-257-3166
Website: www.washingtonhouse.net

This Bucks County landmark dates back to 1742 when "Main Street" was a Lenne Lenape Indian trail and then a stagecoach line between Philadelphia and Bethlehem. Known today for warm hospitality, intriguing seasonal menus and a thoughtfully chosen wine list, The Washington House is still the home of convivial good times and memorable cuisine. Proprietors William Quigley and Elayne Brick proudly celebrate the restaurant's 25th Anniversary in 2010! Executive Chef Andrew Loeffler's seasonal menus burst with flavors and visual appeal as demonstrated in this popular French Lentil dish.

Jumbo Sea Scallops over Sautéed French Lentils with Pine Nuts and Sun-Dried Cherries

Lentils

2/3 c. dried lentils (French green)
1/2 tsp. ginger
1/2 tsp. cinnamon
1/4 tsp. salt
8 grinds fresh pepper

Lemon butter sauce

1 c. white wine
1 lg. shallot, diced
Juice from 1 lemon
1/2 c. heavy cream
1/2 lb. butter, chilled and cubed

Entrees

Recipe continued on next page

Recipe continued:

Scallops
>   16 jumbo sea scallops, approx. 2 oz. each
>   4 Tbsp. olive oil, preferably Greek Extra Virgin
>   1/4 c. toasted pine nuts
>   1/2 c. chopped sun-dried cherries
>   2 c. baby spinach
>   8 basil leaves, julienned
>   4 oz. goat cheese

Directions:

Prepare lentils ahead. Rinse dried lentils; combine in saucepan with 1 1/3 cups water. Add ginger, cinnamon, salt and pepper. Cook until tender and set aside. Water should be almost completely absorbed into lentils.

Prepare Lemon Butter Sauce just before you serve: In a saucepan combine wine, shallots and lemon juice. Reduce by 1/2. Add cream and reduce again by 1/2 volume. Remove mixture from heat and slowly whisk in the cold butter until all is emulsified. Keep sauce in a warm, but not hot, spot before serving.

Heat sauté pan with 2 tablespoons of olive oil. Lightly salt and pepper sea scallops, then sear until golden brown on both sides. Remove and keep warm. Heat remaining olive oil in pan; add cooked lentils, cherries, pine nuts, basil leaves and spinach; cook for 1 1/2 minutes or until spinach is wilted. Crumble in goat cheese and divide mixture among 4 plates. Top with 4 scallops and drizzle each with Lemon Butter Sauce. Serves four

Entrees   *Submitted by: Alyson Nelson, Marketing & Production Coordinator*

353 Main Street
Gaithersburg, MD 20878
Phone: 301-977-1011 Fax: 301-977-5595
Website: www.vasilisgrill.com

Vasilis Mediterranean Grill is a family-owned restaurant where you're welcomed with a smile and treated to an authentic taste of Greece. Owners Bill and Julie Hristopoulos are hands-on restaurateurs, using the freshest ingredients to personally prepare their own extraordinary recipes. They opened their first establishment in 1993 and moved to the current location on Kentland's Main Street in 2002, designing the new restaurant from the floorboards up to capture the spirit of their native country. Traditional Greek food in ample portions and at reasonable prices, served by a friendly, knowledgeable staff – it all adds up to a dining experience that makes customers feel like family and brings them back week after week.

Shrimp Saganaki (Garithes Saganaki)

1 1/2 lbs. large shrimp, shelled and deveined, tail on
3-4 Tbsp. fresh lemon Juice
1/4 c. olive oil
1 bunch scallions, thinly sliced
2 garlic cloves, peeled and minced
4-5 pepperoncini peppers, minced
2 c. chopped fresh plum tomatoes
1/2 c. seafood stock or fish stock
1 tsp. dried Greek oregano
1 c. Greek feta, crumbled
1/4 c. ouzo
1-2 Tbsp. chopped fresh parsley
Salt, pepper to taste

Directions:

Clean the shrimp and sprinkle with lemon juice. Let them stand in a bowl until the sauce is ready. Heat the olive oil in a large skillet and sauté the garlic, scallions, and pepperoncini peppers until wilted. Add the tomatoes and seafood stock, and simmer for 15 minutes. Drain the shrimp and add them to the skillet. Add the Greek feta, Greek oregano, and ouzo and cook the shrimp for about 5 minutes, or until pink. Season with salt and pepper, sprinkle with fresh parsley. Serve and say opaa!!!

Entrees   *Submitted by: Vasilis Hristopoulos, Owner*

201 Main Street S.E.
Minneapolis, MN 55414
Phone: 612-312-2000
Fax: 612-259-0191
Website: www.vicsdining.com

A classic dish with a twist. Vic's Restaurant is on the Minneapolis Riverfront. We have the entire downtown skyline for your enjoyment. Featuring steaks, seafood, salads and lighter fare.

Sea Bass Wellington with Roasted Red Pepper Beurre Blanc

10 4-6 oz. fresh sea bass fillets (1" thick)
Kosher salt and pepper to season the sea bass
2 Tbsp. whole butter
1 Tbsp. fresh garlic, minced
1 Tbsp. fresh shallots, minced
1 c. button mushrooms, sliced

1 tsp. nutmeg
1 tsp. Old Bay Seasoning
1 c. white wine
Juice of 1 lemon
4 sheets frozen puff pastry (2 boxes)
Egg wash (1 egg, 1/4 c. milk)

Directions:
In hot sauté pan, add butter, garlic, and shallots. When caramelized add mushrooms, and seasonings. Cook until soft. Add wine and lemon juice; let reduce by half. Using a wire whisk, mash mushrooms until smooth and spreadable. Set aside. Cut thawed puff pastry into 20, 4 inch squares. On 10 squares (bottoms) spread mushroom mixture leaving a 1/2 inch border on all sides. (Save 1/4 of mushroom mixture). Lightly season sea bass fillets with salt and pepper. Place on 10 pre-mushroomed bottoms. Brush egg wash on edges of the bottoms. Place a small dollop of remaining mushroom mixture on top of sea bass. Place top puff pastry square on and lightly press edges together with fingers. Press dinner fork around edges. Place Wellingtons on an oiled sheet pan about 2 inches apart. Bake in preheated 375° oven for 20 minutes. Slice on an angle, finish with the Roasted Red Pepper Beurre Blanc. (Recipe on next page.) Enjoy with your friends and enjoy life to the fullest! Serves 10

Entrees   **Recipe continued on next page**

Recipe continued:

Roasted Red Pepper Beurre Blanc

2 Tbsp. whole unsalted butter
2 shallots, diced
1 c. white wine
3 c. heavy whipping cream
2 sticks whole unsalted butter, softened
Juice of 2 lemons
1 red pepper, roasted, peeled, cleaned and diced
2 tsp. kosher salt
1 tsp. white pepper

Directions:

In small sauce pan, on high heat, sauté shallots in 2 tablespoons of butter. When lightly browned, add white wine. Reduce wine until very little liquid remains. Turn heat down to medium and add cream. Bring cream to a boil, reduce heat to low; let simmer 5 minutes. Remove from heat and slowly add butter in small pieces using a wire whisk. Add lemon juice, peppers and seasonings. Keep warm until served in a double boiler if desired.

Entrees

Submitted by: Doug Pittman, Executive Chef, General Manager

Wagoner's Main Street Cafe

112 S. Main Street
Wagoner, OK 74467
Phone: (918) 485-3668

Mike still unlocks the door at 5:30 a.m. in case we're busy in back. Floyd Young usually sits in the third or fourth booth on the right in Wagoner's Main Street Cafe every morning, greeting practically everyone who walks through the front door. He knows practically everyone, and except for the occasional newcomer to the cafe, they know him. His hands and body are bent from a lifetime of hard work, but his mind is as keen as a newly-honed knife.

Easy Lasagna Bake

2 lb. ground beef
2 lg. jars of favorite spaghetti sauce
6 oz. tomato paste
16 oz. cottage cheese
16 oz. ricotta cheese
1/4 c. parmesan cheese
4-5 c. mozzarella cheese, shredded
Salt & pepper
2 – 16 oz. bowtie or penne pasta
Salt & pepper

Directions:
Preheat oven 350°. In a large pan bring salted water to boil. Add pasta and cook till semi-firm. Drain and set aside. Cook ground beef till done. Drain and rinse, then put back in pan. Add spaghetti sauce and tomato paste. Bring to boil, then remove from heat and add pasta, cottage cheese, ricotta cheese, parmesan cheese and 3 cups of mozzarella. Stir well and pour into greased pan. Cover the top with the remaining mozzarella. Set on cookie sheet and bake 35-45 minutes or until it bubbles. Remove from oven and let sit for 10 minutes before serving. Serve with a large salad and garlic toast.

Entrees   *Submitted by: Darlene Burke, Owner*

967 Main Street
Willimantic, CT 06226
Phone: 860-423-6777
Fax: 860-450-0794
Website: www.willibrew.com

The Main Street Café opened in 1991 and is now located in the Willimantic Brewing Co., a living landmark restaurant and pub brewery housed in an historic granite and limestone 1909 U.S. Post Office Building. When used as a post office our pub was the customer lobby and the private dining room housed the postmaster's office. Our dining room, from where you can view our 7 barrel brewery, was the post office work room.

Parmesan Encrusted Tuna with Beer Butter

4 – 8 oz. yellow fin tuna steaks
1 c. plain bread crumbs
1 Tbsp. fresh parsley, chopped
1 Tbsp. dried oregano
1 Tbsp. dried basil
1 tsp. dried thyme
1/4 c. grated parmesan cheese
Salt & pepper to taste
1/4 c. milk
1 c. seasoned flour
2 eggs, lightly beaten with a splash of water
1 Tbsp. olive oil
1 Tbsp. butter

Recipe continued on next page

Recipe continued:

Beer Butter

    1/2 c. unsalted butter, softened
    2 Tbsp. margarine, softened
    2 Tbsp. light brown sugar
    1 Tbsp. honey
    Pinch ground nutmeg
    Pinch ground cinnamon
    1 oz. quality beer; red, amber, or golden ale

David, Kim and Will

Directions:

With an electric mixer or beater, combine butter and next five ingredients on medium speed. Increase speed to high and slowly add beer. Mix for two minutes until fluffy. Place butter in the center of a piece of parchment paper or plastic wrap and roll into a log. Refrigerate for at least one hour. Preheat oven to 400°. Combine bread crumbs and next six ingredients in a large bowl, set aside. Set up a breading station by placing milk, then seasoned flour, then egg mixture, then bread crumb mixture, side by side in separate bowls. Dip each steak into milk, flour, egg and bread crumb mixture. Refrigerate breaded steaks for at least 30 minutes. Heat olive oil and butter over medium-high heat. Sear tuna steaks on one side for two minutes, flip and cook three minutes more. Transfer to oven and finish for five minutes for medium-rare or until desired temperature is reached. Cut four quarter-inch slices from butter log and top each steak with one. Serve tuna steaks with roasted garlic mashed potatoes and sautéed garlic spinach. Serves four.

Our post office-themed menu is overflowing with mouth-watering selections, featuring over 100 items, some of which are made with the beer brewed in-house. We brew over a dozen different handcrafted styles of beer each month and have won the distinguished award of 2010 Best Beer Bar in America.

Entrees   *Submitted by: David Wollner, Proprietor*

11 E. Main Street
Mooresville, IN 46158
Phone: 317-834-3900
Website: www.zydecos.net

We are Zydeco's, the world famous Cajun restaurant in beautiful downtown Mooresville, Indiana. We offer classic south Louisiana cuisine, Cajun and Creole as well as chef's exciting specials. Enjoy dishes such as red beans and rice, jambalaya, alligator, frog legs, etouffee, shrimp, oysters and crawfish. It's all served up in a festive Mardi Gras atmosphere.

Crawfish Pie

Pate Brisée
(basic crust)

3 1/2 c. flour
2 sticks butter, frozen and sliced into pats
Pinch salt
1/2 c. cold water

There are entire symphonies written about crawfish pie. Well, maybe there is one song somewhere that mentions it. Anyway, here is my favorite crawfish pie recipe, and there should be a song written about it. It has tons of crawfish tail meat, andouille and cheese. It has heavy cream, corn, wine and butter, carbohydrates and fat galore and it has a whole bunch of crawfish on top to scare the kids and neighbors. If you try to jam anything else in here, I think it will explode in some kind of stupendous chain reaction. I wouldn't recommend anyone eat like this everyday, of course, but just this once, treat yourself to a classic New Orleans dish. Serve with a nice, light spinach salad and a cold diet drink to alleviate the guilt.

Directions:
Place 3 cups of flour into a food processor. Add the butter and salt and pulse on and off 2 times. Add the chilled water and pulse a final time. Use the remaining flour to lightly dust a work surface. Transfer the dough to the work area. Form and press the dough into a ball, then flatten it out slightly to make a disk. (Do not knead or overwork the dough.) Wrap the dough in wax paper and allow it to rest for 30 minutes.

Entrees   **Recipe continued on next page**

Recipe continued:

Pie filling

1 Pâte Brisée (recipe previous page)
1 ear of corn
1 c. diced onion
1/2 c. diced celery
1 c. diced green bell pepper
1 Tbsp. dried thyme leaves
3 cloves garlic, minced
1 tsp. salt
1 tsp. black pepper

1 bay leaf
4 Tbsp. butter
1 Tbsp tomato paste
1 Tbsp hot sauce
1/4 c. heavy cream
1 lb. boiled crawfish tail meat
2 c. Shrimp Stock
1 lb. boiled red potatoes, cubed
1/2 c. dry white wine

3 Tbsp. flour
1 lb. Andouille sausage, cubed
1 lb. whole boiled crawfish
1 lb. shredded mozzarella cheese
1/2 c. diced green onion
1 Tbsp. paprika

Directions:

Preheat oven to 350°. On a lightly floured surface, quarter the prepared Pâte Brisée dough and roll it out into 4 equal rounds. Place the pastry in 4 ovenproof soup bowls; allow the dough to hang over the edge of each bowl. Tear the dough around the bowls, making a decorative edge. Blind bake the pastry crusts in the 350° oven for 20 minutes or until golden brown.

Scrape or cut the corn kernels off of the cob into a small bowl. Set aside. In a large sauté pan, sauté the onion, celery, bell pepper, thyme, garlic, salt, pepper and bay leaf in 4 tablespoons of butter. Add the tomato paste and cook for 1 minute. Add the corn, hot sauce and cream and simmer for 3 minutes. Add the crawfish tail meat and simmer for 1 minute. Add the shrimp stock, potatoes and wine and bring back to a simmer. Sprinkle the flour over the mixture, cover with a lid and cook for 3 minutes. Remove the bay leaf and stir. The mixture should have a thick consistency. If not, continue to simmer with the lid off until it thickens up. Stir in the andouille.

Preheat the broiler. Spoon the mixture into the blind-baked pastry bowls. Cover with whole crawfish and shredded cheese. Brown the bowls under a broiler until the cheese is hot and bubbly. Serves 4. Top each crawfish pie with green onion and paprika. Serve and enjoy!

Entrees   *Submitted by: Leonard Carter Hutchinson, Ph.D. Chef and Co-Owner*

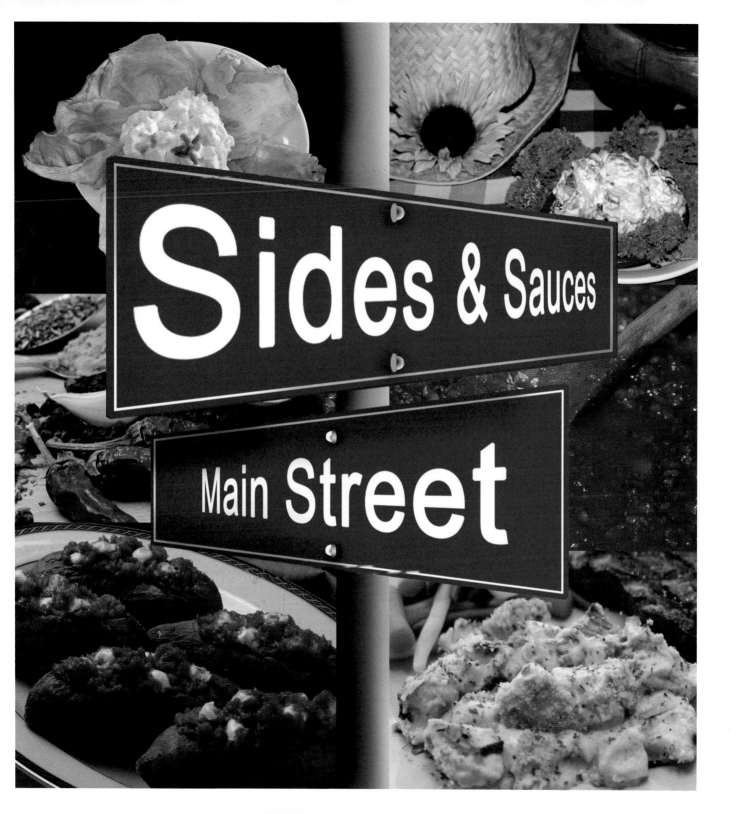

363 Main Street
Jerome, AZ 86331
Phone: 928-634-7087

Photo provided by:
Ron Chilston Photography

We know you have many choices when it comes to restaurants in the small historic town of Jerome, Arizona. 15.quince Grill and Cantina welcomes you into a warm and artistic atmosphere so that you may enjoy your meal. Our menu contains a fusion of home made foods with Native American, Spanish & Mexican influences. The owner, Vlad and his employees invite you in to savor our unique blend of New Mexican Cuisine.

Jerome, Arizona

Traditional Green Chile Sauce

(This is a traditional sauce made in homes throughout New Mexico for generations.)

2 Tbsp. vegetable oil
1 Tbsp. unbleached flour
1/2 med. onion, chopped
1 clove garlic, minced
1 lb. pork, cubed
1 tsp. granulated garlic
1 tsp. salt
3 lbs. roasted hatch green chile
2 c. water

What is New Mexican Cuisine? New Mexican Cuisine comes from a unique blend of influences. New World corn, beans, and chiles combined with Old World garlic and onions; Spanish, Mexican, and Native American cooking approaches simmering together for 500 years to create regional flavors so distinctive they are known the world over.

Directions:

Heat 1 tablespoon of oil in saucepan over low heat. Add onion and minced garlic. Cook until transparent. Add pork and seasonings. Brown pork over medium heat. Stir in green chile and water. Bring to a boil. In a separate skillet, heat 1 tablespoon of oil over low heat. Add flour to make a roux. Stir roux until golden brown. Add to sauce. Cover and simmer over low heat 10 to 15 minutes. Makes approximately 1 1/2 quarts.

Sides & Sauces   *Submitted by: Vladimir Costa, Owner*

165 Main Street
Annapolis, MD 21401
Phone: 410-269-6737
www.ChickandRuths.com

Here at Chick & Ruths, we enjoy life with great food fun and the best service anywhere!

Chick and Ruth Levitt moved from Baltimore to Annapolis with their three children in August of 1965. In taking over a sandwich shop on Main Street, Chick was to institute something that had diminished through the years. Most people had forgotten and young people have never known the "Ma & Pa" establishments. This "unique" delicatessen not only serves quantities of quality food, but also quantities of genuine friendship that have lasted through the years. This is due to Chick's love for people, concern for people, and interest in people.

Deli Fries

6 potatoes
Vegetable oil
14 oz. bowl of chopped onions
Salt and pepper to taste

Chick and Ruth are now gone, but their memories and traditions live on with their son Ted and his wife Beth. They wish to thank their friends for their patronage in the past. They hope to continue to serve their usual fare of wholesome food, friendship, and lodging in the future.

Directions:
Wash potatoes really well and boil with skins on until soft, about 45 minutes. Remove from water and let cool slightly. Slice potatoes really thin like potato chips, leaving peelings on. Put large iron skillet on stove and coat bottom of pan with vegetable oil. Turn heat on high. Fill the bottom of the pan with a layer of sliced potatoes. Continue adding potatoes until they are about 2 inches high in the pot. Pour the chopped onions on top of the potatoes. Sprinkle salt and pepper over all. When bottom layer has browned, turn potatoes with a spatula. Do not turn the heat down. When all potatoes have browned, remove and serve.

Submitted by: Ted Levitt, Owner

301 Main Street
P.O Box 51
Crossett, AR 71635
Phone: 870-304-3504
Fax: 870-304-3484

I was born and raised in Possum Valley, Arkansas. Everything is prepared by hand, from scratch. I love the Lord, people, singing, cooking and eating. I can do all at the same time, in that order. God has blessed.

Western Bean Casserole

2 lb. hamburger
1 bell pepper
1 med. onion
Salt and pepper to taste

4 cans Ranch style beans w/ jalapeno peppers
2 bags Knorr Spanish Rice
4 c. water

Directions:
Brown hamburger with bell pepper and onion. Drain grease, then add salt and pepper. Place in baking dish and add beans, rice and water. Mix with the meat mixture. Bake at 400° for 45 minutes until rice is tender. Stir loose from pan and garnish with grated cheddar cheese before serving.

Broccoli Rice Chicken Casserole

4 skinless/boneless chicken breasts
Butter
Montreal Steak Seasoning
1 onion, diced

1 med. bell pepper
2 carrots, julienne
2 pkg. Knorr Rice/Chicken/Broccoli
4 c. chicken broth

Directions:
Cube chicken and season with Montreal Steak Seasoning; sauté in butter until done, then set aside. Sauté onion, bell pepper, and carrots in butter until tender. Add packages of Rice/Chicken/Broccoli, chicken broth and bring to a rolling boil. Cover and let sit until rice is tender, approximately 15 minutes. Mix rice mixture and chicken breasts together, garnish with steamed broccoli flowerets. Cover, bake at 350° until hot and ready to serve.

Sides & Sauces   *Submitted by: Becky Roberts, Owner*

117 Main Street
Greenwood, MS 38930
Phone: 662-455-9575
Website: www.deltabistro.com

Taylor Bowen Ricketts, a Mississippi native, graduated from the University of Mississippi with a BA in Fine Arts with an emphasis in Painting. After graduation she helped friends open several restaurants in Oxford including City Grocery as well as The Harvest Café, and The Bottletree Bakery. Taylor and her husband, Darby, partnered with friends to open several iconic Oxford restaurants. They opened Proud Larry's, Yocana River Inn, and Jubilee. Taylor sees the culinary arts as another medium and creative outlet, like painting. She continues to immerse herself in both mediums, and her artwork is as much sought-after as her food. Taylor Ricketts and her family moved to Greenwood, Mississippi and became the proprietors of Delta Fresh Market. Her newest role is chef de cuisine at Delta Bistro. The menu reflects her creativity, and she paints each item with flavor as well as color. Taylor has supplemented her kitchen experience with classes from the Culinary Institute of America – Greystone.

Roasted Tomato Sauce

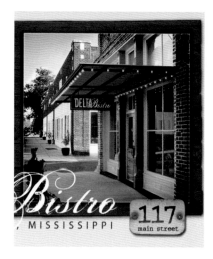

5 lb. tomatoes
1 Vidalia onion
1 red bell pepper
1 poblano bell pepper
1 fresh jalapeno
10-12 whole garlic cloves
3 bay leaves
1 Tbsp. basil

1 tsp. thyme
1/2 tsp. fennel seeds
1/2 tsp. oregano
1 Tbsp. salt
1 tsp. red chili pepper flakes
3 c. red wine
1 lb. butter

Directions:

Rough chop the tomatoes, onion, peppers and jalapeno. Toss all ingredients together and spread in a casserole pan. Roast at 450° for 45 minutes or until desired brownness. Remove from oven and let cool. Puree in food processor. Put into a stock pot and add red wine and butter to it. Simmer on low heat for one hour. Stir occasionally. Can be canned or stored in refrigerator. This is a good multi-purpose sauce with many uses. We use it for pasta, pizza, and salad dressing. It is good to make in the summer time when fresh tomatoes are plentiful.

Sides & Sauces   *Submitted by: Taylor Bowen Ricketts*

4 Main Street
Kennebunk, ME 04043
Phone: 207-985-0050
Website: www.duffyskennebunk.com

Duffy's Tavern & Grill is located in Kennebunk's historic Lafayette Center (formerly the Kesslen Shoe Company). The space, complete with exposed beams and large windows overlooking the Mousam River and Mousam River Dam, exudes a raw mill feel while providing 21st century comforts. We whip up our Italian Cheese Potatoes for special events and to accompany specials on random Friday and Saturday nights. Guests enjoy a change of pace from traditional mashed potatoes. These pair particularly well with steak and chicken entrees.

Italian Cheese Potatoes

4 Tbsp. butter
4 Tbsp. flour
3 c. milk
1 Tbsp. Italian seasoning
1 Tbsp. garlic powder
2 c. shredded cheddar cheese
1/2 c. grated Parmesan
3 lb. potatoes, peeled, cubed and cooked
1 c. seasoned bread crumbs

Directions:

In a medium sauce pan, use the butter and flour to make a roux. Slowly add the warm milk. Stir until thickened. Add seasonings and cheeses to the sauce pan, stirring constantly until melted. In a 9x13 pan, combine the potatoes and the cheese sauce. Top with bread crumbs. Bake at 350° for 30-45 minutes. Serves 6-8.

Sides & Sauces   *Submitted by: David "Duffy" Cluff, Owner*

329 S. Main Avenue
Bolivar, MO 65613
Phone: 417-326-4100

Kathy's PASTA

Gnocchi

2 lb. potatoes
2 eggs
2 3/4 c. flour
1/2 tsp. salt

The charm of Kathy's Pasta dates back to the grand opening on March 23, 1994. Originally located at 434 South Springfield Street, Kathy Gifford began her venture small; with mainly carry-out, seating for 20 and only 8 items on the menu. Within a year, customer demand enlarged the seating to 40. Kathy expanded the menu, and a full-service restaurant was born. In April of 1997, Kathy and her husband, Larry, purchased the building at 329 South Main, the present location. With seating for 97, a full-selection menu and catering services, Kathy's Pasta is proud to offer the Bolivar area a unique Italian dining experience, while maintaining the quiet charm of the early days. It is our goal to continue to offer the best homemade food, friendly service and fair prices for the years to come.

Directions:

Peel and cube potatoes and boil. Drain and toss over low heat until dry. Mash until smooth. Beat in 2 eggs, add salt. Blend in flour to make soft dough adding another 1/4 cup flour if necessary to keep from sticking. Take a 3 inch ball and roll into a 1/2 inch tube, cut into 1 inch pieces and roll with a fork. Cook in salted boiling water a few pieces at a time. When they rise to the surface, they are done. Keep warm in buttered dish in oven. Serve with Italian sauce or grated parmesan.

In October of 2002, Kathy's expanded to add a stylish banquet room including a deck for dining outside. Patrons can also dine around the fountain out front. We hope you enjoy your visit and your meal, because we look forward to seeing you again!

Submitted by: Kathy Gifford, Owner

667 Main Street
Woodland, CA 95695
Phone: 530-666-4400
Website: www.ludys.com

Ludy's Main Street BBQ started in 1994, when gourmet chef Paul Ludovina returned to his home town of Woodland, CA after spending 16 years in Santa Barbara fine-tuning his craft. Since then, Ludy's has served the Greater Sacramento area for more than a decade and a half, serving up our slow-smoked barbeque both in our restaurant and catered all around California. With close to thirty years of culinary experience, Paul has turned Ludy's into a state-wide caterer from the comfort of a modest, small town establishment.

Ludy's Potato Salad Recipe

8 red potatoes, diced into 1/2 inch cubes
1/2 c. diced pickles
1/2 c. diced olives
2 c. diced celery
1/2 Tbsp. garlic powder
1 Tbsp dill weed
1/2 Tbsp black pepper
1 Tbsp salt
2 Tbsp. mustard
1 1/2 c. mayonnaise

Directions:
Place diced potatoes in boiling water until fork tender. Once potatoes are done, remove from water and let cool. Combine the pickles, olives, celery, garlic powder, dill weed, black pepper, salt, mustard, mayonnaise and enjoy!

131 S. Main Street
Memphis, MO 63555
Phone: 660-465-2688
Fax: 660-465-2687
Website: www.southmainstreetcafe.com

Chef David Snodgrass and wife Jeanne own and operate Main Street Cafe in the small Northeast Missouri town of Memphis where they prepare food fresh, and in season, work to procure ingredients from local producers and growers. Before settling in Memphis, Chef Dave worked for nearly 20 years in all styles of restaurants throughout the United States. This experience along with Dave's love of cooking allows for an unexpected variety on a small town menu. Favorites include such diverse options as the Philly Cheese Steak, Hummus Focaccia Sandwich, Black Bean Quesadilla, Spinach Salad with hot bacon dressing, and Reuben. The Stuffed Baked Sweet Potato is a popular special side.

Stuffed Baked Sweet Potato

6 sweet potatoes
1/2 c. brown sugar
1 c. cream cheese
Dash of cinnamon

1/2 c. chopped pecans
Dash of nutmeg
1/2 c. chopped dates

Directions:
Preheat oven to 350°. Scrub and wrap sweet potatoes in foil. Place in oven for approximately 25 minutes. Potatoes need to remain firm; time will vary slightly depending on size of potato. While potatoes are cooking, place remaining ingredients in a large mixing bowl. Pull the sweet potatoes from the oven and immediately make a slit lengthwise in each one. Hollow out with a spoon (leave enough to maintain the shape of the potato) and place the scooped out potato with other ingredients. Mix until nicely blended. Refill potato halves with mixture, allowing to mound slightly in the center. Place potatoes back in oven and bake for an additional 15-20 minutes. Potatoes are best if baked just prior to serving. To prepare in advance complete the above steps without the final baking, cover and refrigerate. Remove and bake 20 minutes before serving time.

Sides & Sauces   *Submitted by: David Snodgrass, Chef/Owner*

NORTH MAIN BBQ

406 N. Main Street
Euless, TX 76039
Phone: 817-267-9101
Fax: 817-684-8120
Website: northmainbbq.com

Founded in 1981 by Hubert and Dollie Green, Ray Green, and Eddie Kelsey. North Main BBQ, "Home of the World's Best Ribs" is backed with 23 years of barbeque experience. North Main BBQ serves the "World's Best Ribs," provides great customer service, and prices that can't be beat! Through our commitment, experience and expertise, North Main BBQ has established a relationship with our customers that will last a lifetime.

Teriyaki Sauce

1 c. water
1 c. soy sauce
1 1/2 c. brown sugar
(enough to soak up liquid)

3 cloves fresh garlic, minced
1 Tbsp. fresh ginger root, minced

4 oz. pineapple juice
2 oz. Jack Daniels Whiskey

Directions:

Mix all ingredients together. Pour into container and refrigerate. Use as needed. Great with beef, pork, chicken or fish.

Sweet Meats

Pork ribs, St. Louis ribs or back ribs
Secret spice (available on our website)
Hickory smoke

Directions:

Sprinkle rub (secret spice) on ribs and pat. Smoke with hickory at 250° for about 3-4 hours.

Sides & Sauces   *Submitted by: Hubert & Ray Green, Owners*

76 Main Street
Providence, RI 02903
Phone: 401-331-0003
Website: www.parksideprovidence.com

The Parkside Rotisserie and Bar is a Manhattan-style bistro centrally located in the heart of Rhode Island's capital city, Providence. Serving lunch and dinner daily, the Parkside is surely a fantastic choice anytime. The Parkside offers a wide array of upbeat foods ranging from spicy crab cakes to grilled tenderloin and Portobello salad. There are also several innovative pasta dishes as well as the Parkside's signature rotisserie meat items and daily specials. The Parkside's unique atmosphere is accented by an open kitchen where guests can enjoy watching our talented culinary staff prepare all of the enticing entrees found on the menu. Join us at the Parkside for a relaxing dining experience that is "casual elegance."

Zippy Green Sauce

1 c. fresh basil (packed)
1 oz. flat parsley (packed)
4 Tbsp. Dijon mustard
1 1/2 oz. balsamic vinegar

1/2 c. olive oil
3-4 med. garlic cloves
1/3 c. Pignoli Nuts (Pine nuts)

Directions:
Combine the basil and flat parsley in with the pine nuts; pulse a few times in a food processor. (If you are using walnuts instead of pine nuts and they are not already chopped, pulse them a few times first, before adding the basil.) Add the garlic and pulse a few times more. Place Dijon mustard in with balsamic vinegar and pulse a couple of times. Slowly add the olive oil in a constant stream while the food processor is on. Stop to scrape down the sides of the food processor with a rubber spatula until blended and makes a paste. Add a little freshly ground black pepper to taste. Makes 1 cup. We serve this with our rotisserie marinated chicken (our signature dish), but it can be used on any meats, vegetables, salads, or even pasta.

Sides & Sauces   *Submitted by: Adam Vargulish, General Manager*

256 E. Main Street
Apopka, FL 32703
Phone: 407-880-3351
Website: www.porkiesoriginalbbq.com

Porkie's Original BBQ in Apopka serves up Florida's best ribs, chicken and smoked ribeyes with a side of antique toys, memorabilia and family fun. The aroma of Porkie's Original BBQ is an appetizing welcome as you enter this quaint eatery located in the heart of Apopka on Main Street and can be smelled a mile away.

Our owners traveled Tennessee, Alabama, Georgia and the Carolinas searching for the perfect BBQ flavor before creating their own signature sauces and spices. All their sauces are original recipes and are made from scratch which seems to be a common thread at Porkie's. Our Brunswick Stew and Jim's Dirty Taters are just a couple of the original family recipes you won't find anywhere else. And don't forget the Homemade Banana Pudding made fresh daily! Porkie's Original BBQ is truly Florida's Best Barbeque, so come on in for some great food and family fun!!!

Jim's Dirty Taters

3 lb. red skin potatoes (diced in 1/4 in. pieces)
2 Tbsp. butter
2 oz. olive oil
2 Tbsp. crushed garlic

3 Tbsp. Lawry's garlic salt
1 Tbsp. salt
1/4 tsp. pepper
1 c. diced onions

Directions:
Mix all ingredients into a 12 inch baking pan and stir evenly. Roast in a 375° preheated oven for 50 minutes, stirring every 15 minutes.

Submitted by: Steve White, Owner

409 Main Street
P.O. Box 7
Bancroft, NE 68004
Phone: 402-648-7458

The Country Pub has been serving food and spirits to Northeast Nebraska for 30 years. Current owners and operators, Aaron and Nikki Peirce, have created a menu mixing traditional with new by serving a variety of burgers, sandwiches, and salads, with noon and evening specials. Along with beef, pork, chicken, and seafood entrées, everything is made with the individual in mind.

Creamy Corn

1 1/4 lb, frozen whole kernel corn
6 oz. softened cream cheese
8 oz. whipping cream
1 Tbsp. sugar
(more or less depending on how sweet you want it to be)
1/2 stick butter
Salt to taste

Directions:
Combine all ingredients in a small roaster and set oven at 200° until it is heated through to 165 degrees, stirring periodically.

Sides & Sauces   *Submitted by: Aaron Peirce, Co-Owner*

69 Main Street
Poca, WV 25159
Phone: 304-204-4700
Fax: 304-204-4701

The Hungry Hound is a small town Hot dog and Wing joint that strives to serve fun food that is consistently good. Home of the original "Flat Dog" (a dog that is grilled and pressed in seasoned butter and fixed your way). We also have other menu favorites including Burgers, Philly's, BBQ, ice cream and much, much more. Although this recipe is not on the menu YET, it is a family favorite.

Cheesy Garlic Pasta with Asparagus

1 lb. penne Rigate pasta
1 c. butter
1/4 c. olive oil
1 tsp. red pepper flakes

8-10 garlic cloves
1 bunch fresh asparagus
6 oz. Asiago cheese
6 oz. shredded parmesan cheese

Directions:
Fill pot with water (approximately 16 cups), bring to a boil, add pasta and cook until tender, then strain. In large skillet, melt butter over low heat; add olive oil and pepper flakes. Chop garlic fine and cut asparagus into bite size pieces. Add garlic to melted butter and oil, and sauté until tender, then add asparagus and cook to a bright green. (Do not overcook). Pour strained pasta into a large mixing bowl and add the butter, garlic asparagus mix, stir well, add cheeses and mix. Ready to serve, goes great with grilled chicken and crusty bread. Enjoy! Yields 6-8 servings.

Sides & Sauces   *Submitted by: David and Kelly Bays, Owners*

122 E. Main Street
Anamosa, Iowa 52205
Phone: 319-462-5533
Website:
www.tylcranddowningseatery.com

Tyler & Downing has been doing business in Anamosa, Iowa since 1904. The restaurant, Tyler & Downing's Eatery, was started (2004) from the tradition of serving our community, as four generations of our family have done for over 100 years. Dirk A. (D.A.) and Brenda K. Downing, fourth generations, are the owners.

The legacy of family and tradition is the reason behind offering an old and simple recipe for Sweet Hot Mustard. It was Dirk's Great-Great Aunt Hattie Leech's (1848-1916) recipe. We share it with you now and hope you call it "Aunt Hattie's Mustard," as we have for over 120 years. It is incredible with smoked ham, deli sandwiches or any cured meat. It will add life to a bratwurst, wieners or burgers. Wherever you might use mustard, try it. It will be delicious!

Aunt Hattie's Sweet Hot Mustard

4 tsp. Coleman's dry yellow mustard
(no substitute, if can't find Coleman's, don't make it)
4 tsp. sugar
1/4 tsp. salt
1 tsp. cider vinegar
2-3 tsp. cold tea

Before the restaurant, our family store...1934

Directions:
Mix first four ingredients together, then add the tea slowly, to get the consistency you desire. IMPORTANT: Let stand, covered, overnight. (This makes a small batch. Just increase proportions to make more or less.)

Sides & Sauces   *Submitted by: Dirk A. Downing, Owner*

2001 Main Street
Claridge, PA 15623
Phone: 724-744-2907

Hours:
Monday - Saturday: 11am – 12 midnight
Sunday: 11am – 10pm

Customers love this restaurant! They say Zackel's has the best fish sandwich, prime rib, pizza and wings around. It's also a cool place to just hang out. Although it is a little off the beaten path, it is definitely worth the drive.

Spaghetti Sauce

1/2 c. olive oil
1 1/4 Tbsp. extra virgin olive oil
12-14 oz. fatty pork (from pork butt or neck bone)
3 oz. garlic, chopped
1 lg. onion, chopped
1/4 green pepper, diced
1 lb. ground beef, cooked and drained
2 Tbsp. salt
1 Tbsp. black pepper
1 Tbsp. Italian seasoning
1-2 bay leaves
1/4 sprig parsley, chopped
1/4 sprig basil, chopped
1 28 oz. can Tomato Magic® (ground tomatoes)
1 14.5 oz. can Red Gold® (whole peeled tomatoes)
1/2 gal. water

2 tsp. dried rosemary leaves
1 28 oz. can tomato paste

Directions:

Brown the fatty pork in 1/2 cup of olive oil; once well browned, remove bones from meat. In the same pan, add 1 1/4 tablespoons of extra virgin olive oil and garlic, sauté until medium brown, then add onion and green pepper and let brown slightly. Add cooked ground beef, seasonings, both cans of tomatoes and a half gallon of water (squish whole tomatoes in your hand.) Stir the mixture and low boil for 30 minutes. Add rosemary leaves. Finally, add tomato paste to thicken. Yields approximately 1 gallon.

Sides & Sauces *Submitted by: Bob Oliver, Chef*

Breads & Breakfast

Main Street

ANDY'S CAFÉ

227 S. Main Street
Independence, OR 97351
Phone: 503-838-1696
Fax: 503-838-0567

Andy's Café has had the privilege to serve our patrons for the past 14 years. Andy and his wife Denice have spent nearly 30 years collectively in the restaurant industry. Located in a small picturesque town of about 8,000 at the end of the Oregon Trail, we feature breakfast and lunch menus as well as catering many events, large and small. Fun, family oriented and friendly with as wonderful and witty a clientele as can be found anywhere on the planet! Join us!

Our Signature Spinach Scramble

2 c. fresh baby spinach leaves
1/2 c. fresh chopped tomatoes
3 eggs beaten, we use cage-free brown eggs
Asiago cheese

Directions:
Scramble above ingredients, then fold in 1/4 cup of fresh grated medium Asiago cheese. Serve with our homemade hash brown potatoes with onions and northwest hazelnut toast. Just before serving, sprinkle a little Asiago cheese over the top. Zesty, colorful and pleasing to the senses.

Breads/Breakfast   *Submitted by: Andy and Denice Scott, Owners*

608 Main Street
Mediapolis, IA 52638
Phone: 319-394-3370

Apron Strings opened in 1988. It has been known for serving all sandwiches on homemade buns which Martee, the owner, makes daily. Many people order them for all occasions, and she has made millions of these.

Overnight Homemade Rolls

1 pkg. yeast
4 1/4 c. warm water
1 c. butter
1 Tbsp. salt
2 c. sugar
4 eggs
14-16 c. flour

Directions:
Dissolve yeast in 1/4 cup warm water. Mix remaining water, butter, sugar and salt in large bowl. Add dissolved yeast to this mixture along with eggs. Mix well. Add flour until not sticky. Knead a little. Start this at 2:00 p.m. Cover and let rise. At 6:00 p.m. punch down. Let rise until 9:00 p.m. Punch down. Make into rolls and place on greased pans and leave on counter overnight. Bake at 6:00 a.m. at 350° for 12-15 minutes. Recipe makes 45 large buns or 90 small buns.

Breads/Breakfast   *Submitted by: Martee Woodruff Murguia, Owner*

D'Vine

He is D'Vine and
We are the branches

Soulfood & Catering

207 Main Street
Biloxi, MS 39530
Phone: 228-374-0910
Fax: 228-374-0970

D'Vine was a promise to me from God 20 years ago. I believed God that He would give me my dream in owning a restaurant. I was a troubled teen and when I gave my life to Him and had faith, here I am.

Hot Water Cornbread

2 c. cornmeal (Self-Rising)
1 1/2 c. flour
1/4 c. sugar
3 c. water
2 lg. eggs
3 c. cooking oil

Directions:
Mix cornmeal, flour, and sugar together in large bowl. Add water and egg into dry mixture. Add more water if needed. Pour oil into large frying pan and heat. Pour 1/4 cup of mixture into pan to form 6 small circles. Cook for 3 minutes on each side until done. Repeat process until all batter has been cooked in the oil.

Breads/Breakfast   *Submitted by: Norma Nelson, Owner*

158 E. Main Street
Newark, DE 19711
Phone: 302-737-6100
Fax: 302-737-6199
Website: www.klondikekates.com

Located in the center of life on Main St. in Newark, Delaware, Klondike Kate's Restaurant & Saloon serves both local families and nearby University of Delaware students alike. The combination of Klondike Kate's historical charm with its modern business philosophy has helped to make Klondike Kate's a staple in the Newark community for over 30 years. One of the oldest buildings on Main Street, Kate's Victorian architecture mixed with the youthful energy of the staff and guests makes for a very desirable atmosphere and uniquely rich culture.

Eggs Chesapeake

8 eggs
3 Tbsp. white vinegar
1 lb. lump crab meat
1/2 c. mayonnaise
2 Tbsp. parsley
1/3 c. Japanese bread crumbs

1 Tbsp. dry mustard
1 Tbsp. Old Bay seasoning
1 egg
16 oz. drawn butter
4 egg yolks
2 Tbsp. white wine

2 tsp. lemon juice
1 tsp. Tabasco
1 tsp. Worcestershire
Salt and pepper to taste
4 English muffins

Directions:

To make the crab cakes, mix the mayonnaise, parsley, mustard, Old Bay and egg. Fold in crab meat and bread crumbs. Form into 3 ounce cakes and sauté over medium high heat until golden brown. This will take about 4 minutes per side. To make the hollandaise sauce, start with the white wine. Put over high heat in a pan and reduce by half. In a bowl, whip the egg yolks with the white wine reduction over medium heat. Continue to whip until yolks are thick. Remove from heat and slowly add drawn butter. When all the butter is incorporated, add lemon, Tabasco, Worcestershire, salt and pepper. To poach eggs, bring 2 quarts of water and white vinegar to a boil. Lower the temperature to a simmer and drop egg in water out of the shell. Cook for 3 minutes until semi firm. Brown crab cakes and set on English muffin. Place poached egg on top of the crab cake. Top with hollandaise sauce and serve.

924 Main Street
Waterboro, ME 04087
Phone: 207-247-5222

Our story goes as follows: I'm Lois, and I'm Shelly, and we are two small town girls that just happened to meet and become friends. Lois is from Hollis, and Shelly is from Waterboro. We met while working for a local restaurant a few years back. Soon we discovered that between us, we could do just about anything in the kitchen. If one of us had never cooked a particular recipe, you could bank the other one had. And the rest is history.

Blueberry Stuffed French Bread

You will need one recipe of white bread:

5 1/2 to 6 1/2 c. of flour	2 1/4 c. milk	1 Tbsp. shortening
1 pkg. active dry yeast	2-3 Tbsp. sugar	1 1/2 tsp. salt

Directions:

Place 3 cups of the flour into a large bowl, along with the package of yeast and set aside. Combine milk, sugar, shortening, and salt in a small sauce pan and heat until warm. Add the warm milk mixture to your flour mixture and beat on low speed for about 1 minute, gradually adding as much flour as you can with a wooden spoon. Turn dough onto a lightly floured board and knead in more flour until you have a stiff dough. Spray a large bowl with cooking spray and place dough in bowl. Let dough rise in warm place until double in size. When doubled in size remove from a bowl and cut dough in half.

While dough is rising, prepare filling as follows:

2 Tbsp. melted butter	2 c. chopped walnuts	1 tsp. cinnamon
4 c. well-drained blueberries	1 c. brown sugar	

Directions:

Melt butter and set aside. Combine next 4 ingredients together in a bowl, then divide into two bowls. Once dough has doubled in size, cut the dough in half. Roll each half to approximately 8x12. Brush each one with melted butter. Cover each half with blueberry ingredients to 1/4 inch of the edge of dough, fold ends in 1 inch and roll into log. Place in greased bread tin. Bake at 350° for 30-40 minutes. Let cool overnight. Slice 1 inch thick and dip in French toast batter and grill.

Breads/Breakfast   *Submitted by: Lois Merrifield & Shelly Nelson, Co-Owners*

3066 Main Street
Tannersville, NY 12485
Phone: 518-589-6101
Website: www.krookedcafe.com

When you fall in love with this area, and Maggie's cooking, let her cater your wedding next to a waterfall, or throw a surprise birthday bash for your best friend. Let her cater an intimate dinner for two, or a spectacular gala for two hundred people. Maggie would love to work with you to create a very special event. And if you need any kind of information, directions to Windham or Woodstock, where to find horses to ride, water to windsurf or antique stores to rummage, just ask Maggie, or any one of her staff.

Krooked Rancheros

1 English muffin
3 eggs
1/2 red onion, chopped
1/4 of green, yellow & red pepper

1 scotch bonnet pepper, chopped
1 whole tomato, sliced
Chopped cilantro
1 slice American cheese (or your choice)

Directions:
Toast English muffin. Grill eggs over easy and put on top of English muffin. Grill onions and peppers and place on top of eggs. Put a sliced tomato over veggies, then top tomato with a slice of cheese. Garnish with cilantro. Melt in oven for 10 minutes at 375° or under broiler.

Breads/Breakfast   *Submitted by: Maggie Landis, Owner/Chef*

914 Main Street
Bridgeport, NE 69336
Phone: 308-262-1033

We modeled the restaurant after a small cafe called Ryden's Border Store and Cafe on the Canadian border of Minnesota along the North Shore of Lake Superior. I used to work there as a short-order cook. The job that started out as a favor for a friend turned into a part-time seasonal job for 5 seasons. I enjoyed it so much that I tried to capture the thrill of a small restaurant after a family move to Western Nebraska. Some days I feel like I created a monster, but overall I love what I do and enjoy the satisfaction that old fashioned meals bring to my customers. I truly feel that I have the best customers in town and we all look forward to our days together.

"Ryan's Garbage Omelet"

3 eggs
Fresh ground sausage
Bacon
Ham
Sautéed green peppers
Tomatoes
Onions
Mushrooms
3 oz. American cheese

All produce is hand picked fresh each day from the grocery store across the street. We pay slightly more than direct from the distributors, and we have virtually no waste due to spoilage. I have a small staff of only 4 employees, and we are all cross trained to fill in anywhere needed. All the staff treat my two sons, Tommy, age 7 and Wyatt age 5, like their own children.

Directions:
Cook sausage, bacon, and sauté all other ingredients and set aside. Blend the eggs in a blender, this adds air to the eggs making a lighter and fluffier omelet. Pour mixture onto a flat-top grill, cook 1 minute, add ingredients. Grill on medium heat, "roll" omelet in thirds, then finish cooking by steaming the omelet under a lid. Serve with homemade hash browns (not frozen store bought) and toast with jelly. Can also be served with green chili.

Breads/Breakfast   *Submitted by: Ryan and Michael Nelson, Owners*

FAMILY OWNED AND OPERATED
Pennsylvania Dutch - With A Southern Touch

Miller's Bread - Basket
"Your Family Restaurant"

483 Main Street
Blackville, SC. 29817
Phone: 803-284-3117
Mon - Sat 11am - 2pm
Thur & Sat 5pm - 8pm

Remember the song "Oh Cast Your Bread Upon The Waters" and it shall return unto you after many days! Bread is a wonderful way to share, by giving it as a gift or sitting down for dinner and fellowshipping. Breaking bread together is used as a remembrance of Our Savior's Love for us in giving His life for our salvation at Communion time. Uncle Ray's White Bread was developed to taste like Grandma's sour dough bread, but without the starter carry over! It has been a favorite along with other flavors like wheat, butternut, Cinnamon-Raisin, Cheddar Cheese, Garlic-Onion, etc. Served at Millers Bread-Basket!

Uncle Ray's White Bread "Our Daily Bread"

(Can be doubled, or work as Dinner Rolls)

1/2 c. warm water
1 Tbsp. yeast
1 c. sour milk
1/8 c. shortening, melted

1/4 c. mashed potatoes
1 tsp. salt
1/2 c. sugar
4 c. bread flour

Directions:

Can be started in a Kitchen Aid Mixer with a hook attachment, but the last of the flour must be kneaded by hand (caution, do not overload mixer). Combine warm water, a pinch of sugar, and the yeast. Set aside. Combine the sour milk (sweet milk with 2 teaspoons vinegar added) vegetable oil or melted shortening in a mixing bowl. Add mashed potatoes (instant potatoes will work), salt, sugar, and 2 cups of bread flour. Slowly add yeast on top, while mixing at slow speed. Slowly add approximately 2 more cups of flour. Knead the last of the flour until bread dough has reached desired consistency. Place dough in a buttered bowl and let it rise in a warm location until it has doubled in size. Divide dough into two loaves and place in loaf pans. Bake at 350° till golden brown.

Breads/Breakfast   *Submitted by: Uncle Ray and Susie, Owners/Manager*

PUTAH CREEK CAFE

1 Main Street
Winters, CA 95694
Phone: 530-795-2682

Good Morning! That's how we start our day at Putah Creek Cafe, bright and early. And when you start your day with us, we hope to be the part of your morning that gets you started and going for a great day. We will do it the only way we know how - with fresh ingredients, quality preparation and the best and friendliest service around. Our commitment to making your visit to our restaurant an enjoyable eating experience is something we at the Cafe take very seriously. We're here to serve you the All-American Breakfast and Lunch seven days a week.

Corned Beef Hash Patties

7-8 lb. corned beef, raw
5 oz. bacon grease
1/2 c. chopped onion
2 1/2 c. chopped green pepper
3 c. russet potatoes, peeled, cut in small cubes,
   par boiled till soft
1 c. beef broth or broth from the corned beef
3 tsp. kosher salt
3 tsp. black ground pepper

Directions:
Place the corned beef in a pot and cover with plenty of water. Bring the water to a boil then turn down the heat to a simmer. Cover the pot and cook for up to 2 hours, adding more water if needed. Continue to cook until the beef is tender. Remove the corned beef from the pot and chill. Save 1 cup of the broth. Cut the corned beef in small pieces and feed them through a grinder with a fitted plate with large holes, or chop in a food processor.

    Recipe continued on next page

Recipe continued

While the beef is chilling, in a large sauté pan add the bacon fat then the onions and peppers; cook until tender. Remove and chill the vegetables. In a large bowl add the onion mixture, ground corned beef, potatoes, and broth. Sprinkle with salt and pepper to taste. The mixture should be just wet enough to form patties; add more broth if needed. Weigh out each patty to 4 ounces and form in round or oval shapes about 1/2 inch thick, place on a sheet pan and chill. Cook on a greased griddle until lightly brown on both sides. The corned beef can be frozen for future use.

We at Putah Creek Cafe have the best selections of the "American Lunch Classics:" great soups and salads, sandwiches and burgers. One of our daily specials is a freshly prepared batch of corned beef made from scratch. It is a favorite with local and visiting guests. John & Melanie have owned the Putah Creek Cafe for 20 years. It has a reputation for serving comfort breakfast and lunch entrees along with freshly made desserts such as pies, cakes, cupcakes, cookies and bread pudding. Local farm produce, freshly ground coffee, fresh orange juice and apple juice set this restaurant apart from other eateries. Just added are dinner entrees with a wood burning pizza oven that sits outside the cafe. So whether you're here with friends, family or business associates, we are sure you'll enjoy our large and distinctive menu. And yes, we have "PUTAH CREEK CAFE" to go." So relax and enjoy your dining experience. We'll take good care of you.

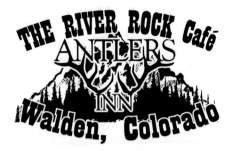

460 Main Street
Walden, CO 80480
Phone: 970-723-4670
Fax: 970-723-3352

River Rock Café is a traveler's treasure. Located in northern Colorado, we are a gateway to a unique experience… always ready with a cup of coffee and a smile. Our Inn is open year-round. Affordable luxury.

Rocky Mountain French Toast

24 slices Texas toast
12 eggs
3 Tbsp. vanilla
4 c. crushed frosted flakes
1/2 c. crushed almond slivers

Toppings
Raspberry sauce
Whipped topping

Directions:

Beat eggs and vanilla together. Dip bread into egg mixture and then roll into frosted flakes and almond mixture. Heat griddle to 350°. Place toast on griddle and cook until golden brown and crunchy. This is a slow cooking French toast. DO NOT RUSH IT or it will burn. Top with sauce, almonds and garnish with whipped topping.

Breads/Breakfast   *Submitted by: Stacey Gollobith, Manager*

Established 1989

701 N. Main Street
Coupeville, WA 98239
Phone: 360-678-3239
Fax: 360-678-3005

The County Deli has been in operation since 1989. It's a family owned and operated deli/restaurant. We have been recognized by several national publications – the latest being "Coastal Living" magazine. We are world famous for our fresh roasted turkey sandwiches, our home-cooked dinner menu and our to-die-for "English custard" bread pudding.

Aegean Quiche

8 raw eggs
3/4 c. sour cream
1 lb. frozen spinach (thawed & drained very well)
1 c. Greek feta cheese crumbles
1/2 c. parmesan cheese
1 sm. tomato, sliced thin
1 deep dish frozen or homemade raw pie crust

Directions:
Beat raw eggs and sour cream until well blended; set aside. Drain spinach WELL (put through a strainer, pushing down with a towel or paper towels). Spread the spinach throughout the pie crust. Next crumble the feta cheese on top of the spinach. Lay the tomatoes in a few nice circles around the top of the quiche. Pour in the egg mixture slowly. Sprinkle with the parmesan cheese and bake for 35-45 minutes at 375°. This is ALWAYS a sell-out at the Deli. Serves 6.

Breads/Breakfast   *Submitted by: Maureen Hummel, Creator & Head Chef*

312 E. Main Street
Bozeman, MT 59715
Phone: 406-587-3973
Fax: 406-586-5410

The Nova Cafe, located in the heart of historic downtown Bozeman, Montana, is locally owned by Serena Rundberg and serves up the best breakfast in town!! Our unique and delicious breakfast and lunch menu is offered daily. The Nova Cafe desires to enrich the lives of its guests, employees and community. We strive to be an integral part of our community by supporting local artists, farmers, producers and other local businesses.

Wild Alaskan Smoked Salmon Hash

2 lbs. diced red potatoes
1 lb. smoked wild Alaskan salmon
1/2 c. plus 2 Tbsp. extra virgin olive oil
1/2 c. diced white onions
1 tsp. fresh minced garlic
2 stalks diced celery
1 diced red bell pepper

1 oz. fresh dill
4 Tbsp. small capers

1/2 c. diced green onions
1 tsp. black pepper

Directions:

Prepare all of your vegetables: dice onions, celery, red peppers, potatoes, and green onions.
Parboil potatoes in 12 cups of salted water for approximately 20 minutes (until they're soft but not mushy); strain and set aside. While the potatoes are cooking, separate the chunk of smoked salmon, making sure to remove any bones and skin. Preheat olive oil on medium-high heat in large stainless pan, then add onions and sauté until soft. Next add garlic, celery, and red bell pepper and sauté those until soft, approximately five minutes (they should be soft but not soggy). Lower the heat, add diced red potatoes, and lightly stir so that the olive oil coats everything. Cook on low for approximately ten minutes, stirring frequently. Add the separated smoked salmon, 1/2 ounce of the fresh dill, capers, and most of the green onions. Mix well and cook for another five minutes until mixture is warmed all the way through. This may be refrigerated for later use. Spoon mixture into a skillet with preheated olive oil. Brown hash and plate it. Top with sour cream and garnish with fresh dill and green onions. May be served with two eggs any style and toast. Serves six.

Breads/Breakfast   *Submitted by: Serena Rundberg, Owner*

181 S. Main Street
Toledo, OR 97391
Phone: 541-336-3272
Fax: 541-336-1943

These Apple Rolls are just like my Grandma used to make. They are wonderful warm or cold. My husband likes them warm with a scoop of vanilla ice cream.

Grandma's Apple Rolls

1 rich pie dough, rolled out
6 finely chopped apples
1 c. sugar
Cinnamon to taste

Rich Pie Dough
3 c. flour
1 tsp. salt
1 1/2 c. shortening
1 egg
1 Tbsp. vinegar
1/2 c. water, a little at a time

Syrup
1 c. sugar
1 c. water
2 Tbsp. butter
Dash of cinnamon and salt

Directions:

Make dough: Mix all ingredients, using a little water at a time, until soft dough is made. Roll dough out. Mix chopped apples, sugar and cinnamon. Spread apple mixture over dough. Gently roll up. Slice dough approximately 1 1/2 inches thick; should have 12 rolls. Carefully place in 9"x13" baking pan, leaving space between them. Boil syrup ingredients together for 5 minutes. Pour over rolls. Bake at 375° for 45 minutes.

Breads/Breakfast   *Submitted by: Gail Wood, Owner*

119 Main Street
Albion, RI 02802
Phone: 401-333-1143

A family owned diner nestled in the quaint town of Albion, RI serving up breakfast, lunch, seafood and homemade daily specials. "A place where customers truly feel like part of the family." Also on the menu is award winning Gifford's Ice Cream & Richie's Real Italian Ice as well as homemade pies & puddings prepared by owners Terri Kadisevskis and Jocelyn Kondrotas.

Country Biscuits and Sausage Gravy

4 c. self rising flour
1 Tbsp. baking powder
1 Tbsp. sugar
2/3 c. shortening
2 c. buttermilk (reserve some to brush tops)

Sausage Gravy Mix
1 stick of butter
1/2 c. all-purpose flour
48 oz. half and half
12 fully cooked sausage links, cut into chunks
Salt, Pepper, Crushed Red Pepper & Onion Powder

Directions:
Mix ingredients together, but do not knead. Roll out dough 1 inch thick. Cut into rounds and brush tops with buttermilk. Bake at 400° for 15 minutes. For gravy, melt butter in a pot on medium heat and add flour slowly, whisking till thickened. Then gradually add half and half, whisking constantly as it comes to a boil. Add salt, pepper, crushed red pepper and onion powder to taste. Lower heat and simmer for 15 minutes. Meanwhile, lightly brown the sausage in a frying pan. Add sausage to gravy mix and let simmer another 15 minutes. To plate, cut 2 biscuits in half and place open on a plate. Ladle gravy mix over biscuits and enjoy!

Breads/Breakfast   *Submitted by: Terri Kadisevskis and Jocelyn Kondrotas, Owners*

Desserts

Main Street

831 Main Street
Brookville, IN 47012
Phone: 765-647-3300

Aromas Café & Deli was founded in 2006 and is owned by Dave, Sherrie and Tia Wolff. This dessert is best served with ice cream or Café Mocha Latte.

Café Mocha Tart

1 pie crust
1/3 c. chocolate chips
3/4 c. chopped walnuts
3 Tbsp. margarine
4 oz. espresso
1/3 c. light brown sugar
1/2 c. light corn syrup
2 eggs
1 tsp. vanilla

Directions:
Heat oven to 350°. Fit pie crust into a 9-inch tart pan. Mix all ingredients and fill the tart pan. Bake for 30-35 minutes. Cool before cutting.

Desserts   *Submitted by: Sherrie & Tia Wolff, Owners*

4143 W. Main Street
Dothan, AL 36305
Phone: 334-699-8646
Fax: 334-699-1380

Bishop's Home Style Cooking, owned by Tim and Kate Bishop, is well known in the community as a place to take your family for good home cooking. The menu has a variety of items from which to choose, and the portions are large. They also are known for catering events around the area. Their Carrot Soufflé is a local favorite.

Carrot Soufflé

26 oz. frozen carrots
1/2 c. sugar
1 1/2 tsp. baking powder
1 1/2 tsp. vanilla
1 1/2 c. flour
4 eggs
6 Tbsp. margarine, softened

Directions:
Boil carrots until extra soft. Drain the water, then add sugar, baking powder and vanilla. Mix well. Add flour and continue mixing to a smooth consistency. Add eggs, beating until mixture is smooth. Finally, add margarine and mix until consistency is smooth. Bake at 325° for 40-45 minutes. It should set up just like a pie.

Submitted by: Tim Bishop, Owner

315 Main Street
Malvern, IA 51551
Phone: 712-624-8082

Classic Café is a family owned and operated restaurant in Malvern, Iowa. They have specialty coffees, smoothies, full bar, and a full service restaurant with daily specials. Darren Bartley is the owner/chef and his sister, Alicia Bartley and brother in-law, Brad Hagen are his partners. They have a large garden which produces much of the fresh produce for the café.

Hot Chocolate Cake

1 c. chocolate chips
1/2 lb. butter, unsalted
5 egg yolks
1 1/4 c. sugar
1 1/4 c. flour
1/4 c. cocoa powder
1/2 Tbsp. baking powder

Directions:
Melt chocolate chips and butter together in a double boiler. Stir to combine and set aside to cool to room temperature. In a large bowl, whip egg yolks and sugar until airy. Sift flour, cocoa and baking powder into the mixture and continue mixing it. Fold chocolate mixture into the egg and flour mixture until just combined. Do not over mix! Place in oven safe dish and bake for 8-10 minutes in a 400° oven. Cake should be firm on top, and watch so it doesn't burn. Top with vanilla ice cream and enjoy!! (We use individual coffee cups at the restaurant.) Be sure to remind your guest that the cup is very warm. Yields: 14-6 oz. servings.

Desserts   *Submitted by: Darren Bartley, Owner/Chef*

11 Main Street
Bennington, NH 03442
Phone: 603-588-6888

Common Place Eatery has been on Main Street in Bennington, New Hampshire for twelve years. It is a family run business with a casual atmosphere for the entire family. Everything is homemade here, and the Prime Rib is the best around!

Double Chocolate Chip Brownie Pie

10 inch single pie crust, your favorite recipe
1 c. margarine, melted
2 c. sugar
1/2 c. cocoa

1 1/3 c. all purpose flour
4 eggs
2 Tbsp. vanilla extract
6 oz. pkg. chocolate chips

Directions:
In a large bowl combine margarine, sugar, cocoa, and flour. Add eggs one at a time. Add the vanilla, and fold in the chocolate chips. Pour into 10 inch deep dish pie shell. Bake in a 350° oven for 25-30 minutes. Crust will be golden brown. You can substitute chocolate chips with white chocolate chips or peanut butter chips. You can also add nuts.

Desserts

Submitted by: Bernetta MacKenzie, Owner

332 Main Street
Conway, SC 29526
Phone: 843-248-3321
Website: www.cradys.com

What began as a small coffee shop has now evolved into a small town Bistro with a "Big City" style and attitude. When you walk into the restaurant, you may feel as if you have just stepped off the streets of Manhattan, or into a beautiful café in Europe…yet, you are on Main Street, in Conway, South Carolina. Crady's began as an answer to prayerful dreams in October of 2001, by Barbara Crady Whitley and her family as a tribute to Barbara's mother, Najgy Crady. In three metamorphoses since then, beginning with a very small coffee shop, to a lunch destination, and finally, to fine evening dining, CRADY'S has become synonymous with quality: from its metropolitan décor to eclectic low country cuisine, scrumptious handmade desserts and friendly, excellent service.

Southern Caramel Cake

1 c. unsalted butter or margarine
2 c. granulated sugar
4 eggs
1 c. sour cream
1/2 c. whole milk
2 3/4 c. all purpose flour
1/2 tsp. salt
2 tsp. baking powder

Cooked Caramel Icing:
4 c. sugar
(Remove 1/2 c. and place in a heavy bottomed sauce pot)
1 c. whole milk
1 c. unsalted butter
1 tsp. baking soda
2 tsp. cider vinegar

Desserts

Recipe continued on next page

Recipe continued

Directions:

Place the butter and sugar in a mixing bowl and mix until light and creamy, about 5 minutes. Add eggs, one at a time, mixing well after each addition. Meanwhile, mix sour cream and milk. Set aside. To egg, sugar, and butter mixture, add 2 cups flour, salt and baking powder. After this has been incorporated, add the sour cream, milk mixture and mix until well blended. Add the remaining 3/4 cup flour and mix well. Do not over mix.

Place the batter into four 9" round cake pans which have been buttered and floured, or sprayed with a baking spray. Bake at 350° for 18-25 minutes. Let cool in pans about 10 minutes and ice with a cooked caramel icing. For icing: In a large sauce pot, place the 3 1/2 cups of sugar, milk, and butter. Cook over medium heat until mixture comes to a boil. Set aside while the 1/2 cup of sugar, in the second sauce pot, becomes an amber liquid over medium heat.

Be careful while pouring the sugar syrup into the butter, sugar, milk mixture. Stir to incorporate. Then do not stir again. Bring mixture to a softly rolling boil and cook until temperature reaches "soft ball stage" on a candy thermometer. Remove from heat. Slowly add baking soda while stirring carefully. Add cider vinegar and stir until mixture becomes thick enough to spread on baked, cool layers.

Crady's still holds true to our "small" roots, and wants all who come in to share their time dining with us to feel as if they are enveloped into warm and welcoming arms. Come in for a Taste of CRADY'S... located in the heart of Historic Downtown Conway, South Carolina.

Desserts   *Submitted by: Heather Whitley, Manager*

901 Main Street
Timber Lake, SD 57656
Phone: 605-865-3351

Timber Lake is a small town where the only things they eat are beef and potatoes. We try to make different things, hoping they will try them.

Tiramisu Layer Cake

1 (18.25 oz.) pkg. white cake mix
1 tsp. instant coffee powder
1/4 c. brewed coffee
5 Tbsp. coffee flavored liqueur
8 oz. container mascarpone cheese

3/4 c. confectioner's sugar
2 c. heavy cream
2 Tbsp. unsweetened cocoa powder
1 (1 oz.) square semisweet chocolate

Directions:
Preheat oven to 350°. Grease and flour 3 – 9 inch round cake pans. Prepare the cake mix according to package directions. Divide two-thirds of batter between 2 pans. Stir the instant coffee powder into remaining batter and pour into remaining pan. Bake for 20-25 minutes or until toothpick comes out clean. Let cool in pan for 10 minutes, then turn the cake out onto wire rack and cool completely. In a measuring cup, combine the brewed coffee and 1 tablespoon of the coffee liqueur; set aside. In a small bowl, using an electric mixer set on low speed, combine the mascarpone, 1/2 cup confectioner's sugar, and 2 tablespoons of coffee liqueur. Beat just until smooth. Cover with plastic wrap and refrigerate. In a medium bowl, using an electric mixer set on medium speed, beat the cream, 1/4 cup confectioner's sugar and 2 tablespoons of coffee liqueur until stiff. Fold 1/2 cup cream mixture into the filling mixture. Place one plain cake layer on a serving plate. Using a thin skewer, poke holes in the cake about 1 inch apart. Pour 1/3 of the reserved coffee mixture over the cake, then spread with half of the filling mixture. Top with coffee flavored cake layer; poke holes in the cake. Pour another third of the coffee mixture over second layer and spread with remaining filling. Top with remaining cake layer, poke holes in cake. Pour the remaining coffee mixture over the top. Spread the sides and top of cake with frosting. Place the cocoa powder in a sieve and lightly dust the top of the cake. Garnish with the chocolate cube. To make the chocolate curls use a vegetable peeler and run it down the edge of the chocolate square.

Submitted by: Ranae Hack, Owner

4 Main Street
Kennebunk, ME 04043
Phone: 207-985-0050
Website: www.duffyskennebunk.com

Duffy's Tavern & Grill is located Kennebunk's historic Lafayette Center (formerly the Kesslen Shoe Company). The space, complete with exposed beams and large windows overlooking the Mousam River and Mousam River Dam, exudes a raw mill feel while providing 21st century comforts. Cheryl's homemade apple crisp is a signature dessert that guests crave. The sweetness of the topping, and the tartness of the apples marry to create a gooey, yummy dessert.

Cheryl's Homemade Apple Crisp

Base
20 Macintosh Apples
1 c. all purpose flour
2 c. sugar
2 tsp. cinnamon

Topping
1 lb. softened butter
2 c. brown sugar
4 c. Quaker Oats
2 tsp. cinnamon
1 c. all purpose flour
1/2 c. sugar

Directions:
Peel and slice the apples into large chunks. Add the dry ingredients and mix well. All the apples should be covered in the dry ingredients. In a separate bowl, combine the topping ingredients, mixing well by hand. Place all the apples in a 13x9 pan, and distribute the apple topping evenly. Be careful not to compress the topping on top of the apples too much; they will melt together while cooking. Cook on 350° for 45-50 minutes. Serve warm with vanilla ice cream; enjoy! Serves 10-12.

Desserts   *Submitted by: David "Duffy" Cluff, Owner*

305 Main Avenue
Winnetoon, NE 68789
Phone: 402-847-3321

We are on Main Street in a little town in northeast Nebraska. "The World's Only Winnetoon." Our Mother started the business in 1975 and my sister Barb and I (Linda) own the business now. Our motto is, "Taste the Home cooked Delight in every bite at Elaine's." We say, "Come at noon or by the light of the moon, come real soon to Elaine's in Winnetoon." We have a Salad Bar that has real homemade salads in it. This recipe is featured every Tuesday evening on our salad bar, when we make homemade Chicken Fried Steaks and Real mashed potatoes and gravy.

Mom's Bread Pudding with Caramel Sauce

4 c. dried bread or rolls
4 eggs
1 c. sugar
6 c. milk
1 tsp. vanilla

Caramel Sauce
1/4 c. butter
1 c. brown sugar
2 Tbsp. cornstarch
1 tsp. vanilla
2 c. half and half

Directions:
Cut dried bread or rolls in 1 inch pieces. Cover the bottom of a greased 9x13 pan. Beat eggs, add sugar, milk, and vanilla. Beat well and pour over dried crumbs. Baked at 350° for 45 to 60 minutes or until a knife comes out clean. For Caramel Sauce: Put butter in a microwave safe bowl and melt. Add brown sugar, cornstarch, and half and half. Beat well and heat for 4 minutes. Stir and microwave for 2-4 minutes until thickened. Add vanilla to mixture. Serves 12 to 14.

Desserts   *Submitted by: Barbara Boggs and Linda Kallhoff, Owners*

925 N. Main Avenue
Choteau, MT 59422
Phone: 406-466-3311
Website: www.elkcountrygrill.com

Follow your dreams, as it could be an interesting experience! We've wanted to own a restaurant for the longest time. Finally we had an opportunity to move back home and do just that. The restaurant business has been a rewarding one, and the things we've learned have been good and bad, but we are still glad we followed our dream.

Bread Pudding with Rum Sauce

4 c. cubed bread
1/3 c. raisins
3/4 c. brown sugar
2 c. milk
4 eggs
1 1/2 tsp. vanilla
1/2 tsp. cinnamon

Rum Sauce
1 1/2 c. brown sugar
3/4 c. butter
1/2 c. whipping cream or
half and half
1/2 Tbsp. flour
1 Tbsp. real rum

Directions:
In the mornings I usually don't have dried out bread, so I cube my bread and put it in a 13x 9 pan, then place in oven for 10 minutes at 350°. Mix up brown sugar, milk, eggs, vanilla and cinnamon. After the 10 minutes, pull the pan out, add raisins, and the rest of the mixture. Bake for 45 minutes or until you can stick a knife in and have it come out clean. For rum sauce: In a sauce pan, put brown sugar, butter, cream and flour. Stir over medium heat until mixture starts to bubble. Take off heat and stir in rum. Cut Bread Pudding into 9 servings, place in a bowl or on a plate then add rum sauce to it. Add some ice cream, and they'll love it.

Desserts   *Submitted by: Rose Crawford, Owner*

Elsie's Diner

300 W. Main Street
Albion, IL 62806
Phone: 618-445-2441

Elsie's Diner is named after owner Mary Borowiak's mom and best friend, Elsie Jones Tourville. Elsie's Diner seats 70 and is decorated in country style. They serve family meals with a fast food style appeal.

Eclairs

1 c. water
1/2 c. real butter
1/4 tsp. salt
1 c. flour
4 eggs
1 12 oz. tub of Cool Whip
1 8 oz. pkg. cream cheese
2 3.4 oz. pkg. instant vanilla pudding mix
3 c. cold milk

Directions:

In medium sauce pan, heat and bring water, butter and salt to a boil. Add flour and stir until smooth ball forms. Remove from heat and let stand 5 minutes. Add eggs one at a time, beating well with wooden spoon. Beat until smooth. Spread into 9x13x2 baking dish. Bake at 400° for 30-35 minutes. Take out and let cool completely. In mixing bowl, barely mix pudding and milk. Add softened cream cheese and blend until smooth. Spread over "puff." Refrigerate for 20 minutes. Spread over whipped topping and drizzle with chocolate topping. Keep refrigerated.

Desserts   *Submitted by: Mary Boworiak (In loving memory of my Mom and my best friend)*

433 Main
Northport, AL 35476
Phone: 205-247-7773
Website: www.fifthandmain.biz

Downtown Northport
247-7773

As you approach Fifth & Main in downtown Northport, you can't help but be charmed by the giant fork and spoon flanking the sign on the corner of the building. Veteran restaurateur Carrie Fitts opened her newest establishment in early 2010. The menu changes daily and includes a variety of made-from-scratch soups and scrumptious desserts, all rendered with love and attention to detail. The dining room is intimate, currently seating around forty patrons, and you will likely meet Carrie's husband, Lewis, as he is often found washing dishes in the back. Lunch is served from 10:30-2:30, Tuesday through Saturday. Fifth & Main is a welcome addition to the shops and galleries of downtown Northport.

Lemon Squares

1 c. all-purpose flour	2 eggs, slightly beaten	1/2 tsp. baking powder
1/2 c. butter	1 c. granulated sugar	1/2 tsp. salt
1/4 c. confectioners' sugar	2 Tbsp. all-purpose flour (optional)	2 or 3 Tbsp. lemon juice Confectioners' sugar

Directions:

Preheat oven to 350°. Mix 1 cup flour, butter, and 1/4 cup confectioners' sugar. Press into 8x8x2 inch pan, building up a 1/2 inch edge. Bake 20 minutes. Beat remaining ingredients until light and fluffy. Pour over hot crust. Bake about 25 minutes longer or just until no imprint remains when lightly touched in center. Cool; sprinkle with confectioners' sugar, if desired, and cut into squares. Yield: 2 dozen.

Desserts   *Submitted by: Carrie Fitts, Owner*

133 E. Main Street
Hixton, WI 54635
Phone: 715-963-4031
Website: www.bluecollarcafe.com

Nestled comfortably in Hixton, Wisconsin lies an American cafe and Gourmet jam producer. Our award winning spicy jams have traveled the globe tingling taste buds and warming hearts. Our cafe offers a sanctuary for the hungry travelers offering good old American fare.

Blue-Collar Brownies with a Kick

3 eggs
2 c. sugar
1 1/2 tsp. vanilla extract
1/4 c. melted shortening
1/2 c. butter, melted
1 1/2 c. all purpose flour
3/4 c. baking cocoa
1 1/4 tsp. salt
1/2 c. strong decaf coffee
1 jar of your favorite Spicy Blue Collar Jam

Aaron, Nika, Sue and Ritch

Directions:

In a mixing bowl combine eggs, sugar, vanilla and coffee. Make sure coffee has cooled so as to not cook the eggs; mix well. Add butter and shortening. Sift flour, cocoa and salt into egg mixture and mix well. Grease a 13x9 inch pan. Pour half of the batter in the pan and spread it out to the edges of the pan. Spread a layer of jam on top of the batter, then spoon the remaining batter over the top of jam. Bake at 350° for 30 minutes or until a tooth pick comes out with moist crumbs. Cool in pan and enjoy!

Desserts   *Submitted by: Nika Charles, Chef*

905 N. Main
Harrison, AR 72601
Phone: 870-741-4690
Fax: 870-741-7976
Website: www.homeyhearthbakery.com

Homey Hearth is celebrating 20 years of service to Harrison, Arkansas. Clarence Yoder started the restaurant as a source of supplemental income, but with the baking skills of his wife, Barbara, it soon became their main source of income. They use recipes from their home and extended family. Visit them at their website.

Quick and Easy Peach Cobbler

2- 29 oz. cans of sliced peaches in syrup
1 c. sugar
1 c. milk
1 c. self rising flour

Directions:
Preheat oven to 350°. Grease a 9x13 baking pan, then pour in the peaches. In a small mixing bowl, combine sugar, flour and milk. Pour mixture slowly over peaches, covering them completely. Bake 45 minutes to 1 hour until top is golden brown.

Desserts   *Submitted by: Kimberly Lloyd, Baker*

4015 E. Main Street
Danville, IL 61834
Phone: 217-446-2120
Fax: 217-446-3866
Website:
www.iandistatelinetavern.com

At the I & I State Line Tavern, we present this recipe so you can get your sweet treat while keeping your blood sugar as level as possible without sacrificing your health and digestion. Agave is a plant based low glycemic syrup that tastes like honey. Stevia is a green leafed herb from South America that has no calories and when used with agave, has a super sweet taste with no bitter aftertaste. Cinnamon, when combined with carob, is a great energy elixir for women and is a circulatory and metabolism-boosting spice. Raw tahini is a sesame butter high in polyunsaturated fats and an awesome source of iron.

Organic Fudge Truffles

(Sugar free, wheat & gluten free in only 90 seconds)

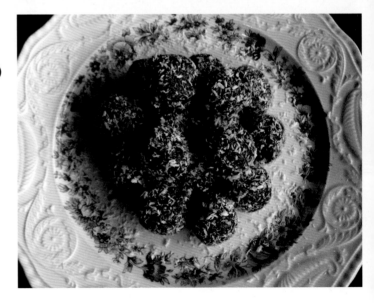

    1 Tbsp. organic unsweetened almond milk
    2 tsp. organic agave
    1 dropper of organic chocolate liquid stevia
    1 rounded Tbsp. organic raw tahini
    2 rounded Tbsp. organic carob powder
    1/2 tsp. organic cinnamon
    1 tsp. organic vanilla

Directions:
Blend all the ingredients with a wooden spoon in a glass bowl. Form into a ball and roll in organic hemp seeds or organic unsweetened coconut.

Desserts   *Submitted by: Teresa Wright, Owner*

Additional Recipe

Organic Brownies

(Sugar free – Wheat free)

    1/4 c. plus 2 Tbsp. organic agave
    2 organic omega 3 eggs
    1 1/2 Tbsp. organic vanilla
    3/4 c. organic Medjool dates
    1/2 c. organic unsweetened almond milk
    15 oz. can organic black beans, drained
    1/2 c. organic raw tahini (no salt added)
    3 droppers liquid organic stevia
    2 tsp. organic cinnamon
    3/4 c. organic roasted carob powder
    1/2 c. gluten-free baking powder
    1 tsp. baking soda
    1 tsp. xanthan gum
    3/4 c. organic unsweetened carob chips
    1/2 c. organic walnuts, almonds, or pecans, chopped

Directions:

Preheat oven to 350°. Using food processor, add agave, eggs, and vanilla. Puree until mixed. Add dates and almond milk and puree until well blended. Add in carob powder and pulse slowly until mixed. It will now begin to look like a brownie mix. In a separate bowl, blend flour, baking powder, baking soda, and xanthan gum. Slowly add prepared flour mixture into food processor. Pulse until blended. The brownie mixture will still appear very thick. Add chips and pulse a few times. Transfer mixture to an 8 x 8 pan that has been sprayed with cooking spray and lightly floured with buckwheat flour. Use a small amount of spray oil on your spatula for easier spreading. Spread the brownie mixture evenly and sprinkle your choice of chopped nuts on top. Bake at 350° for 45 minutes. Yield: 16 brownies.

Vegan Note: To make this recipe vegan, substitute for each egg 1 ounce of organic silken tofu, pureed or 1 tablespoon of ground organic flax seed in 3 tablespoons of water.

Desserts   *Submitted by: Teresa Wright, Owner*

Jo's

School House Café

409 Main Street
Hecla, SD 57446
Phone: 605-994-2345

I opened Jo's Schoolhouse Café in the fall of 2007. We are located in the lunchroom of the Hecla School which closed in 2002 due to declining enrollment (so there was little remodeling to do).

Rhubarb Custard Pie

1 1/2 c. sugar	**Pie crust**	**Crumb Topping**
1/4 c. flour	4 c. flour	1 c. flour
3 eggs	1 12 oz. can 7-Up	1/2 c. oleo
1/4 tsp. nutmeg	2 c. Crisco	1/2 c. brown sugar
Dash salt	Salt	
4 c. rhubarb		

Directions:

Combine pie crust ingredients and divide into 4 balls. Roll out one ball for each crust and place in 9 inch pie plate. Combine pie filling ingredients and pour into unbaked pie crust. Then combine topping ingredients and cover the filling with them. Bake at 400° for 50 minutes.

Gramma Janice's Strawberry Dessert

Crust	**Filling**
1/2 c. butter	10 oz. pkg. thawed strawberries
1/4 c. brown sugar	2 egg whites
1 c. flour	1 Tbsp. lemon juice
1/2 c. pecans	1 c. sugar
	1/2 pt. Cool Whip
	1 tsp. vanilla

I love to cook and have a very large cookbook collection. Hecla is a very small farming community in northeast South Dakota, so a lot of my restaurant fare is hearty South Dakota cooking - meat and potatoes - the Rhubarb pie is a hit during the summer.

Directions:

Combine crust ingredients and bake on cookie sheet for 20 minutes at 300°. Stir during baking to retain crunchy texture. Reserve 1/3 of crust for topping and put remaining amount in bottom of 9x13 inch pan. Combine first 4 ingredients of filling and beat for 20 minutes. Then fold in the Cool Whip and vanilla. Pour on top of the crumb crust and cover with remaining crumbs. Freeze.

Desserts

Submitted by: Jo Landreth, Owner

504 E. Main Street
Everett, PA 15537
Phone: 814-652-2314

Established in 1942, Kelly's Scenic View Restaurant is located in Everett, PA, nestled in the heart of the Alleghenies. Kevin and Sallie Smith have owned the business since 1981. Kelly's is well known for our home style cooking, Friday night fish fries, affordable pricing and friendly service. We offer a full menu of breakfast, lunch and dinner items and can accommodate approximately 150 people.

"Our Own" Oatmeal Pie

2 eggs
1/2 c. white sugar
1/2 c. brown sugar
1/2 c. butter
1 c. coconut
3/4 c. oatmeal
3/4 c. white corn syrup
1 c. milk
1 tsp. vanilla

Directions:
Combine eggs, sugar, corn syrup and butter. Mix 2 - 3 minutes. Add oatmeal alternately with milk and mix 1 minute. Add coconut and vanilla. Pour into unbaked pie shell and bake 45 minutes at 350°.

Desserts   *Submitted by: Kevin & Sallie Smith, Owners*

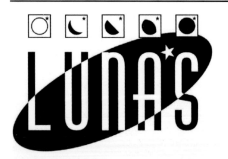

200 Main Street, Hunt Tower
Gainesville, GA 30501
Phone: 770-531-0848
Fax: 770-532-4120
Website: www.lunas.com

Luna's Restaurant, located on Main Street in Gainesville, Georgia, has been a local favorite since 1997. Chef Albert Luna is a graduate from Johnston and Wales and has been Executive Chef for Luna's since 2000. Chef Albert brings a gourmet twist to classic continental fare. Luna's also boasts private dining facilities and an eclectic piano lounge.

Flan

10 Tbsp. sugar
5 tsp. water
28 oz. sweetened condensed milk
28 oz. evaporated milk
5 lg. egg whites
2 1/2 tsp. vanilla extract
10 oz. cream cheese

Directions:
Preheat oven to 300°. Caramelize sugar by heating in a sauce pan with water on low heat and put in the greased cups equally. Mix rest of ingredients well and pour into cups equally over caramelized sugar mixture. Bake for 45-60 minutes (cooking times may vary) in water bath (put the cups into a larger pan with water filled up to almost the rims of the cups) till you have a consistency of "JELLO" and let cool. To Serve: Sit custard in hot water to release caramelized sugar and take a knife and gently scrape along the side of the bowl to release the Flan. Turn bowl upside down on serving plate, pour the caramelized sugar over the flan and garnish if desired with fresh berries. Yield 10 servings.

      Submitted by: Albert Luna, Executive Chef

611 S. Main Street
Midland, TX 79701
Phone: 432-682-5970

For seven years, April Haynie had worked as a waitress for Cowboys Cafe (now Main Street Diner) along with another waitress, Catherine "Cathy" Pool when "Cowboys" closed down. April and Cathy leased the building in March of 1999, renamed it, bought some groceries and went to work. Cathy Pool retired due to health issues in 2007. Located on Main Street in Midland, Texas, they serve a majority of the oilfield employees and working class people of Midland and surrounding communities. The menu consists of breakfast, burgers and home cooked lunch specials, such as hand-breaded chicken-fried streak, meatloaf, pork roast, Mexican casserole, liver and onions, real mashed potatoes and homemade desserts!

5 Layer Dessert

1 c. flour
1/2 c. pecans
1/2 c. soft oleo
1 13 oz. Cool Whip
1 c. powdered sugar
1 8 oz. cream cheese
2 sm. pkg. instant chocolate pudding
2 sm. pkg. instant French Vanilla pudding

Directions:

Mix flour, pecans and oleo well. Pat into a 9x13x2 pan. Bake 20 minutes at 375°. Cool. Mix half of the container of Cool Whip, powdered sugar, and the 8 ounce package of cream cheese together. Spread on the baked crust. Mix chocolate pudding according to directions and spread over the cream cheese layer. Mix French Vanilla pudding according to directions and spread on top of chocolate pudding. Top with remaining Cool Whip.

Desserts   *Submitted by: April Haynie, Owner*

MERMAID CAFE
OLDINLET BOOKSHOP AND B&B

HOMER, ALASKA

3487 Main Street
Homer, AK 99603
Phone: 907-235-7649
Website: www.mermaidcafe.net

This is a very special sorbet. It is made using only local raspberries, sugar and local award winning Raspberry Melomel Mead from the Ring of Fire Meadery. Simple and easy to prepare it exemplifies the use of local products and partnerships between local businesses.

Raspberry Melomel Sorbet

2 1/2 c. Raspberry Melomal Mead
1/2 c. water
1 c. sugar
4 c. raspberries

Directions:
Mix mead, water and sugar in a medium saucepan. Bring to a boil, add raspberries. Remove from heat. Cover and let stand for 10 minutes. Pass through a fine mesh strainer with a flexible rubber spatula. Discard seeds. Chill thoroughly, then freeze in ice cream maker according to manufacturer's instructions.

Desserts   *Submitted by: Michael Hiller, Owner*

584 S. Main Street
P. O. Box 455
LaBarge, WY 83123
Phone: 307-386-2103
Website: www.historicmoondancediner.com

My husband, Vince Pierce and I purchased and relocated the Moondance Diner in the summer of 2007, weeks before it was to be demolished for new construction on its former site. Located in lower Manhattan, New York it was featured in the first Spiderman, Sex and the City, and Friends. It was an integral part of New York for almost 80 years. After a lot of time, money and patience, the Moondance Diner shines brightly in La Barge, Wyoming.

Classic Custard Bread Pudding with Rum Sauce

8 large butter croissants
(cubed to 1" pieces)
14 med. eggs
3 c. heavy whipping cream
4 c. whole milk
2 1/2 c. vanilla sugar
(We infuse our sugar with a vanilla bean for flavor.)
1 Tbsp. real vanilla extract

Moondance

Directions:
Preheat oven to 350°. Spray a full size restaurant pan with non-stick coating. In a large mixing bowl, whisk eggs. Add cream, milk and vanilla sugar. Combine ingredients well. Add vanilla extract and stir. Add the cubed croissants and let mixture rest for 15 minutes. Meanwhile, place a full size cookie sheet or jelly roll pan in oven and add water until it reaches about half way up the sides. Pour the bread pudding into the restaurant pan and place inside the jelly roll pan. This will create a steam bath. Bake for about 45 minutes or until set. Allow to cool before slicing into 15 squares.

Desserts

Recipe continued on next page

Recipe continued

Rum Sauce

   1/2 c. brown sugar
   1/2 c. vanilla sugar
   1/2 c. heavy whipping cream
   1 tsp. light corn syrup
   1 Tbsp. rum (any high quality)

Directions:

Rum Sauce: In a heavy sauce pan, combine first 4 ingredients. Bring to a boil. Remove from heat and add rum. Mix together. Cook and top bread pudding with sauce and whipped topping. Yield 15 servings.

Our motto is simple… "We proudly serve fresh, hand-patted-burgers, hand-cut-fries, hand-dipped ice cream, and hand-made desserts; including the Classic Custard Bread Pudding."

We have an eclectic group of patrons, including some who frequented the Moondance Diner while it was in New York City, some from other countries, and some who have just crossed the street. We would love to meet you; stop by for a visit and experience the magic.

572 Main Street
Pine Mountain, GA 31822
Phone: 706-663-4647

Moore's Whistling Pig Cafe is located in the heart of Pine Mountain, Georgia. We are located on Main Street and have been in business for 10 years. The cafe is locally owned and operated by family members. The Cafe is known for its outstanding BBQ Pork Sandwiches, Ribs, Fried Green Tomatoes and a secret recipe - rich black rib sauce. All menu items are homemade, from the fresh hand-patted burgers to the hand-peeled potatoes for homemade fries. Moore's Whistling Pig Cafe is open Monday through Saturday from 10 AM until 3 PM and also offers catering for special events.

Key Lime Cake

1 box lemon cake mix
3 oz. pkg. lime jello
3/4 c. orange juice
5 eggs
1 tsp. vanilla
1 c. canola oil

Frosting
1/3 c. lime juice
1 box powdered sugar
8 oz. cream cheese
1 stick butter, softened

Directions:
Mix cake mix, jello, orange juice, eggs, vanilla, and oil together. Bake in 2 or 3 layer 9 inch pans for 25 minutes at 350°. While cakes are warm, mix lime juice, 3 tablespoons powdered sugar and drizzle over warm layers. Let Cool. For icing, mix 1 stick butter, cream cheese and remaining powdered sugar. Ice cake. Enjoy!

Submitted by: Susie and Robert Moore, Owners

3757 Main
Keokuk, IA 52632
Phone: 319-524-6467
Website: www.ogosrestaurant.com

Ogo's is locally owned and operated by Kevin and Lori Gregory. Many people ask where we got the name, Ogo's. It is short for "Oh Great One" and is also a nickname for Kevin, that was given to him by students when he was a DARE teacher for the Clark Co. MO Sheriff's Office, in which Gregory also served as County Sheriff in the late 1990's before he and Lori opened Ogo's in 2001. Ogo's is popular with families and seniors because of the homemade food, like Kevin's Meatloaf and other foods that his mother passed on to him. The Hawaiian Wedding Cake is by far the most popular and requested recipe for our restaurant. If ever in Keokuk, remember to stop by Ogo's where you come as a customer and leave as a friend.

Hawaiian Wedding Cake

2 c. flour
2 c. sugar
2 tsp. baking soda
2 beaten eggs
1/4 bag finely diced walnuts
1/4 bag coconut
1 can pineapple

Icing

8 oz. cream cheese
1/2 c. butter
1 tsp. vanilla
3/4 c. powdered sugar

Photo provided by: Ed Vinson Photography

Directions:
Mix first 4 ingredients together, then stir in walnuts, coconut, and pineapple. Pour in prepared pans and bake 30 minutes at 340 °. For icing, combine all ingredients and put on cake after it has cooled.

Desserts   *Submitted by: Kevin and Lori Gregory, Owners*

2530 Main Street
Yakima, WA 98903
Phone: 509-453-8485

Old Town Station is a locally owned family business that is proud to have been serving visitors and the people of Yakima Valley since 1979. We offer breakfast, lunch and dinner. We have delicious homemade desserts. With our fresh home cooked meals, great service and reasonable prices, everyone comes back for more.

Bread Pudding with Homemade Cinnamon Sauce

1 loaf white bread
7 scrambled Eggs
1 1/2 qt. non-dairy creamer
1 1/2 c. sugar
1/8 c. vanilla
1 Tbsp. nutmeg

Directions:

Cut up bread and place in bottom of pan. In separate bowl, mix eggs, creamer, sugar, vanilla and nutmeg together until smooth. Pour over bread in pan. Make sure all bread gets covered. Let stand 5 minutes before cooking. Place in 300" oven. Cook for 25 minutes, turn pan around, cook for 25 more minutes. Serves 10-12 people.

Cinnamon Sauce

3 3/4 c. sugar
1/2 c. flour
1/8 c. apple cider vinegar
1/2 c. brown sugar

3/4 c. margarine
1 Tbsp. cinnamon
5 c. water

Directions:

Place water in pan and add sugar and flour, mix well. Bring to boil, stirring constantly. Turn heat down and let simmer for 5 minutes. Remove from heat. Stir in vinegar and brown sugar, melt butter in microwave and slowly add to sauce. Add cinnamon and stir well. Store in refrigerator.

Desserts   *Submitted by: Shawnda Petersen, Manager*

943 N. Main Avenue
Springfield, MO 65802
Phone: 417-866-8744

Pappy's Place has stood at this location since 1904. While now housing a bar/restaurant, the store first began as a family-owned shoe repair shop. Shortly after that, the owners opened a grocery store and kept it that way until the 1920s. New owners opened a cafe on the property in 1924. Following Prohibition, the cafe applied for a beer-by-the-drink license. This license, which is still held by Pappy's, is the oldest continuous license in Springfield. Pappy's Place may be old, and not very well-known, but it is a place of character. The people are friendly, the food is good and the beer is cold. A casual atmosphere makes for a laid-back time. For many people, it is a place of good memories.

Vegan Peanut Butter Pie

16 oz. silken tofu
1 c. peanut butter
3/4 c. sugar
2 Tbsp. soy milk
2 tsp. vanilla
2 Tbsp. molasses
1 graham cracker crust

Directions:
In a large mixing bowl, whip ingredients together until smooth and pour into the pie crust. Chill and garnish with Chocolate Syrup, then Serve!

Desserts   *Submitted by: Chef Scott Keese*

PARAGON CAFE
Where the coffee is still .50 cents

107 Main Street W
Mohall, ND 58761
701-756-6415

The Paragon Cafe was established in 1945. Connie Peterson is the 4th owner, operator, and manager of the business. The restaurant is open 7 days a week: Monday – Friday from 5:30 am to 2:30 pm. They close at 1:30 pm on Saturday and Sunday. Breakfast and lunch are served. They are known for their omelets, burgers and old fashioned tomato soup which is served every Friday. The slogan is "Where the coffee is still 50 cents." These Raisin Bars are a community favorite. Not only do they serve them in the restaurant, but Connie also takes them to church socials and other community gatherings.

Raisin Bars

2 c. raisins
1 c. coffee
1 tsp. cinnamon

1 tsp. nutmeg
1 tsp. cloves
1 c. sugar
1/2 c. margarine

1/2 tsp. soda
(dissolved into 1/2 c. warm water, mix well)
2 c. flour
1 tsp. baking powder

Directions:
Place raisins, coffee, spices, sugar and margarine into a pan. Bring to a boil and boil for 3 minutes; cool, then add soda dissolved in warm water, flour and baking powder. Spread into a greased 10x16 jelly roll pan. Bake at 350° for 30 minutes or until done. Cool and frost.

Carmel Frosting

1/4 c. margarine
1/3 c. cream

3/4 c. brown sugar
1/2 tsp. vanilla

1 1/3 c. powdered sugar

Directions:
Combine margarine, cream and brown sugar and bring to a boil for 1 minute, then cool. Add vanilla and powdered sugar. Stir till creamy and frost bars.

Zucchini Jam

6 c. zucchini   6 c. white sugar   1 can crushed pineapple (and juice)   6 oz. box of red Jello

Directions:
Peel and shred zucchini. In saucepan, combine zucchini, sugar and pineapple; boil 6 minutes. Add Jello, stir well to dissolve the Jello. Pour in jars and seal.

Desserts   *Submitted by: Connie Petersen, Owner*

Parkview Restaurant

1615 W. Main
Corning, AR 72422
Phone: 870-857-6884

We are a small sit down and dine restaurant, you get waited on at your table. We serve breakfast, lunch, and dinner with lots to choose from. We are open 7 days a week: Mon-Sat 5:30 am - 9:00 pm, and Sun 5:30 am - 2:00 pm.

Quick Crust Cobbler

3 c. sugar
3 c. flour
2.1/2 c. milk
1/4 c. baking powder
Fruit of your choice

Directions:
Mix sugar, flour, milk and baking powder. Melt 1 stick of butter in cake pan. Pour batter and add fruit of your choice. Bake 30.minutes at 375°.

Desserts   *Submitted by: Brenda Eason, Dinner Cook*

323 Main Street
Vincennes, IN 47591
Phone: 812-886-5146
Fax: 812-886-9184

Since May 20, 1996, Becky and Bill have offered a personalized style of dining to downtown Vincennes. Becky Pea, a native of Vincennes, graduated from Purdue and Johnson and Wales Universities in Restaurant management and Baking and Pastry Arts. Bill, from AuGres, Michigan, served 4 years in the Marine Corps and also graduated from Johnson and Wales University. With their cheesecakes, specialty tortes and gourmet foods, they have pleased many palates.

Peanut Butter No-Bake Cookies

4 c. sugar
1 c. milk
1 c. melted margarine
1 1/3 c. peanut butter

1/4 tsp. salt
1 tsp. vanilla
6 c. oatmeal

Directions:
Boil first 3 ingredients for 3 minutes. Take off heat and add next 4 ingredients. Immediately spoon mixture on parchment paper to desired size. Cookies will harden as they cool.

Chocolate No-Bake Cookies

4 c. sugar
1 c. milk
1 c. melted margarine
1/2 c. cocoa

1 c. peanut butter
1/4 tsp. salt
1 tsp. vanilla
6 c. oatmeal

Directions:
Boil first 4 ingredients for 1 minute. Take off heat and add next 4 ingredients. Immediately spoon mixture on parchment paper to desired size. Cookies will harden as they cool.

Desserts   *Submitted by: Becky and Bill Stenger, Owners*

910 N. Main Street
Oshkosh, WI 54901
Phone: 920-233-5565
Fax: 920-230-7456

Pilora's Café takes a new and unique approach to dining out. We've mixed coffee house with restaurant and have come up with a great combination. We have a strong focus on tasty vegetarian options, healthy meatier options and original breakfasts.

Cherry Pecan Bread Pudding

8 c. cubed bread
3 Tbsp. melted butter
3/4 c. sugar
4 eggs
2 c. milk
2 tsp. vanilla
1 c. dried cherries
1/2 c. pecans

Directions:
Cut bread into cubes (we use a rosemary olive oil bread) and place in large mixing bowl. Melt butter. Put in mixer and add vanilla and sugar. Mix thoroughly, then add eggs. Mix for 2 minutes on medium-high speed so that mixture is slightly thickened. Slowly stir in milk. Pour mixture over bread and stir. Let sit 5 minutes. Stir in cherries and pecans. Pour mixture into an ungreased 9" x 13" pan. Sprinkle with cinnamon sugar. Bake at 350° for 35 minutes. Bread should be slightly brown, and center should be firm. Serve with ice cream.

Desserts   *Submitted by: Paula Tellock, Owner*

10 N. Main Street
Berlin, MD 21811
Phone: 410-641-2131

A one of a kind, Rayne's Reef is a historic old fashioned soda fountain established for over 100 years and nestled within Berlin's town center. The landmark eatery has been the backdrop for such notable movies as "Tuck Everlasting" and "Runaway Bride." Rayne's serves locals and visitors old fashioned hamburgers and hand-dipped milkshakes as well as a complete breakfast and lunch menu. With its beginnings as a luncheonette and soda fountain, originally operated by the Rayne and Connelly families, this restaurant has served as an ever present and popular meeting place for all of the town's people. Long a landmark within the town, today, under the ownership of the Queen family and having recently undergone extensive architectural restoration, it proudly stands ready to serve you!

Black and White Malt

4 scoops vanilla ice cream
1 1/2 c. milk
3 Tbsp. chocolate syrup
2 Tbsp. malted milk powder

Directions:
Combine all ingredients in a blender, blend until no white is showing and enjoy!

Desserts   *Submitted by: Ryan Brewington, Manager*

116 W. Main Street
Northville, MI 48167
Phone: 248-773-7671, Fax: 248-773-7581
Website: www.redpepperdeli.org

At the Red Pepper Deli, we strive for a tasty and healthy lifestyle. By keeping this pie raw, we are saving important enzymes and nutrients. With this you can get your sweet treat without sacrificing health and digestion.

Raw Apple Pie

Crust
- 2 c. walnuts
- 1/2 c. dates
- 1/2 c. unsweetened coconut

Filling
- 4 med. apples peeled, cored & sliced (combination of sweet & tart apples)
- 3 Tbsp. lemon juice, divided
- 1/2 c. raisins, soaked in warm water
- 1/2 c. dates, soaked in warm water
- 2 med. apples, peeled, cored and chopped rough (combination of sweet & tart apples)
- 1 tsp. apple pie spice

Directions:

For crust: Use food processor with metal "S" blade. Pulse all crust ingredients to make a crumble. Do not allow it to form a paste. Form into pie plate and freeze until filling is prepared. For filling: Place sliced apples in a bowl and mix in 2 tablespoons of lemon juice and set aside. Drain raisins and dates well. In a food processor with metal "S" blade, process raisins, dates, chopped apples, remaining lemon juice and apple pie spice until it forms a paste. Incorporate paste and sliced apples. Place in crust and spread evenly over crust. Serves 8 people generously.

Desserts   *Submitted by: Carolyn Simon, Owner*

Rt. 114 Main Street
East Burke Village, VT 05832
Phone: 802-626-3514

Nick and I as owners of a small, causal, fine dining restaurant, take pride in everything being fresh and homemade. We make all of the desserts, ice creams and sorbets. We make all of our sauces to order. We also make all of our salad dressings, our most popular dressings are the Poppy Seed and Maple Balsamic Vinaigrette made with local Vermont maple syrup.

Annie's Famous Carrot Cake

2 c. flour	1 1/2 c. vegetable oil or canola oil	***Cream Cheese Frosting***
2 c. sugar	1 tsp. vanilla	12 oz. cream cheese
1/2 tsp. salt	2 c. finely grated carrots	6 c. confectioner's sugar
1 tsp. baking soda	1 c. drained crushed pineapple	12 Tbsp. soft butter
2 tsp. cinnamon	1 c. shredded sweet coconut	Walnuts
3 eggs	1/2-3/4 c. chopped walnuts	

Directions:

Preheat oven to 350°. Spray 3 – 8 inch pans, line bottoms with parchment and spray again. Whisk first 5 ingredients together. Stir in the remaining ingredients, put in prepared pans and bake about 25-35 minutes, checking and rotating after 15 minutes. Let cool on racks about 20 minutes. Run a knife around the edges. Cool on wire racks until completely cool. While cooling, prepare the frosting.

For frosting: With a mixer on medium speed, whip butter and cream cheese until well combined. Gradually add sugar. If it is too stiff, add a little milk. Let rest at room temperature until ready to frost the cake. Put a layer on a plate and frost. Repeat until all 3 layers and sides have been frosted. You can put walnuts on the sides of the cake for decoration. Refrigerate if you are not going to use it right away. Remove from refrigerator at least 1 hour before serving.

Desserts   *Submitted by: Annie Lachance, Owner/Baker*

ROARING
20'S
ICE
CREAM
PARLOUR

301 W. Main
Flushing, MI 48433
P.O. Box 175
Phone: 810-659-2660
Facebook page:
Roaring 20's Ice Cream Parlour

Hot Fudge Sundae

1 med. homemade waffle bowl
3 oz. thick creamy hot fudge
6 oz. vanilla ice cream
2 oz. whipped cream
2 Tbsp. crushed nuts
1 cherry

The Roaring 20's is known for its homemade waffle cones, and waffle bowls made right on the premises. We offer 40 different flavors of hand-dipped ice cream, 11 different flavors of soft serve ice cream, shakes, malts, old-fashioned sodas, coolers, banana splits, sundaes, slushes, ice cream flurries, slush freezes etc., and an outside picnic area for you to enjoy your treat.

Directions:

In a medium waffle bowl or regular bowl, drizzle 1 ounce of Hot Fudge in the bottom of your bowl; add a 3 ounce scoop of vanilla ice cream. Top the ice cream with 1 ounce of Hot Fudge. Add another 3 ounce scoop of vanilla ice cream; top it with 1 ounce of Hot Fudge. Add 2 ounces of whipped cream, then drizzle Hot Fudge across the top of the whipped cream. Sprinkle crushed nuts on top and add a cherry. For a different twist, add a banana and crushed cookies. Serves one.

Mint Chocolate Chip Flurry/Malt

4 oz. milk
2 Tbsp. malt powder
6 oz. mint chocolate chip ice cream
3 Tbsp. crushed M&M's
2 oz. Whipped cream

Directions:

Pour milk in a mixing glass or blender and add malt powder. Stir or blend until smooth. Add 6 ounces of mint chocolate chip ice cream and 3 tablespoons of crushed M&M's. Blend until it reaches a smooth, thick consistency. Scoop out and put it in a cup. Top with whipped cream and M&M's, and eat with a spoon.

Desserts

Submitted by: Joanie Fagan, Owner

RUBY LENA'S TEAROOM AND ANTIQUES

Historic Downtown Branson

224 W. Main (Hwy 76)
Branson, MO 65616
Phone: 417-239-2919
Fax: 417-338-0119

As the owner, we strive to make sure we serve our "guests" fresh food, homemade desserts, along with quality and presentation. As the guests come into our 100 year old house, they will find décor of vintage and Victorian style, along with vintage tablecloths, napkins and dishes to serve them. We want to bring back the memories of when grandma used to bake, the aromas and happy times as a kid. So, after 30 years being a broker-owner in Real Estate, I'm now a "tearoom" mom. I was raised on a farm and loved to bake, so this was my dream. I've been blessed to meet so many guests who have truly enjoyed our "tearoom" in the downtown historic district of Branson, Missouri. They have thanked us for being here! This recipe is one of our favorite desserts served daily, alamode.

Warm Baked Fudge

4 eggs
2 c. sugar
1 c. melted butter
1/2 c. flour

1/2 c. cocoa
2 tsp. vanilla
1 c. chopped pecans

Directions:

Cream eggs and sugar. Add melted butter. Sift flour and cocoa together and add to mixture. Add nuts and vanilla. Pour into 9x12 inch greased pan. Set in a pan of hot water and bake at 325° for 45 minutes to 1 hour or until crusty on top and soft inside. Serve warm with your favorite cup of tea or coffee, or maybe a scoop of ice cream and garnish with a maraschino cherry. Serves 8 to 12.

Desserts   *Submitted by: Bobbi Helms, Owner- Hostess*

201 W. Main Street
Ronceverte, WV 24970
Phone: 304-647-4700
Fax: 304-647-5983

This charming Corner Grill serves up history along with some good home cooking. People seem to enjoy a good pork loin, turkey and dressing, pot roast, ham, fried chicken and mashed potatoes and gravy. "The basics have worked well for us over the years. We try to keep everything as nearly homemade as we can." When it comes to desserts, customers and staff alike line up for a sampling of the brownies, fudge and cookies.

Piña Colada Pie

2 6 oz. graham cracker crusts
1 can Eagle Brand condensed milk
2 8 oz. pkg. softened cream cheese
20 oz. can Dole crushed pineapple,
well drained (discard juice)
1 lg. tub Cool Whip

Juice of one lemon
1 t. vanilla
1 c. chopped pecans
1 c. flaked coconut
2 Tbsp. toasted coconut for topping

Directions:
Combine milk, cheese, pineapple, vanilla and lemon juice. Fold in nuts and coconut. Add Cool Whip and fold to blend. Divide into shells. Add toasted coconut and chill for 3 hours. Enjoy!

Desserts   *Submitted by: Mike Rodoussakis, Owner*

Salem Cross Inn
RESTAURANT & TAVERN

260 W. Main Street, P. O. Box 553, West Brookfield, MA 01585
Phone: 508-867-2345, Website: www.salemcrossinn.com

A family run restaurant since its opening in 1961, Salem Cross Inn has established a reputation as one of the finest restaurants in New England. Situated on 600 acres in central Massachusetts, the Inn is one of the finest examples of colonial restoration in the United States and is listed on the National Register of Historic Places. Home of "The Best Apple Pie in New England" contest, we'd like to share this recipe for the award winning Honey Apple Pie. This pie is made using the freshest ingredients available including apples from our local orchards. Guests who visit the Fireplace Feast help peel the apples with an antique apple peeler and corer and learn some of the secrets to rolling out a perfect crust.

Honey Apple Pie
"The Best Apple Pie in New England"

Pie Crust
   5 c. flour
   1 3/4 c. shortening
   1/4 c. sugar
   1 tsp. salt
   1/2 tsp. baking powder
   1 egg, beaten
   1 Tbsp. cider vinegar
   Water

Desserts

Recipe continued on next page

Recipe continued

Directions:

<u>For crust:</u> Combine flour, sugar, salt and baking powder. Cut in shortening until consistency of small peas. In a measuring cup, put in beaten egg, vinegar and enough water to make 1 cup of liquid. Add gradually to dry ingredients. Press to make a ball, then divide into 4 equal parts. Yields 4 crusts. Dough may be frozen for later use if only making one two-crust pie.

Pie Filling

6-8 Rome apples peeled and sliced
1/3 c. honey
3 Tbsp. sugar
2 Tbsp. cornstarch
1 tsp. cinnamon
1/4 tsp. salt
3 Tbsp. melted butter

Directions:

<u>For filling:</u> Mix honey, sugar, cornstarch, cinnamon, salt and butter in large bowl. Add sliced apples and toss until well coated. Roll out the bottom pie crust, place into a buttered, 10" pie pan and fill with apple mixture. Roll out top crust, place over apples, flute the edges together and vent the top. Place in the center of a 350° oven for approximately 1 hour or until bottom crust is light brown and top crust is golden brown.

Helpful hints: To make an extra crispy top crust you can brush the top of your pie with an egg wash and then sprinkle the entire top with a light coating of sugar and cinnamon. Save extra pieces of pie dough as treats for the kids. Simply put all extra dough pieces together in a ball and roll out into an oval. Cut 1" strips the long way on the oval and sprinkle with sugar and cinnamon. Place individual strips onto a cookie sheet (with parchment paper) and bake for 10 minutes at 350° or until golden brown.

132 S. Main Street
Thayne, WY 83127
Phone: 307-883-2510

Located in Thayne, Wyoming, the Star Valley Grille at the Cheese Factory has served generations of Star Valley families. From our popular appetite-pleasing Mozzi Burger, with smoked ham, Applewood bacon, baby portabella mushrooms, Mozzarella and Swiss cheese to our array of Star Valley cheese, our menu has something to please everyone. Established in 1925 and reestablished in 2008, The Star Valley Grille at The Cheese Factory is steeped in history, tradition and flavor. Won't you join us?

Star Valley Apple Crisp

Main

5 c. peeled, sliced green apples
3 tsp. water
1/2 c. sugar
1/2 tsp. cinnamon
2 Tbsp. flour

Topping

3/4 c. oatmeal
3/4 c. flour
3/4 c. brown sugar
1/4 tsp. baking soda
1 cube melted butter

Directions:

Combine main items in a mixing bowl. Mix well, pour into small baking dish (double recipe for 9x13 pan). Mix topping items and evenly cover the apple mixture. Bake at 350° for 45 minutes or until golden brown. Served well a la mode!!

Desserts   *Submitted by. Jared Zebe, General Manager*

SUNNySide CaFé

2130 N. Main
Mtn. Grove, MO 65711
Phone: 417-926-5471

Sunnyside Café is locally owned and operated. In addition to serving delicious buffets, we have a large selection of items on our menu to choose from including some of the best steaks in the area. We also have a private dining room for large groups or special occasions. Come in and experience some down-home cooking.

Wagon Train Sheet Cake

2 sticks butter
1 c. water
4 Tbsp. cocoa
2 c. flour
2 c. sugar

1 tsp. baking soda
1/2 tsp. salt
2 eggs, lightly beaten
1/2 c. sour cream or buttermilk
1 tsp. vanilla

Directions:

Place butter, cocoa and water over medium heat and bring to a boil. Pour over the flour and sugar and mix well. Add all the other ingredients and mix well. Pour into well-greased and floured cookie sheet pan (15 1/2 x10 1/2). Cookie sheet pan must be a deep cookie sheet pan. Bake at 350° for 23 minutes. Ice cake while it is still hot. Make frosting five minutes before cake is finished.

Chocolate frosting

1 stick butter
4 Tbsp. cocoa
6 Tbsp. milk

1 lb. box powered sugar
1 c. pecans, chopped
1/2 tsp. vanilla

Directions:

Mix together butter, cocoa and milk. Cook over medium heat and bring to a boil. Remove from stove and add sugar, nuts and vanilla. Mix well and pour over cake.

1032 S. Main Street
Woodstock, VA 22664
Phone: 540-459-5886
Website: www.sunrise-cafe.webs.com

My restaurant Sunrise Cafe is located at 1032 South Main St. in Woodstock, Virginia. My family has had a business at this location since 1945 when my father came home from WWII and purchased the property. It has undergone changes over the years, adapting to changes in the family and the community. At first it was a tavern, then a family diner and now a sandwich shop and bakery. The following recipe is my latest attempt to set the world (well, maybe Woodstock) on fire....

Grasshoppers...a cookie

1 c. salted butter, room temp.
3/4 c. light brown sugar
3/4 c. sugar
2 eggs
1 tsp. vanilla flavoring
Few drops green food color
3/4 tsp. salt
1 tsp. baking soda
2 3/4 c. all purpose flour
10 oz. bag crème de menthe flavor baking chips
(Andes brand)

4 oz. semi sweet chocolate chips
4 oz. chocolate almond bark candy coating

Directions:

Mix first six ingredients in mixer until creamy. Blend next four dry ingredients together in large bowl. Add wet to dry and stir with spoon until well incorporated. Portion with cookie scoop and place on parchment lined cookie sheet. Bake for 18 minutes at 325°. Cool at least an hour, then melt (use microwave oven or double boiler) chocolate chips and coating together. Dip each cookie halfway in coating. Place on wax paper to dry.

Desserts   *Submitted by: Tammy Nottingham, Owner/Chef*

21 W. Main Street
Mesa, AZ 85201
Phone: 480-461-9529
Website: www.sweetcakescafe.com

Sweet Cakes Café is a quaint Café on Main Street in Downtown Mesa. Often called a 'Chick Place' because it is a wonderful place for women to enjoy a fabulous lunch with friends and spend a few hours 'talking about important stuff!' We have been featured on TLC's "Best Food Ever" in the Bodacious Bakeries episode aired in May 2010.

Gooey Sweet Cake

2 boxes yellow cake mix
2 eggs
1 c. margarine
16 oz. cream cheese
4 eggs

6 1/2 c. powdered sugar
1 1/2 tsp. vanilla
1 1/2 c. chopped pecans
2 1/2 c. powdered sugar

Directions:
Mix cake mix, eggs and margarine together. Press in bottom of large cake pan (1/2 sheet pan). In mixing bowl, blend cream cheese, eggs, powdered sugar and vanilla together. Spread that over the cake mix crust. Mix pecans with remaining powdered sugar and sprinkle that on top. Bake at 350° for one hour or until firm and golden brown.

Desserts   *Submitted by: Kellie Huntington, Manager*

ROADHOUSE
LODGING • MEALS • BAKERY

talkeetna, alaska

13550 E. Main Street
Talkeetna, AK 99676
Phone: 907-733-1351
Website: www.talkeetnaroadhouse.com

The Roadhouse, built between 1914-17, is one of the oldest establishments still in operation on Main Street in "Beautiful Downtown Talkeetna." Our kitchen is open to the public and we've become famous for our breakfast, hearty soups, home baked breads and genuine frontier hospitality. Our bakery produces all sorts of treats each day such as pies, a variety of cinnamon rolls, cookies, cakes and brownies.

Blueberry Rhubarb Pie (BluBarb!)

Crust...yields five discs of pie dough
1 lb. unsalted butter
5 c. flour
1 tsp. salt
2 tsp. sugar

Directions:
Cut butter into all ingredients, using your fingers or a pastry cutter. Work quickly but gently until butter and flour are crumbly. Add cold water in small amounts, gently stirring until dough holds together (refrain from over-stirring). Form dough into a ball then divide into five equal discs.

Desserts

Recipe continued on next page

The historic end-of-the-road town of Talkeetna is known today throughout the world as the base for international climbers making their way to climb Denali (Mt. McKinley), North America's tallest peak. Denali and the other peaks of the Alaska Range offer a magnificent backdrop for this picturesque town of around 800 people, located about two and a half hours north of Anchorage and halfway between Anchorage and Denali Park entrance both by rail and road.

recipe continued

Filling

    8 c. rhubarb, chopped in half-inch pieces
    3 c. frozen blueberries
    1/2 c. white sugar
    1/2 c. brown sugar
    1/2 c. flour
    pinch of salt
    1/4 tsp. nutmeg

Streusel

    1 1/2 lb. butter
    5 c. flour
    2 c. white sugar
    2 c. brown sugar

Directions:

Streusel: Combine all ingredients, cutting butter in and working with fingers until well incorporated. Yields plenty and can be frozen for use on more pies or muffin tops. Putting it all together: Roll out the disc of dough; place in greased 8" pie tin and crimp. Combine all Filling ingredients in a bowl, toss to coat, and empty into pie shell. Top with a generous clumping of streusel. Place on a sheet pan and put in 350° oven. Set timer for 25 minutes. When timer goes off, tent with foil and set timer for one hour. Pie needs to be "bubbling" within an inch of the center. Depending on the speed of your oven the pie may need to bake covered for an additional thirty minutes, then the foil taken off for an additional 25 minutes in order to "dry" it out. Foil can be taken on and off as needed to regulate cooking versus browning too fast. Pies need a solid hour to cool before cutting into.

Desserts   *Submitted by: Trisha Costello, Owner*

300 Main Street
Montesano, WA 98563
Phone: 360-249-4131
Fax: 360-532-0516

The Bee Hive Restaurant originated in 1934, when Mom and Pop Gunn and their daughter, Gladys, affectionately known as B.B., placed a large army tent on a vacant lot and sold a mouthwatering hamburger and a cup of hot coffee for 25¢. Eventually, the tent was replaced with the current building. Jack Mempa, a real character who loved people, fine clothes and cars, purchased the restaurant in 1966, and built an addition to include a cocktail lounge. The Bee Hive was truly a buzzin' with locals and tourists alike. Ill health forced Jack to sell in 1997, to Ralph and Paul Larson, a father and son team of local restaurateurs. The restaurant still maintains a1950's charm. All time favorites include homemade pies and rolls.

Bee Hive Bread Pudding with Amaretto Sauce

2 c. milk
1/4 c. butter
4 eggs
1 c. sugar
1 tsp. vanilla
6 c. bread, cubed
2 tsp. cinnamon
1 c. raisins

Amaretto Sauce
2/3 c. sugar
1/3 c. butter
1/3 c. buttermilk
2 tsp. corn syrup, light
1/4 tsp. baking soda
2 Tbsp. amaretto

Directions:
Beat eggs, milk, butter, sugar and vanilla together. Add bread. In separate bowl, mix raisins and cinnamon. Add raisins and cinnamon to bread mixture. Spray 9x13 inch pan with PAM. Place pan in water bath and bake 40-50 minutes at 350°. Place the sauce ingredients in a saucepan and bring to a boil. Continue boiling 5 minutes, until it becomes a caramel brown. Serve the warm sauce over the bread pudding and place a dollop of whipped cream on the top. Serves 12.

Desserts

Submitted by: Sue Larson, Owner

practicing the art of food

534 Main Street
Plattsmouth, NE 68048
Phone: 402-296-3373

The Chocolate Moose has been open for almost 8 years now in the charming town of Plattsmouth, Nebraska, about 15 miles outside of Omaha. Kit Ostaseski is the chef/owner and describes the cafe as an eclectic gourmet cafe. The name is a play on words coming from her favorite dessert, chocolate mousse, and she thought it fitting to give one of her signature mousse recipes for this book.

Caramel Chocolate Mousse

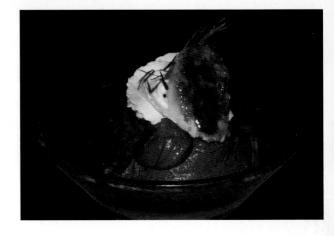

2 oz. caramel
10 oz. semi-sweet chocolate
1 1/2 c. heavy cream
1 tsp. instant coffee
1 Tbsp. brandy or cognac
4 egg yolks
2 egg whites
2/3 c. heavy cream
1 tsp. vanilla extract

Directions:
Place the caramel and chocolate into a food processor and process until finely chopped. Heat the cream in microwave for 2 minutes until hot and pour into processor; while still running add the coffee, brandy, and yolks (one at a time) and run until smooth. Pour into a glass bowl and cool slightly. Whip the whites until firm but not stiff. Whip the remaining heavy cream with the vanilla until firm. Fold the cream into the chocolate mixture followed by the whites. Thoroughly blend and cover with plastic wrap for at least 6 hours. Scoop out the mousse into martini glasses and decorate with shaved chocolate. Serves 8 to 10.

Desserts   *Submitted by: Kit Ostaseski, Owner/Chef*

700 Main Street
Louisville, CO 80027
Phone: 303-666-8020
Website:
www.thehuckleberry.com

Located in Historic Downtown Louisville, Colorado, The Huckleberry is in an historic building dating back to 1894. Originally the town's Post Office, our building has also served as a bank, a pharmacy, and two different restaurants. Today, the Huckleberry serves breakfast, lunch and dinner in an atmosphere of fun, creative comfort. Our food is created to be FUNKY COUNTRY - real food you recognize and love with a modern twist. We've taken American Classics and added a hint of culinary sophistication to appeal to a wide variety of discerning palates. At The Huckleberry, there's something for everyone!

Peach Huckleberry Pie

1 1/2 c. huckleberries or blueberries, frozen
4 1/2 c. peaches, frozen
Lemon zest – 1/2 lemon
1/3 c. cornstarch
1 tsp. ginger powder
1 1/3 c. sugar

Crust
2 c. all purpose flour
1/4 c. sugar
1/2 tsp. salt
1/2 c. butter
1/3 c. cold water

Directions:
Place all filling ingredients in a large round pan and cook on low heat, stirring frequently until all ingredients thicken. Cool rapidly. Meanwhile, mix all the dry crust ingredients into large mixing bowl. Cut butter into chunks and add to ingredients. Add water slowly until all ingredients form a ball. Roll out into two pie crusts. Pour cooled filling into bottom pie crust. Brush the inside crust with egg wash and place egg wash side down. Then crimp edge of pie. Cut holes in crust to ventilate. Egg wash and sprinkle with sugar. Bake at 300° for 45 minutes, until golden brown.

Wagoner's
Main Street Cafe

112 S. Main Street
Wagoner, OK 74467
Phone: (918) 485-3668

Mike still unlocks the door at 5:30 a.m. in case we're busy in back. Floyd Young usually sits in the third or fourth booth on the right in Wagoner's Main Street Cafe every morning, greeting practically everyone who walks through the front door. He knows practically everyone, and except for the occasional newcomer to the cafe, they know him. His hands and body are bent from a lifetime of hard work, but his mind is as keen as a newly-honed knife.

Strawberry Banana Pie

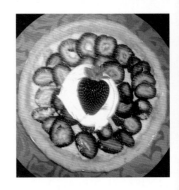

2 3/4 c. milk
1/4 c. cornstarch
3/4 c. sugar
1/4 c. melted margarine
6 10-lg. strawberries
1 lg. banana

1 tsp. vanilla
1 9-inch baked pie shell
Cool Whip
Yellow food coloring
Waxed paper

Directions:

Put first 4 ingredients in a heavy sauce pan. Mix well. Begin cooking on medium heat and bring to boil while stirring. Continue stirring while mixture boils for 1 minute. Remove from heat, add vanilla and stir. Slice banana and arrange slices in bottom of pie shell. Pour filling over the banana and cover with wax paper. Chill. Before serving, remove waxed paper and place sliced strawberries on top of filling. Top with Cool Whip and serve. This is a customer favorite. They call ahead to save their slice.

Floyd discusses not only issues of the world today, but also tells tales of his days as a student in a one-room school house out west of town or perhaps what the weather was like on a particular day 50 years ago. He recalls who the members of the Anti-horse thief Association and the day they strung the wire to bring electricity to the country homes out west of town. If someone finds an old picture and wants to know about it, Floyd is the person who can likely tell them. Just check with him in that third or fourth booth on the right. He's the tall, lanky one with great stories to tell. This piece was written by another unique person, Liz McMahon, who usually sits in the sixth or seventh booth on the right. It's the people who keep Main Street Cafe alive and well.

Desserts   *Submitted by: Darlene Burke, Owner*

1021 N. Main Street
Sweetwater, TN 37874
Phone: 423-351-9900
Fax: 423-351-9911

Stop and enjoy our made from scratch Southern favorites at Walker's Family Restaurant such as Pinto Beans and Cornbread with Country Ham, Fried Catfish and our famous BBQ ribs, Brisket and Pulled Pork. Among our many other offerings are mouthwatering burgers and hand cut steaks. And last but definitely not least, finish off with one of our homemade desserts and hand dipped ice cream.

Apple-Cinnamon Bread Pudding with Brown Sugar Glaze

1 loaf white bread (approx 2 lbs)
4 lg. eggs
2 c. whole milk
1 c. sugar
3 Tbsp. ground cinnamon
3 c. apples (approx. 3-4) peeled, cored and sliced

Brown sugar glaze
2 c. brown sugar
1 1/2 c. water

Directions:
Cut bread into 1 inch cubes and place in a large mixing bowl. In a separate bowl, whisk together milk, sugar, eggs and cinnamon. Add the slices of apples and pour over the bread. Mix well by hand until combined. Mixture should be moist but not soggy. Adjust by adding more bread if too wet, and adding milk if too dry. Place mixture in a greased 11x14 baking pan and bake at 325° until golden brown and firm to the touch. While baking, make the glaze. Combine sugar and water in a small sauce pot and bring to a slow simmer. Cook for about five minutes and remove from heat. Sauce will thicken as it cools. Once pudding is finished baking, top with glaze, then let it rest at room temperature for approximately 30 minutes before cutting into squares. It can also be served hot from the oven. Once fully cooled, your leftovers can be wrapped and refrigerated for up to a week, or frozen for up to 3 weeks. Brown sugar glaze should remain at room temperature.

Submitted by: Chef Don Walker

RECIPE INDEX

SIDES AND SAUCES

Recipe Index continued on next page